3106494900

£19.50

# PSYCHOLOGY AND MUSIC

## THE UNDERSTANDING
## OF MELODY AND RHYTHM

D1745249

# PSYCHOLOGY AND MUSIC

## THE UNDERSTANDING
## OF MELODY AND RHYTHM

B
8.64
TIG

Edited by

## Thomas J. Tighe
*University of Connecticut*

## W. Jay Dowling
*University of Texas at Dallas*

WITHDRAWN

from

STIRLING UNIVERSITY LIBRARY

**LEA** LAWRENCE ERLBAUM ASSOCIATES, PUBLISHERS
1993   Hillsdale, New Jersey          Hove and London

78455
4.95

3106 4949

Copyright © 1993, by Lawrence Erlbaum Associates, Inc.
All rights reserved. No part of this book may be reproduced in
any form, by photostat, microfilm, retrieval system, or any other
means, without the prior written permission of the publisher.

Lawrence Erlbaum Associates, Inc., Publishers
365 Broadway
Hillsdale, New Jersey 07642

**Library of Congress Cataloging-in-Publication Data**

Psychology and music : The understanding of melody and rhythm / edited
  by Thomas J. Tighe, W. Jay Dowling.
     p.    cm.
  Includes bibliographical references and index.
  ISBN 0-8058-0145-6 – ISBN 0-8058-0128-6 (pbk.)
    1. Music–Psychology.  2. Melody.  3. Musical meter and rhythm.
  I. Tighe, Thomas J.  II. Dowling, W. Jay.
    [DNLM: 1. Cognition.  2. Music–Psychology.  ML 3830 U55]
  ML3830.P897  1993
  781.2–dc20
  DNLM/DLC
  for Library of Congress                       92-4661
                                        CIP

Books published by Lawrence Erlbaum Associates are printed on acid-free
paper, and their bindings are chosen for strength and durability.

Printed in the United States of America
10  9  8  7  6  5  4  3  2  1

233521

# Contents

     Go Together
     *Caroline B. Monahan*                                    121


**PART III   DEVELOPMENT OF MUSCIAL PERCEPTION**
             *Thomas J. Tighe*                                155

     The Music Listening Skills of Infants
7    and Young Children
     *Sandra E. Trehub*                                       161


8    Children's Muscial Cognition and Taste
     *Arlette Zenatti*                                        177


9    Development of the Perception of Musical Events
     *Anne D. Pick & Caroline F. Palmer*                      197


     Epilogue
     Implications for Contemporary Musical Practice
     *Jon H. Appleton*                                        215


     Author Index                                             221


     Subject Index                                            225

# *Preface*

This volume grew out of a symposium organized by the editors several years ago for the American Association for the Advancement of Science (AAAS). The intent of that symposium was to inform interested colleagues from other scientific disciplines of the fascinating new developments in the scientific study of music perception and cognition. As is typical for AAAS symposia, the aim was to bring together leading investigators in the field to overview, in essentially nontechnical terms, the major findings and issues. The idea was to make accessible to an audience outside the field of specialization (in this case, scientists from many disciplines) advances in our understanding of the biological and psychological bases of music perception. Strong interest and positive response to the symposium prompted the idea of a similar mode of communication to a still larger audience, and thus the idea for this volume was born.

The aim here remains to communicate the new developments and findings stemming from the tantalizing interaction of the objectivity of science and the subjectivity of music. Music is, of course, an intensively perceptual and cognitive experience, and experimental psychology has its historical base in the scientific analysis of perception and cognition. Progress in the understanding of perception and cognition has been so marked and far reaching as to have engendered the growing recognition of a new area of specialization under the term *cognitive science*. This book reports outcomes from application of the techniques and findings of cognitive science to the perception and comprehension of music, with particular emphasis on the perception and understanding of melody and rhythm.

We were fortunate to secure the participation of preeminent investigators covering a variety of approaches to music perception and appreciation. The chapters span studies of music perception by infants (which afford insight into the innate basis of music perception), studies of the developing child's growing assimilation of the cultural norms of music perception, and studies elucidating specific mechanisms whereby adults perceive and encode the structure of music. Although each chapter proceeds from a program of rigorous scholarly work, the book is nevertheless intended for a broader audience than the professional specialist or psychology student. The authors were encouraged to write for the general lay audience and to avoid technical language wherever possible. Further, each of the major sections of the book is preceded by an explanatory introductory overview prepared by the editors.

Our thanks are due to Judith Amsel of Lawrence Erlbaum Associates for her support and encouragement of this project. We hope the fruits of our labors will justify her faith in the volume. We appreciated the careful editing work of Kathryn Scornavacca, whose efforts insured a timely production process. We would also like to acknowledge the contribution of Kirsten DeConti who provided invaluable editorial assistance with skill, care, and unflagging zeal.

*—Thomas J. Tighe*
*—W. Jay Dowling*

# EXPLORATIONS IN MELODY AND TONAL FRAMEWORK

W. Jay Dowling
*University of Texas at Dallas*

As the Gestalt psychologists began reminding us three quarters of a century ago, a melody is not just a collection of independent notes, but an integrated whole whose parts are inseparably related in an organic structure. A change in one part of the melody inevitably affects the way the rest of the melody is perceived. Perceiving a melody invokes a context of actual and possible events that adds meaning to what is heard. Melodies are like sentences in these two respects: Sentences are integrated wholes and not just strings of words; and sentences rely for their meaning on a surrounding context of language structure and usage. Melodies depend on the structural context provided by a musical style. The studies reported in the following chapters involved listeners who grew up in a western European tradition of tonal music, and so focus on that tradition in assessing the ways in which melodies are understood and remembered. Just as with the understanding of sentences, the understanding of melodies requires knowledge that the listener acquires over a long period of time. This knowledge incorporates what the listener knows of the structural frameworks for melodic patterns that are found in the musical culture.

The following three chapters by Dowling, Cuddy, and Bartlett focus on the tonal framework for pitch material in melodies. This tonal framework consists of the *do, re, mi* pitch pattern that

1

underlies the great majority of European folk and nursery tunes, and that can be found in a set of white keys on the piano keyboard. But the tonal framework is much more than a static set of pitches and the intervals between them, as the chapters indicate. The tonal framework defines certain pitches as *stable*—pitches where a melody can come to rest—and other pitches as relatively *unstable* and requiring resolution to more stable ones. An example that pervades these chapters is that of a melody perceived as incomplete because it ends on an unstable pitch. Such a melody leaves the listener hanging, feeling a need for resolution.

The example of the incomplete melody illustrates two things about the tonal framework. It makes clear that the framework establishes unstable and stable pitches, with dynamic tendencies attracting the one to the other. It also makes clear that the listener has knowledge of the framework, based on a lifetime of listening to melodies structured in similar ways. That knowledge is largely implicit. In hearing an incomplete melody that ends on *re* instead of *do*, for example, average listeners do not say to themselves, "That melody ended on *re* and is therefore incomplete." Rather they experience the incompleteness directly and feel immediately the requirement for resolution. Even the listener with considerable training in music, who can subsequently state the reason for the incompleteness, will experience that incompleteness first before the reason occurs explicitly in consciousness. That immediate experience of incompleteness results from the implicit knowledge the listener has of the tonal framework.

The requirement of a large body of implicit (vs. explicit) knowledge indicates another way in which perceiving a melody is like perceiving a sentence. We have much explicit knowledge concerning the words in language. However, when we hear someone speaking in a language that we know, we do not hear a stream of sounds and then attempt to decipher it in terms of our explicit knowledge. Rather, we hear meaningful words and sentences, already interpreted for us via our implicit knowledge base. Using explicit knowledge is slow and clumsy by comparison, as is immediately apparent in those few cases where we are forced to make use of it; for example, communicating in a language that we do not speak well.

The implicit knowledge that we have of the tonal framework is very slowly built up via perceptual learning throughout our lifetime. The chapters provide evidence that mere exposure to music organized in a particular way—Western tonal music for these listeners—is sufficient to induce the auditory system to prepare itself to receive further input conforming to the patterns already experienced. The chapters also provide evidence concerning elaborations of those basic schemes that come about through specialized training in music. The more musical experience the listener has, the more extensive will be the detailed implicit knowledge that listener has of the tonal framework.

The aesthetic implications of implicit knowledge schemes such as the tonal framework are worth noting. In a musical context the tonal scheme defines which pitches are likely to occur and which are not (as Cuddy and Bartlett empha-size), as well as temporal patterns moving from the stable to the unstable and back again. Introducing a pitch foreign to the key defined by the tonal scheme introduces a point of instability that requires resolution, either by a return to the original key or by shifting the tonal center in the direction indicated by the originally foreign note. The aesthetic experience of the listener depends on the stimulus pattern that is heard, setting up a context and then introducing a for-eign element and then resolving the situation. But it also depends on the knowledge of such situations that the listener has derived from countless simi-lar experiences, which defines for the listener what will be heard as a foreign or unstable pitch, and what will count as a resolution. There is a delicate balance here between the rule-governed expected pattern and its violation. Without ex-pectancies based on previously encountered regularities the listener will not register the presence of instability, and if too many instabilities are introduced it will begin to break down the regularity of the stable patterns. On the other hand, if no instability ever appears—if everything always follows the rules—the music will be dull and uninteresting.

# Procedural and Declarative Knowledge in Music Cognition and Education

W. Jay Dowling
*University of Texas at Dallas*

The term *music cognition* can refer to a wide variety of processes that go on when a person listens to music, and so at the outset I place some of those processes in perspective—place them in relation to each other and in relation to the broader context of human cognition. To do this I start with a basic situation in which someone is listening intently to a piece of music, without distractions and without any particular aim except to listen. Even this situation is psychologically complicated, but there are several aspects of it that can be described in a general way. Our listener is very likely consciously attending to the patterns of sound at some structural level: either to the broad, global sweep of the sound textures, or to local details. (It would be hard for us to know, however, to what the listener was attending.) The listener is also likely to be consciously or subconsciously developing expectancies concerning upcoming events in the piece. (We can tell that the listener is doing this if there are occasional surprises in the course of listening.) It also seems likely that the listener will be understanding certain aspects of the musical patterns as the piece progresses, in the sense of noticing consciously (or subconsciously taking account of) points of closure, contrasts among the musical elements, and relations among melodic and rhythmic subpatterns. It might also happen that, following the piece intently and developing expectancies, our listener would begin to generate emotional responses to the music. At least, this is what theories such as that of Meyer (1956) suggest, as well as contemporary psychological theories of emotion (Dowling & Harwood, 1986). (In fact, we might imagine in the absence of such responses that the listener might not have been listening so intently.)

This list of aspects of cognition involved in a basic listening situation suggests a multiplicity of cognitive processes occurring simultaneously. Sometimes those processes are conscious, but at other times they are not. For example, sometimes the expectancies that develop will be conscious, and the listener will be consciously anticipating what will happen next. At other times the listener will not be consciously aware of the expectancies, but will only become aware of having had them as a result of little surprises that occur. This can happen, for example, if a piece fails to end in the expected way (see Fig. 1.1).

Another way in which the cognitive processes differ among themselves is that some of those processes depend more on the knowledge the listener brings to the situation, and other processes depend more on what happens in the musical pattern itself. Clearly the process that develops expectancies must rely on both the listener's knowledge—conscious and explicit knowledge as well as subconscious and implicit knowledge—and the listener's perception of the musical patterns in order to project present patterns into future possibilities.

## PROCEDURAL AND DECLARATIVE KNOWLEDGE

In this chapter I focus on the role of the listener's knowledge in music cognition. In general, knowledge concerning a particular perceptual domain affects the cognition of things in that domain: aiding in the generation of expectancies, facilitating the perception of expected events, and facilitating memory for events that fit the cognitive frameworks of the domain. For example, consider the role of knowledge in solving a perceptual puzzle such as the ''find six lions in the jungle'' type of picture in children's game books. To find the lions you need to (a) know what a line drawing of a lion looks like, (b) know that there are lions to be found, and (c) have some practice discerning lion drawings in confusing contexts.

We can point out two kinds of knowledge that are involved in perceptual tasks such as finding hidden visual figures and listening to parts intertwined in a com-

FIG. 1.1. ''Twinkle, Twinkle, Little Star'' with a normal ending (a) and a surprise ending (b).

plex piece of music. One kind of knowledge is called by psychologists *declarative*. Declarative knowledge is the consciously accessible kind that you can talk about. You can tell someone: "There are six lions to be found here." You can mentally review a list of lion features: large, cat-like creature with furry mane, tawny color, long tail with tassel, and so on. That is all declarative knowledge. But even when you know all this you will still need practice finding the lions before you become rapid and accurate in doing it. In the course of solving a number of problems of this sort you will develop a kind of practical know-how that we call *procedural* knowledge. Procedural knowledge is often consciously accessible only through its results, and not often explicitly present to consciousness as such.

The contributions of declarative and procedural knowledge to perceptual experience can be seen clearly in listener's understanding of spoken language. Knowing in the declarative sense what someone is talking about helps us understand what is being said. But understanding someone speaking requires vast amounts of practice in listening. We have only to try to understand someone speaking an unfamiliar language to appreciate the importance of practice and the procedural knowledge it develops. With a couple of years of academic study of foreign language we can use declarative knowledge to figure out written messages—we can look up unknown words and decipher the syntax in an abstract and formal way. But we will continually have to ask people to speak more slowly, because our procedures for automatic perceptual processing of the speech sounds, so proficient in our own language, are not well-developed. This example points out two important differences between declarative and procedural knowledge. Declarative knowledge is easily and rapidly acquired. (How long does it take to learn that George Washington and Josef Haydn were born in the same year?) But declarative knowledge is relatively slow and clumsy to apply. In contrast, procedural knowledge takes enormous amounts of practice to acquire (as in the example of a foreign language), but is rapid and often automatic in application. *Automatic* here means that it is brought into play in cognitive information processing without conscious intent and without distracting us from attending to other things, including the results of its application.

The roles of declarative and procedural knowledge in cognition have been the focus of a paradigm shift in psychology over the past 10 years or so. When I was in graduate school in the 1960s, models of cognition were heavily based on declarative knowledge. A model of the process of understanding words in a sentence typically contained a module for interpreting speech sounds, turning them into something like a string of representations of letters. Then those strings of sounds would be looked up in a sort of dictionary module and be given a meaning. The meaning they were given would be roughly the same as the meaning the listener would give you in answer to the question "What does X mean?" The process of understanding a spoken word would be conceived of as essentially a two-stage process: procedural interpretation of sounds, followed by accessing declarative meanings of those sounds.

Such a model depends critically on declarative knowledge. Declarative knowledge forms the basis of much of our system of education, both ideologically and economically. We live in a *logocentric* culture, to use Clarke's (1989) term, and we rely heavily on the transmission of information organized in words and symbols embedded in syntactic systems. Our whole method in training the young as well as training the not-so-young is based on the efficient transmission of declarative information to large groups of people at once. The culture is well characterized as logocentric because we tend to think we only really understand something when we can explain it verbally, that is, in an explicit declarative way. Such declarative knowledge can contribute to expectancies. Sometimes the declarative component parallels the procedural, as in the case where we know that at the end of a piece in European tonal music a dominant harmony typically resolves to the tonic, and the violation of that expectation in Fig. 1.1 strikes us on both levels. And sometimes declarative knowledge operates more independently of procedural, as when we know that most classical concertos end with a rondo, and thus expect one at the end of a concerto we have never before encountered.

We contrast this declarative approach with a model of cognition based on a procedural approach. In this model, the brain, faced with patterns of stimulation, finds effective ways to process them. It takes advantage of regularities and redundancies in the patterns. If some pattern elements are predictable, then efficient analyzers will be programmed to be ready for them. Hearing the dominant chord in a particular context sets up a readiness to process the tonic chord more efficiently when it occurs. Note that in the procedural model the same knowledge of the world represented in the declarative model can be represented, but now, that knowledge is represented implicitly rather than explicitly. The listener does not say to himself "Oh, there is a dominant and now I bet there will be a tonic." The listener's experience is one of hearing a dominant chord and then hearing a tonic as its natural resolution. The listener won't be explicitly aware of the expectancies unless those expectancies were violated (as in the example of Fig. 1.1). This implicit knowledge is stored as procedures for handling incoming patterns of stimulation. Stimuli are represented in conscious awareness only after that processing.

What we perceive are meaningful, interpreted musical events, just as in speech where we hear meaningful words and sentences and not a meaningless stream of sounds of which we try to make sense. Just as we perceive an angry face directly, and don't have to think about what emotion the face is expressing, we don't have to cogitate about what emotion is expressed in speech or music, or what thought is expressed in speech. This was pointed out long ago by the gestaltists and is very well captured by Garner's (1966) slogan, "to perceive is to know." That is, we do not perceive uninterpreted sense data and then interpret them with reference to an explicit mental representation (as in the first model), but rather an implicit representation interprets the sense data before we perceive them.

As previously noted, procedural knowledge is built up slowly by perceptual learning and the practice of motor skills (vs. the relatively rapid acquisition of fact), and is stored as implicit sensorimotor schemes, (to use Piaget's 1976 term), as contrasted with explicit representations. And those implicit schemes are automatically invoked by context, as opposed to being under conscious control. Of course, this latter feature confers a great advantage of speed in an immediate situation. We interpret stimuli automatically without consciously thinking about it.

Moreover, not only is a procedural scheme not usually under conscious control, but the declarative level is typically out of touch with the implicit content of the procedural level. The person can't say exactly what it is that they know. Piaget (1976) provided an apt example. He asked adults to describe the order in which you put your hands and knees down when you crawl. Generally, adults can't easily answer that question. To get the answer you have to imagine yourself crawling and retrieve the order of hands and feet. Of course, the motor program is the same for everyone, even for horses, dogs, and cats. It's a very old wired-in program for all four-legged animals. The procedures are stored in the brain but you don't automatically have access to them. Leonard Bernstein (1971) provided an example of musicians from the Vienna Philharmonic. One of them came up to him after rehearsal and suggested some fine points about the interpretation of Viennese waltzes. He said, "You know, Maestro, here in Vienna we stress the second beat in a waltz." Then another one came up and said that the first beat should be stressed and the third beat lengthened. The various musicians in the most eminent orchestra in Vienna had different declarative notions of how to play a waltz, but of course in the performance they all played together cohesively, and, presumably, played Viennese waltzes to perfection.

Among the things that led me to shift emphasis from declarative to procedural knowledge in the understanding of music were two experiments that I carried out over the past few years. These experiments show on the one hand the degree to which perceptual learning sets up pitch coding in the auditory system in terms of a culturally defined framework. The first experiment illustrates the assimilation of the pitches one hears to tonal-scale categories such as those of the piano keyboard. The second experiment goes one step further and shows that with perceptual and motor skill learning, people with only a moderate amount of musical training automatically interpret melodies in terms of tonal-scale categories. This last result provides insight into a process that is crucial in the understanding of musical meaning. The use of expectancies and contextual meanings associated with pitch categories is a major way in which western music is meaningful and has emotional import.

## Experiment 1

Experiment 1 shows that pitches that fall into the cracks in between the standard notes on a piano keyboard are assimilated to the keyboard notes under conditions where pitch processing is hurried (Dowling, Lung, & Herrbold, 1987).
Experiment 1 had to be complicated because pitch perception is generally quite
precise. I needed to contrive conditions where the listeners' pitch processing
would be hurried. Otherwise, they simply would have solved the task quite precisely and not shown the assimilation that I was looking for. To hurry pitch
processing, I hid a target melody in the midst of distractor notes, as the familiar
melody "Twinkle, Twinkle" is hidden in Fig. 1.2. Before performing the main
task in the experiment, listeners need practice with familiar melodies (such as
in Fig. 1.2) to develop their skill in discerning melodies interleaved with distractor notes. After an hour or so of warm-up, listeners are able to focus their
attention on the notes of the target even though distractor notes having the
same loudness and pitch range are interleaved between them.

Figure 1.3 shows a sample trial from this experiment. There is a simple melody, followed by that melody interleaved among distractor notes (presented at
a rate of about eight notes per second). The middle note of the interleaved melody
could move to a new pitch, and it was the subject's task to follow where it moved.
In Fig. 1.3, the possible pitches the target could move to are indicated by horizontal lines. The target could move to semitones that are represented on the keyboard, or to quarter steps in between the keyboard semitone steps. Following
the interleaved pattern, the subject heard a probe tone and had to judge the
pitch of the probe in relation to the pitch to which the target tone moved.

The data obtained from Experiment 1 show the proportion of trials on which
the subjects said "same" when the probe was at different positions relative
to the pitch on which the target landed. The left panel in Fig. 1.4 shows the
data for those trials on which the target landed on a semitone (keyboard) step.
The x-axis represents pitches of the probe relative to the pitch of the target.
Accurate performance will thus lead to the inverted-V pattern we see in Fig.
1.4a, where subjects said "same" most often when the probe really was the
same as the target. In contrast, in the right hand panel (Fig. 1.4b), when the
target landed on a quarter step you can see an inverted-W pattern, indicating
that subjects tended to say "same" more often when the probe was a quarter
step off the pitch of the target, and less often when it actually was equal in pitch.
When it landed on a quarter step, the encoded pitch of the target tended to

FIG. 1.2.  The notes of "Twinkle, Twinkle, Little Star" (open notes) temporally
interleaved with those of "Frère Jacques" (filled notes).

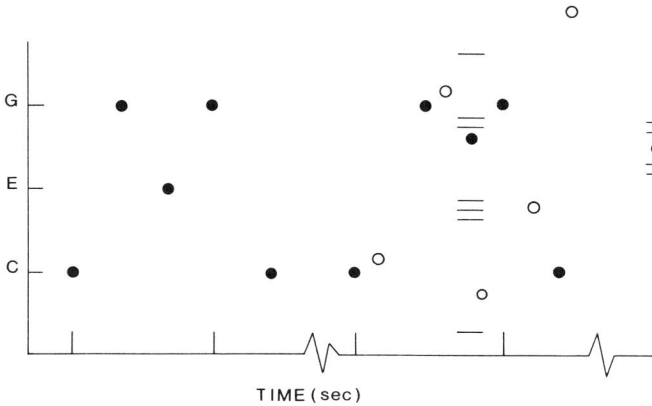

FIG. 1.3. The outline of a trial in Experiment 1. A simple cue melody is followed by the same melody interleaved with distractor notes (open symbols). The middle, target note of the melody can move to a new pitch (indicated by the horizontal lines). Finally, there is a probe tone that may be higher or lower or the same as the new pitch of the target. The subject's task is to judge the pitch of the probe in relation to that of the target.

become assimilated to the neighboring semitone. (The one exception to this generalization is that the quarter step between F and F♯ did not become assimilated to the F♯, which is a noticeably out-of-key pitch in the key of C.)

This is an elaborate task, made difficult by the presence of distractor notes, but the distractors are necessary to force a hurrying of the pitch-encoding mechanisms. I believe that that hurrying is responsible for the assimilation shown

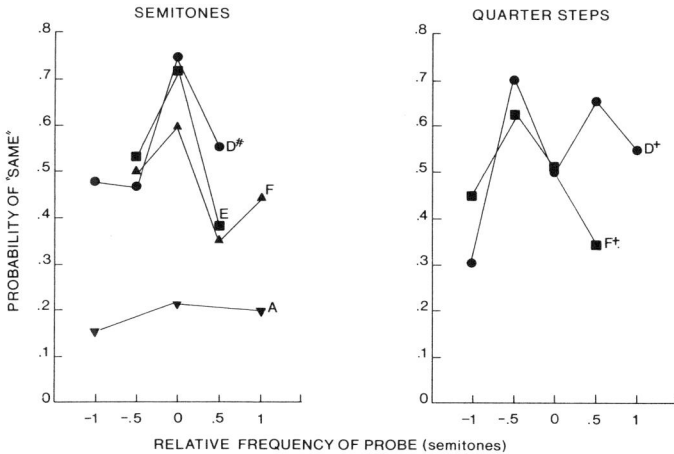

FIG. 1.4. The results of Experiment 1: judgments of the probe tone as the "same" as the target (a) when the target tone fell on a semitone step, and (b) when the target tone fell on a quarter step.

in Fig. 1.4. If we remove the distractor notes, that result disappears, and both sets of data show inverted-V shaped patterns.

There are two important aspects of these results. First, this assimilation appears with musically inexperienced as well as experienced subjects. People who have had no music lessons in their lives show this result just as strongly as people with 5 or 10 years of music lessons. That implies that lifelong perceptual learning just listening to music, over the radio, and so on—music that is all organized in terms of the pitch categories of the keyboard—is sufficient to induce the brain to program itself with these categories. The auditory system then will be able to process the standard categories more efficiently than nonstandard pitches.

A second aspect of the result is that it discloses a relative (vs. an absolute) pitch framework. That is, in a control condition, I transposed the whole experiment up a quarter step so that what had previously been defined as a standard pitch category fell in a crack in the keyboard, and vice versa. The same results appeared. Quarter steps were assimilated to the newly defined semitone steps. The whole system calibrates itself very rapidly to the tuning of whatever instrument or group it is hearing, and then applies its categories in a relative sense rather than in an absolute sense. This result was not a foregone conclusion, as in Western music the categories are now, for the most part, tied to an absolute standard (A = 440 Hz). But the brain seems to operate in terms of relative patterns of categories.

## Experiment 2

Experiment 2 went one step further in disclosing details of the pitch-analyzing procedures people have programmed in their auditory systems (Dowling, 1986). It showed that a moderate amount of musical training—about 5 years of music lessons when a person in their 30s was young—is sufficient for the listener not only to be efficient in encoding standard pitch categories, but also to encode those pitches in terms of contextually determined tonal-scale values. That is, moderately trained listeners encoded pitches in terms of musical meaning. A melody can be encoded quite literally as a sequence of pitch intervals, or it can be encoded in a context-sensitive way as particular pitch levels in a tonal-scale framework. Figure 1.5a shows two ways of encoding the familiar melody "Happy Birthday." Row A of numbers under the tune gives the intervals from note to note in semitones: unison, up two, down two, up five, and so on. Row B gives the notes as pitch levels in the diatonic major scale: 1 = *do*, 2 = *re*, 3 = *mi*, and so on. In line C we suppose that instead of beginning on the fifth degree of the scale (*sol*), "Happy Birthday" begins on the tonic. We could contrive a harmonic context that would pull the listener toward that interpretation of the first phrase of the melody. Of course, the completion of the melody provides

A:  0 +2 -2 +5 -1  -4 0 +2 -2 +7 -2

B:  5 5  6 5 1  7 5 5  6 5 2  1

C:  1 1  2 1 4  3 1 1  2 1 5  4

FIG. 1.5.  The beginning of the tune "Happy Birthday" represented (a) as intervals in semitones between successive notes; (b) as diatonic scale steps in the key of C major; and (c) as diatonic scale steps in the key of G major.

the context that determines pitch encoding shown in Row B of Fig. 1.5. The important thing to note is that the very same melody, with the very same intervals from note to note, can be encoded in different ways depending on how it is heard in relation to the scale framework and the tonic. In Experiment 2, I contrived to produce such a shift in the relationship between a target melody and the tonal context surrounding it. I supposed that if a listener initially encoded the pitches of the melody in terms of tonal scale values, then a shift in that relationship would interfere with later recognition, whereas if the initial encoding were in terms of pitch intervals from note to note, such a shift would not affect performance.

Figure 1.6 shows some sample trials from this experiment. I used a chordal context introducing the melody to establish the relationship between the pitches of the melody and those of the tonal-scale framework. Test melodies were always transposed to a new pitch level. On some trials the test melody retained the same relationship to the tonic that it had originally (as in Fig. 1.6b compared with Fig. 1.6a), whereas on other trials the test melody shifted in its relationship to the tonic (as in Fig. 1.6d). The subject's task was to say whether the transposition to the new pitch level was accurate; that is, whether it preserved the interval pattern in semitones. When the transposition was inaccurate, one of the pitches in the test melody was changed from its relative position in the original (as in Fig. 1.6c and Fig. 1.6e).

What was important was the relationship of the target melody to its context, which would either be the same (relatively speaking) or different. Three groups of subjects with different levels of musical training performed the task: inexperienced people who had no music lessons in their lives, moderately experienced people with about 5 years of music lessons, and professionals with more than 20 years of intensive experience continuing into the present (composers, orchestra musicians, etc.)

The results are shown in Fig. 1.7. The most interesting aspect of the results is the contrast in performance between the inexperienced and moderately experienced groups. The inexperienced subjects recognized the melodies fairly

FIG. 1.6. Sample trials in Experiment 2 (Dowling, 1986): (a) the introduction of a target melody, preceded by chords; (b) a same-context test containing an exact transposition of that melody; (c) a same-context test with an altered transposition; (d) a different-context test with an exact transposition; and (e) a different-context test with an altered transposition. Chord symbols for the context are written under the score. The melodic interval pattern in semitones appears above the score, and the tonal scale step encoding below the score. Reprinted by permission.

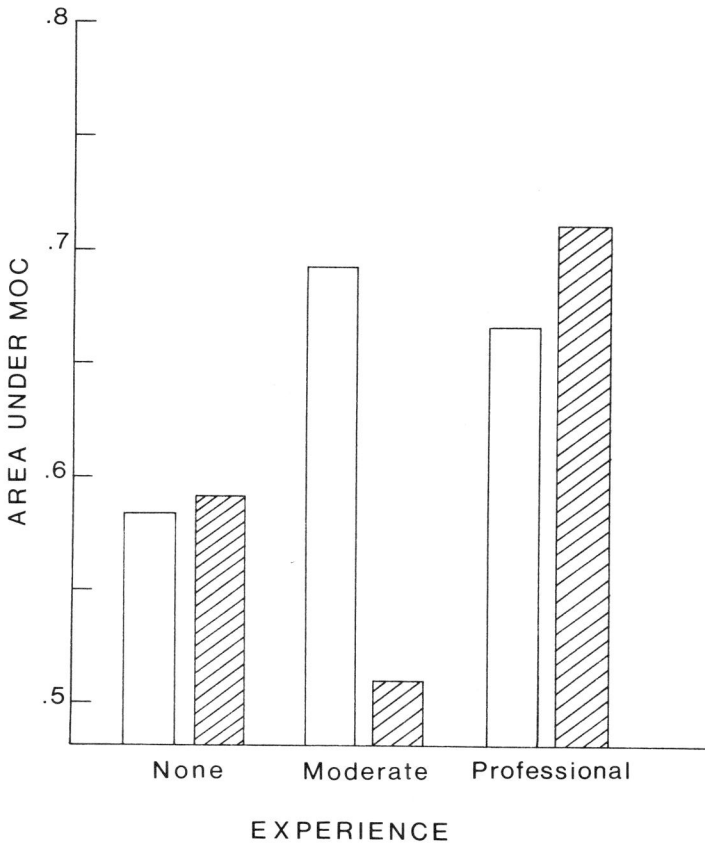

FIG. 1.7. Results of Experiment 2: proportion correct for three groups of subjects (inexperienced, moderately experienced, and professional) with transposed test melodies that were presented with context the same as in the initial presentation (open bars) or shifted (shaded bars) (Dowling, 1986). Reprinted by permission.

accurately, performing distinctly better than chance (which was 50%). These subjects were unaffected by shifts in context—in the relationship between the melody and the tonal-scale framework. They could recognize small changes in the test melodies but did not use a context-sensitive encoding scheme. They literally remembered what they had heard. In contrast, subjects with 5 years of music lessons performed better when context stayed the same, but much worse when the context shifted, in fact, they fell to around chance. That suggests that subjects with a moderate amount of training were automatically encoding the melodies in terms of tonal-scale categories. That scheme worked as long as test items retained the same relative context as the original items.

But when a test item required a different encoding from the original, these subjects were lost. The musical training that they had received was sufficient to program their auditory system with sensitivity to the meanings of pitches in music.

The professionals did much better across the board. In fact, they seemed to have their pitch encoding system under consciousness control. After a couple of sample items at the start of the experiment they would typically say, ''Oh, you want me to ignore the chords around the melody.''

In contrast to the professionals, the moderately experienced subjects definitely did not have explicit declarative access to their pitch-encoding schemes. Otherwise they would have been able to write down what they heard. Typically, people in their 30s who had 5 years of piano lessons as a child are not able to sit down and listen to a melody and write it out. They can't access the declarative encodings of the pitch categories. In fact, declarative access to pitch encoding is usually developed during the first 2 years of conservatory training. Thus this was an implicit coding system that they were using. They would have been very surprised, for example, to be told ''Whenever you hear a melody you automatically encode it in *do-re-mi* categories.'' They would think that that was far more sophisticated than what they did. They were just listening to melodies like everyone else. What the moderately experienced subjects have, then, is an implicit scheme of tonal-scale pitch categories built into their auditory systems, which is essential to musical understanding at the level of pitch coding.

These two experiments, then, disclose two properties of the pitch-encoding procedures in the auditory system. First, the system is programmed by experience to be especially efficient in encoding the set of relative pitch categories that occurs in the music heard by a person throughout the lifespan. When pitch encoding is made to hurry by task demands, other pitches become assimilated to (mistaken for) that prototypical set of pitches. Second, a moderate amount of musical training is sufficient to develop additional sophistication in pitch encoding. Listeners with 5 years of music lessons implicitly encoded pitches in terms of a tonal scale system. This encoding scheme led those listeners to fail to recognize melodies that were identical in interval pattern to targets, but that differed in the scale values of their notes. This result is important for musical understanding because tonal music relies heavily on the stability and instability of the various scale degrees as a structural principle. In both of these cases, what the listeners knew was not something that they were aware of knowing, but rather it derived from knowledge that was implicitly built up in their auditory systems as a response to structural regularities in the music they heard.

## Education

Now I turn to applications to education. The importance of procedural learning to music perception suggests that we should emphasize procedural learning in school for all children, and not just for those taking music lessons. As we saw, moderately experienced subjects have a sophisticated scheme for encoding pitches in terms of tonal meanings. Such a scheme is an important component of musical understanding for music organized in a Western tonal system. We should give as many children as possible as much procedural learning as possible in acquiring listening skills. In particular, we should emphasize procedural learning that involves motor skill acquisition in the process. We should try to have all the students singing as much as possible in school, rather than, for example, memorizing facts. Memorizing facts is good for some purposes, but it doesn't help very much in understanding music. But doing things with music like singing does help.

Having children sing has the added advantage that it is not exorbitantly expensive to implement. When I began to think of this chapter, I thought of a number of very expensive ideas. Then I thought, if instead of *talking* to children, teachers got them *singing* it would help a lot and would produce active involvement. Also, it is fun. It is more fun to sing than to listen to someone lecture.

In terms of the underlying schemes that are important to develop, the particular music that you use is not important. All the music in our culture—pop, rock, classical, nursery tunes, and so on—is organized with basically the same tonal scale system. Singing any of it will continue to program the brain in useful ways.

Now of course we also need to emphasize procedural learning with those who are receiving specialized training in music. We usually try to do this anyway, but I find with my children that they very quickly get bored with the endless repetition that procedural learning requires—practicing scales on the piano, and the like. They don't immediately understand that to get your motor programs and your fingers doing scales and arpeggios you need to do them over and over. Having a declarative understanding of the notes and intervals of a D♭ major scale is not sufficient to actually get your motor system to produce it smoothly and accurately. That they can grasp the structure of one of the pieces they are learning at a glance, but that it takes hours of practice before they can play it well, is very frustrating. Therefore, in my experience, one simply has to use every motivational device available to get them to keep at it through periods of frustration at the slowness of acquisition. But as with all learning, it is best not to rely very much on external rewards. One thing that is worth at least a try is to present things in terms such as: "Practicing scales for two octaves out of this book is a grown-up thing to do. When you are old enough you will get to practice those kinds of scales." That works up to a point.

We should not be misled into thinking that imparting declarative knowledge helps people much in understanding music. It can help in the later stages, as with the professionals in Experiment 2, who were able to bring their procedures under declarative control. But during the early stages of learning, the emphasis should be on building schemes that later can be brought under declarative control. Students can't use elaborate declarative structures until they have the basic schemes to deal with the sensory material.

I do not mean to imply that declarative knowledge has no use in music cognition. There are a couple of uses of declarative knowledge that should not be overlooked. A little declarative input is enough to serve these needs, so we should not overdo it.

1. One thing declarative input can do is provide a scheme for organizing experiences. It provides a map of the territory. For example, if you like a piece by Handel, and you know Handel is a baroque composer and you know Vivaldi is a baroque composer, then you are likely to guess that you would like a piece by Vivaldi. So when you go to the record store for more Handel CDs but they are out of Handel, you can get Vivaldi instead and likely be satisfied.

2. Declarative knowledge also suggests a context in which things should be heard. It includes knowledge about style that says this and this go together, so use similar modes of listening to them. Declarative knowledge can also enrich the context with verbal associations. If you are listening to a requiem mass and you know the text refers to the last trumpet, then that enhances the experience when you hear trumpets. Declarative knowledge tells you what the music is supposed to mean in relation to things outside the music.

In conclusion, I think we need to find ways to balance what I see as an overemphasis in our educational system on declarative knowledge and its acquisition especially in music and the arts, and to move in the direction of enhancing procedural learning. It is via the automatic procedures we develop that in a very fundamental way we perceive and understand the world. With music, this can be done quite effectively, I think, by engaging all the students actively in perhaps simply having them sing rather than talk about music.

# REFERENCES

Bernstein, L. (1971). Quoted in program notes to R. Strauss *Der Rosenkavalier* (CBS recording M3K 42564), p. 7.
Clarke, E. F. (1989). Issues in language and music. *Contemporary Music Review, 4*, 9–22.
Dowling, W. J. (1986). Context effects on melody recognition: Scale-step versus interval representations. *Music Perception, 3*, 281–296.
Dowling, W. J., & Harwood, D. L. (1986). *Music cognition.* New York: Academic Press.
Dowling, W. J., Lung, K. M.-T., & Herrbold, S. (1987). Aiming attention in pitch and time in the perception of interleaved melodies. *Perception & Psychophysics, 41*, 642–656.
Garner, W. R. (1966). To perceive is to know. *American Psychologist, 21*, 11–19.
Meyer, L. B. (1956). *Emotion and meaning in music.* Chicago: University of Chicago Press.
Piaget, J. (1976). *The grasp of consciousness.* Cambridge, MA: Harvard University Press.

# Melody Comprehension and Tonal Structure

Lola L. Cuddy
*Queen's University at Kingston, Ontario, Canada*

Three facts about melody and melody comprehension are readily apparent. First, melody is ubiquitous. It is available, in the form of song, to almost everyone from the cradle onward. Appreciation is not limited to specific cultures or a specifically trained group within a culture. Second, our sense of melody is remarkably robust. When a familiar melody is played, we nod with recognition almost immediately, even though the melody may be realized in a form we have never heard before. It may be played on a different musical instrument, or sung in a different pitch register. It may be played at a faster or slower rate (within broad limits). Nevertheless, the identity of the melody is preserved. Finally, melodies can not only be recognized but compared. That is, we can rank melodies along various psychological dimensions such as simplicity (the "catchiness" of a tune), similarity, and preference. This ability to perceive and judge relationships among melodies involves mental activity of considerable complexity, but it is essential to musical understanding. For example, we can better comprehend and enjoy a composer's use of thematic material throughout a piece if we can readily identify the separate themes and recognize them under various musical transformations.

Despite the seeming effortlessness of melody recognition, analysis of the mental processes involved is surprisingly difficult. To begin the inquiry, we must first decide on the perceptual dimensions and the perceptual units to be studied. Here it may seem appropriate to look at the notes contained in a melody, and to conduct the analysis in terms of the physical characteristics of the notes (e.g., the frequency spectrum of each note). This approach, however, immediately runs into problems at the level of psychological analysis. Consider the following simple task: Two melodies are presented in succession, "Twinkle, twinkle, little star" and "Frère Jacques." Most people would easily recognize that the tunes are different, and most people could also name them. But if asked to say whether or not each tune contained the note "middle C," most people would find this a difficult task indeed. A musical note, in isolation, does not seem to possess special perceptual features that can be used to identify the note. Thus, the absolute identification of notes is not likely an important part of the process of recognizing melodies. ("Absolute pitch" among musicians may be an exception, but this ability is too rare to account for the widespread ability of people to recognize melodies.)

More likely, the recognition of a melody involves the recognition of an integrated whole (Dowling, 1991). In defining melody, *The New Harvard Dictionary of Music* (Randel, 1986) adds to the notion of succession of pitches the notion that the succession must contain "coherence" or acceptance of "belonging together" (p. 481). *The Concise Oxford Dictionary of Music* (Kennedy, 1980) further suggests that "long-lived melodies possess the valuable quality of logical organization" (p. 410). These definitions are intuitively appealing, but leave us with the task of specifying the principles of organization, or identifying the properties of note successions that lead to coherence.

Gestalt psychology directly addressed issues of coherence and organization. The Gestaltists were interested in describing the emergent properties of form or organized wholes, where emergent properties were not predictable from the constituent parts. For the Gestaltists (e.g., von Ehrenfels, 1890/1937; Koffka, 1935), melody was a prototypic "good form"; form was conveyed through the relations among the notes, not through their absolute properties.

Gestalt principles point to features of a melody that may be influential in the formation of perceptual groups (Deutsch, 1982). For example, the principles of proximity and similarity suggest that notes will be grouped together on the basis of nearness in pitch, time, loudness, timbre, and so forth. The principles of good continuation and common fate suggest that an ascending or descending pitch contour—notes continuously rising or falling—is a better "gestalt" than a contour that bounces up and down. These proposals have been borne out by empirical findings. Gestalt principles, therefore, may help us identify the low-level features of melodic patterns (Deutsch & Feroe, 1981), but they don't help us fully to capture the critical features implicated in memory that effect comparisons among melodies. Dowling and Harwood (1986) express the problem in this way:

[With respect to principles of perceptual organization], most (but not all) local features of a piece are accessible to the listener without using memory. The organization of local features in music are, for the most part, determined by the straightforward and automatic operation of the listener's sensory systems. In contrast, the apprehension of global features of a piece almost always involves memory for earlier events in the piece (as perceptually organized in terms of local features) as well as knowledge of other pieces in the same style. Thus, the problem of the relationship between human memory and musical form appears. (p. 160)

Given that we agree to pursue an analysis in terms of the global organization of features, we are faced with another problem. The perceptual structures and strategies underlying melody recognition may involve a number of independent, or, alternatively, interacting, features. Melodies convey a great deal of information on several perceptual dimensions—notably, pitch, time, and loudness—and this information is structured in an elaborate manner—yielding, for example, perceptual structures for tonality, rhythm, and dynamics.

A fruitful research tradition—one that I illustrate in this chapter—has been to isolate an individual perceptual dimension for study and to ask how the information along that dimension becomes structured, elaborated, and retained in memory. The dimension isolated for this chapter is pitch, and the particular focus is the elaboration of pitch structures to yield a sense of tonality. Later we may ask how structures combine to form the integrated whole.

This chapter considers the following issue: Not all melodies are equally easy to learn, and a simple pitch alteration in a melody can sometimes have a trivial effect on its recognition and sometimes a devastating effect. We need to go beyond Gestalt principles to explain this finding. What do we "know" about the melodies of our culture that influences how we go about perceiving, learning, and recognizing melodies? The following experiment yields some promising suggestions about where to look.

## THE DISTORTED MELODIES TEST

A series of experiments was conducted that included a test called *the distorted melodies test*. This test examined listeners' ability to recognize slight pitch alterations in melodies. The test was adapted from a previous report by Kalmus and Fry (1980) for thesis research completed in our laboratory (Mawhinney, 1987). Mawhinney was interested in the self-concept of musical ability and asked what kinds of skills were correlated with one's self-rating of ability. Listeners were given a battery of tests, but it is the results of the distorted melodies test that are of particular interest in the present context.

The test consisted of 20 melodies chosen from the folk, popular, and classical repertoires. Each melody was generated by a sine-tone synthesizer, and care was taken to reproduce the tempo and rhythm in which it would normally be played. For five of the melodies, the notes were all reproduced accurately as well. The remaining 15 melodies, however, contained a pitch alteration. This alteration involved lifting or lowering a note, or short sequence of notes, by one semitone, which is the difference between adjacent keys on a keyboard (or, a ratio of two fundamental frequencies of approximately 1.06%). In no case did the pitch alteration change the contour of the original melody.

Mawhinney (1987) tested 40 listeners (university students), each of whom fell into one of four categories: (a) those who reported "low" musical ability and thought they were "tone deaf" as well; (b) those who reported "low" musical ability but thought they were "average" in listening skills; (c) those who reported "high" musical ability and "average" listening skills; and (d) those who reported "high" musical ability and "above average" listening skills. Listeners were also asked to report the extent of their musical training, but it was self-reported ability, not amount of musical training, that determined the assignment to category.

Each listener heard the 20 melodies in a different random order. After each melody was played, the listener was asked to make two judgments. The first judgment was whether or not the melody was familiar. The second was whether or not it sounded correctly played. Listeners were asked to provide the second judgment for all melodies, even those judged unfamiliar.

Mawhinney's (1987) results showed that on the average, listeners within each category said they recognized about 65% of the melodies as familiar. That is, there were no differences among the categories in number of melodies judged familiar. For the judgment of correct playing, however, there was a significant difference among the categories. Average accuracy of detecting whether the melody was correctly played or not improved across the four levels of self-rated ability, from an average score of 59% in category (a) to an average score of 78% correct in category (d). In addition, a significant relationship was obtained between accuracy scores and self-ratings of listening skills even when the influence of amount of formal musical education was statistically eliminated.

Mawhinney's (1987) analysis concentrated on differences among individuals. An alternative analysis is to examine differences among melodies; that is, to treat each melody as if it were a subject, and provide for each melody a score for familiarity and a score for the judgment of correct playing. The results of this analysis were that certain melodies were reliably judged more familiar than others, and certain melodies were reliably assigned higher scores than others for the accuracy with which they were judged correctly or incorrectly played. Moreover, and more interesting, it was not necessary for a melody to be judged familiar in order to receive a high score on accuracy of judgment of correct playing. These results held for all four categories of self-rated ability.

Here is an illustration of these results, with respect to two specific melodies. Almost everyone (38 of the 40 listeners) said they recognized the Beatle tune "When I'm 64." But only four listeners (one per category) correctly detected that there was a mistake in it. Only about half the listeners recognized the tune of the Canadian folksong "Land of the Silver Birch," but 34 of the 40 listeners correctly said there was a mistake in it.

The statistical support for these conclusions was as follows: For judgments of familiarity, correlations were obtained across the 20 melodies for each possible pair-wise combination of the categories. The average correlation was 0.88. A similar procedure was followed for accuracy of judgment of correct playing: The average correlation between accuracy scores for the 20 melodies was 0.77. Both correlations are statistically significant, as were the individual pair-wise correlations. Finally, there was absolutely no statistical relationship between judged familiarity and accuracy of detection. Correlations hovered around 0.0.

How, then, might one account for the differences among the judgments of the melodies? In particular, why did some alterations sound so much more sour than others? (Some listeners physically winced at hearing some of the distorted melodies.) We approach an answer here with caution, because the experiment was not designed to study individual melodies in depth. The search for an answer was motivated by earlier work on melody recognition (Cuddy, Cohen, & Mewhort, 1981; Cuddy, Cohen, & Miller, 1979; Dowling & Harwood, 1986; Edworthy, 1985).

Inspection of the distorted melodies data yielded some hints, and they had to do with the nature of the alteration. For the easiest of all melodies, the "Nova Scotia Farewell," in which the error was correctly detected by 95% of the listeners, and for Beethoven's "Ode to Joy," in which the error was correctly detected by 90% of the listeners, an alteration was made to the most important note of the original melody. This note, in the original, correct, version of the melodies was the tonic or key-note, and in both distorted versions it was altered to a note outside the key of the melody. Difficult melodies (melodies with a low score on accuracy of judgment of correct playing) never contained this kind of distortion. They contained alterations to notes that in the original, correct, version were less important than the tonic note.

It seems, therefore, that the recognition of a distortion of a melody may be related, at least in part, to the role played in the melody by the note that was altered in the distortion. To pursue this notion further, we argue that if our expectations are geared toward notes that are functionally important, and a note or notes occur that do not fulfil this expectation, we are surprised and our attention is alerted. The important factor guiding expectancy is not familiarity with the melody per se, but familiarity with the customs and rules of the Western tonal–harmonic system. Listeners did not have to judge a melody as familiar in order to detect an alteration. Rather, it is the breaking of rules that makes a melody sound distorted. Such a notion is consistent with the ideas expressed by Kalmus and Fry (1980).

Moreover, all listeners, not just the musically trained, in Mawhinney's (1987) sample responded to the alterations in much the same way; some found the task more difficult than others, but they did not respond in a qualitatively different fashion. Even the self-reported "tone deaf," though they made more mistakes in judging accuracy of playing, showed the same pattern of results as the other listeners. Thus, the results offer support for a proposal that the rules of Western tonal music form a kind of implicit knowledge, extracted from experience in a manner similar to the acquisition of natural language syntax (Krumhansl & Keil, 1982). There will be, generally, individual differences in the facility with which the rules governing melodic structure are detected and applied.

In the next section, I describe some experimental work intended to examine further the idea that notes of a melody may be described in terms of tonal function, and to demonstrate the use of a methodology designed to quantify tonal function.

## PROFILE OF A MELODY

A few definitions are necessary at this point. These definitions arise from the theory of tonal music, which provides a terminology and method of analysis applicable to a wide variety of musical styles (Krumhansl, 1983). I do not intend to touch upon the more advanced and somewhat controversial aspects of the definitions, but merely to present those concepts that are applicable to the present experimental research. The most important concept is that notes within tonal music are organized according to a structural hierarchy. From the available pool of tonal pitch materials, certain notes are selected to be of greater importance than others; within this selected subset of important notes, a further division identifies certain members of the subset as more prominent than others, and the process continues until the one note of greatest importance is reached.

The tonal material for Western music is obtained by dividing the octave (frequency ratio 2:1) into 12 equal logarithmic steps called *semitones*. The twelve notes so formed within the octave are shown in musical notation in the top musical staff-line of Fig. 2.1. (The arrangement of Fig. 2.1 was inspired by a diagram by Bharucha, 1984a; I have extended Bharucha's diagram to include the minor key hierarchy.) The notes begin with middle C on the extreme left-hand side of the staff and progress upwards in pitch. On the first staff-line of Fig. 2.1, those notes without a ♯ (sharp) sign in front of them correspond to the white notes on the piano keyboard. Those with a ♯ sign are the black notes that lie between the white notes. The full set of 12 notes is called the *chromatic scale*. An alternative notation of the chromatic scale is shown on the second staff-line of Fig. 2.1. Here the white notes are unchanged but the sharp notes have all been re-notated as flat notes. Each black note, therefore, has two names, and the name that is used in a given music transcription is usually the one that best describes its musical function in the piece.[1]

---

[1]Sharp and flat equivalence applies only to that kind of tuning system called "equal temperament." This is the kind of tuning you typically encounter with keyboard instruments. Other temperaments are possible, and are even encouraged by some theorists. Description of these systems is beyond the immediate concerns of the present chapter.

FIG. 2.1. The chromatic scale, the scales of C major and C minor, the tonic triads for C major and C minor, and the tonic note. The notation of the minor scale is simplified slightly from strict convention. Adapted from Bharucha (1984a) with permission of the author and publisher.

If we extract just the white notes from the top line of Fig. 2.1, we have the diatonic scale of C major shown in the third staff line of the figure. Now, however, the steps between adjacent tones are not all semitones. The steps in ascending sequential order are: whole-tone (2 semitones), whole-tone, semitone, whole-tone, whole-tone, whole-tone; a final semitone occurs between the seventh note of the scale and the first note of the scale in the next octave. This is the pattern doh-re-mi-fa-sol-la-ti-doh. Each note of the major scale has a scale degree associated with it, and the scale degree is denoted by a Roman numeral. The fourth line of Fig. 2.1 shows the scale of C harmonic minor. Note that the C minor scale differs from the C major scale by two important alterations: The third scale degree, E, is lowered to E♭, and the sixth scale degree, A, is lowered to A♭.

These alterations necessarily change the sequential order of whole-tones and semitones from the order generated for the major scale. In addition, there is now an interval of three semitones between the sixth and seventh scale degree.[2]

The fifth and sixth staff-lines of Fig. 2.1 extract, for the major and minor scale respectively, the notes of the tonic triad. These notes are the scale degrees I, III, and V, and in traditional music theory are thought to be more important than the other notes of the scale. The scale degrees I, III, and V have the names *tonic, mediant,* and *dominant* respectively. Finally, to emphasize this system of gradual reduction from the 12-tone set, the bottom line of Fig. 2.1 shows just the tonic note, thought to be the most important note of the tonic triad. The hierarchical arrangement of levels shown in Fig. 2.1 is referred to as the *tonal hierarchy.*

The tonic note is also called the key-note of the scale. Scales in other major and minor keys are obtained by shifting the tonic note to another location and following it by the same sequence of whole-tones and semitones as shown in Fig. 2.1 for the C major and C minor scale.

An experimental technique, the probe-tone method, has been found to be extremely effective in recovering the levels of abstraction described by music theory and summarized in Fig. 2.1. This technique was first described by Krumhansl and Shepard (1979) and has been elaborated by Krumhansl and colleagues in a series of subsequent papers; for a review, see Krumhansl (1990a). In one variant of the technique, a listener is presented with a musical context followed by a probe tone, one of the 12 tones of the chromatic scale (top of Fig. 2.1). The listener is asked to rate how well the probe fits the context in a musical sense. The set of 12 probe-tone judgments is called the *probe-tone profile* for the context.

Krumhansl and Kessler (1982) obtained, from musically trained listeners, probe-tone profiles for various key-defining contexts. These contexts were simultaneous combinations of tones—chords containing the notes of the tonic triad, and key-defining chord progressions called *cadences.* Examples of cadences are found at the ends of chorales or hymns.

The probe-tone profiles for major-key contexts were averaged to form the standardized profile for the major key; similarly, the probe-tone profiles for minor-key contexts were averaged to form the standardized profile for the minor key. Figure 2.2 shows the standardized profile for C-major contexts in the top panel, and the standardized profile for C-minor contexts in the bottom panel (after Krumhansl & Kessler, 1982, Fig. 2, p. 343.) Note that, for both profiles, highest

---

[2]The natural scale of C minor actually has three flats, B♭, E♭, and A♭. It has the same pattern of flats as the scale of E♭ major and is called the relative minor of E♭ major. The form given here, however, the harmonic minor of C, has the seventh degree raised to B natural. This form occurs frequently in tonal music, and was the form used by Krumhansl and Kessler (1982) to obtain the minor key profile (see subsequent text).

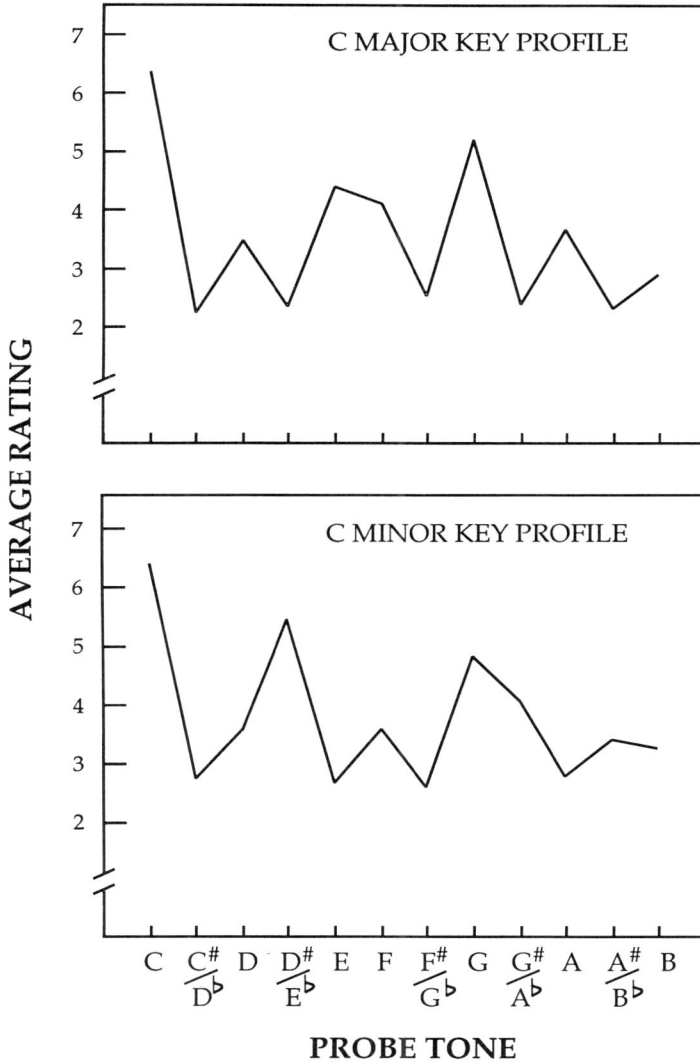

FIG. 2.2.   Tonality profiles for C major and C minor contexts (from Krumhansl & Kessler, 1982). Copyright © 1982 by the American Psychological Association. Adapted by permission of C. L. Krumhansl.

ratings were given to the tonic note, C, followed by the members of the tonic triad, followed by the remaining scale notes, and, last, followed by the notes outside the scale. Thus each experimentally derived profile shows the full distinction between hierarchical levels of structure that is described in traditional music theory.

In our work, we were first interested to discover whether similar profiles could be obtained from contexts consisting of melodies and melody-like fragments. It is possible, we thought, that single-voice melodies are not particularly appropriate contexts for demonstrating psychological evidence of the tonal hierarchy, especially if the listeners are musically untrained. Compared with chords and chord progressions, single-voice melodies place a greater demand on memory. Single-voice melodies lack the vertical (harmonic) structure provided by chords, so that a sense of tonality in melody has to be obtained by detecting and integrating information that unfolds over time. However, as shall be seen, the probe-tone technique provides useful data to address this issue.

The experiment I report next was done in collaboration with J. C. Johnston.

FIG. 2.3. "The March of the King of Laois" as transcribed for use as an experimental context for probe-tone ratings.

We selected and transcribed a short Celtic melody, "The March of the King of Laois." This is a very old tune (probably about 16th century) and we chose it for its simple and unambiguous tonal structure. The notes of the melody cluster about the major tonic triad C-E-G, and there is no change of key throughout the section we presented to the listeners. The melody, as transcribed by Johnston (1985), is given in Fig. 2.3. In the transcription, the melody was simplified by omitting decorative notes and rhythmic variation, so that all notes were of equal length. The melody was played to listeners at a fairly brisk tempo, about five notes per second. The notes of the melody were pure (sine-wave) tones, which have a quality not unlike the flute.

In the experiment, 31 listeners were tested, all university students lacking any formal musical training. Six of the 31 listeners considered themselves "tone deaf." On an initial hearing, no listener recognized the melody, so several playings were presented to familiarize the listener with the melody. Then the listener heard the melody 12 more times in the experimental trials. Each of the experimental trials was followed by a probe tone, as previously described, and the listener rated the probe tone on a 7-point scale of "goodness of musical fit" to the melody.

The tonality profile for the melody is shown in Fig. 2.4. The mean ratings for the 25 "non-tone deaf" listeners are connected by straight lines, and an overall similarity of the profile to the standardized C-major profile derived by Krumhansl and Kessler (1982) is apparent. The correlation between the probe-

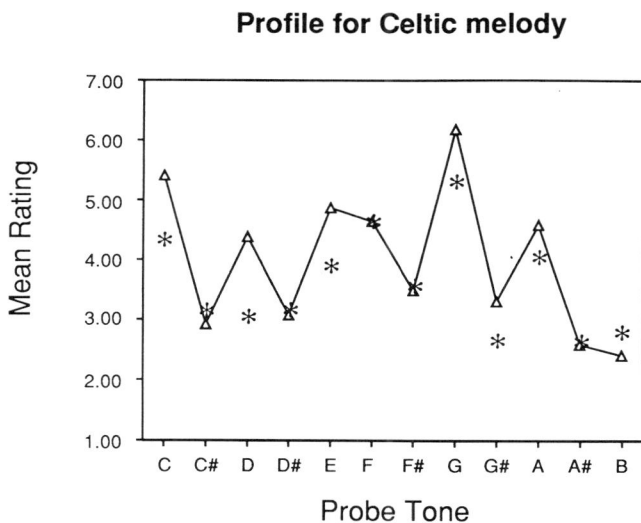

**Profile for Celtic melody**

FIG. 2.4.   Average probe-tone ratings for the melody based on the Celtic tune, "The March of the King of Laois." Connected points are the data for "non-tone deaf" listeners; asterisks are the data for the "tone deaf" listeners.

tone ratings for the melody profile and the probe-tone ratings for the standardized C-major profile was 0.89, a value indicating significantly close agreement.

The main difference between the melody profile and the standardized profile for the major key has to do with the relative assignment of ratings to the tonic C and the dominant G. In the standardized profile, the tonic C is rated higher than the dominant G, in accord with music-theoretic predictions. In the melody profile, the relationship is reversed. Examination of the distribution of notes in the melody reveals that there are about twice as many Gs as Cs—a total of 23 Gs as opposed to 11 Cs (allowing octave equivalence). The ratings obtained for the melody do not capture this degree of difference in frequency of occurrence. Rather, they may represent a compromise between rating tones in terms of two strategies. One strategy is influenced by the relative frequency of occurrence of the notes in the melody; the other is influenced by musical information that C is the tonic of the melody and should be accorded a privileged status. I return to this notion later.

The experiment has demonstrated that musically untrained listeners, therefore, are sensitive to the temporal information conveying tonal structure in a melody. Moreover, the so-called "tone deaf" listeners did not perform very differently on this test. Their data are shown in Fig. 2.4 as asterisks. It can be seen that their profile follows the profile for the other listeners fairly closely. The "tone deaf" did not emphasize the structurally important C and E as strongly as did the "non-tone deaf" listeners and they failed to isolate the scale note D from the nonscale notes on either side of it. In general, the profile recovered from the "tone deaf" may be described as one that conveys tonal structure, but more weakly than for the "non-tone deaf" listeners. The correlation between the probe-tone ratings for the melody profile and the probe-tone ratings for the standardized C-major profile derived by Krumhansl and Kessler (1982) was 0.78, which is respectably high and statistically significant.

In subsequent experiments, Johnston and I collected probe-tone profiles for altered versions of the Celtic melody. In these versions the melody was constructed, not around the major triad, C-E-G, but around either the diminished triad, C-Eb-Gb, or the augmented triad, C-E-G♯. For the two altered versions, the profiles showed that listeners were sensitive to the relative frequency of the notes, but the profiles were less well defined. Listeners were less sensitive to the functional differences between the notes. There may be something special about the major triad pattern C-E-G that enhanced the distinctions in ratings shown in Fig. 2.3. The next section discusses further work with this pattern.

## PROFILES OF MELODIC FRAGMENTS

I mentioned previously that the profile for the Celtic melody may have reflected a balance between the actual frequency of occurrence of the notes in the tune and the musical knowledge that each note within a key has a specific function, or weighting, assigned to it. This is important, because it means that the profile need not be a carbon copy of the frequency of occurrence of the events in a tune. It also means, however, that profiles are influenced by stimulus events.

The next profiles I report were obtained from melodic fragments, and they show further how profiles will shift with the nature of the pattern. The full details of the experiment are given in Cuddy and Badertscher (1987).

The first pattern was based on the major triad (as shown in the fifth staff-line of Fig. 2.1). In the key of C, this pattern was C-E-C-G. The second pattern was the ascending major scale (third staff-line of Fig. 2.1). The third pattern consisted of three notes from the major scale, the seventh, second, and fourth scale degree. In the key of C, this pattern was B-D-B-F. The three tones B-D-F form a triad called the *diminished triad*. On the surface, a diminished triad bears a certain resemblance to a major triad. Obviously, it has the same number of notes; more importantly, both triads in ascending or descending order are built from three nonadjacent scale steps having exactly one scale step in between them. But if you sing the two triads, or play them on the piano, you will hear that they sound very different. The first pattern contains the most important notes of the scale, and it sounds complete. The third pattern contains scale notes, but they are less important. This pattern sounds unfinished and seems to need a completion note. The pattern should sound complete if you follow the pattern with one of the notes of the tonic triad. This is called, in music theory, a "need for resolution."[3]

We tested first- through sixth-grade children, and adults with three levels of musical experience. Each listener rated 12 probe tones for each pattern. Each tone of the patterns and each probe tone was a "Shepard tone" (after Shepard, 1964, 1982), which has an organ-like quality.[4]

The children were told that the experimenter was trying to write a song and needed help with the ending. They were asked to listen to a pattern plus a probe tone and to rate whether it sounded "good" or "bad." Similarly, the adults were asked to rate the "goodness" of the probe tone as the final note of the pattern. A seven-point rating scale was used for both children and adults.

Because no significant differences among the children according to grade level and no significant differences among the adults according to level of musical experience were found, the data are shown averaged across the children's scores and averaged across the adults' scores. The average profiles for the children are shown in Fig. 2.5, and the average profiles for the adults are shown in Fig. 2.6.

---

[3]In music-theoretic terms, the seventh degree (B in the example) has a tendency to resolve to the tonic (C); the fourth degree (F) has a tendency to resolve to the mediant (E in the key of C major, Eb in the key of C minor).

[4]The construction of a "Shepard tone" involves the synthesis of octave equivalents with the amplitude of each component determined by a Gaussian envelope. The goal was to emphasize pitch class and de-emphasize pitch height (see Shepard, 1964, 1982). The tonal function of each note is discernible, but its octave location is ambiguous.

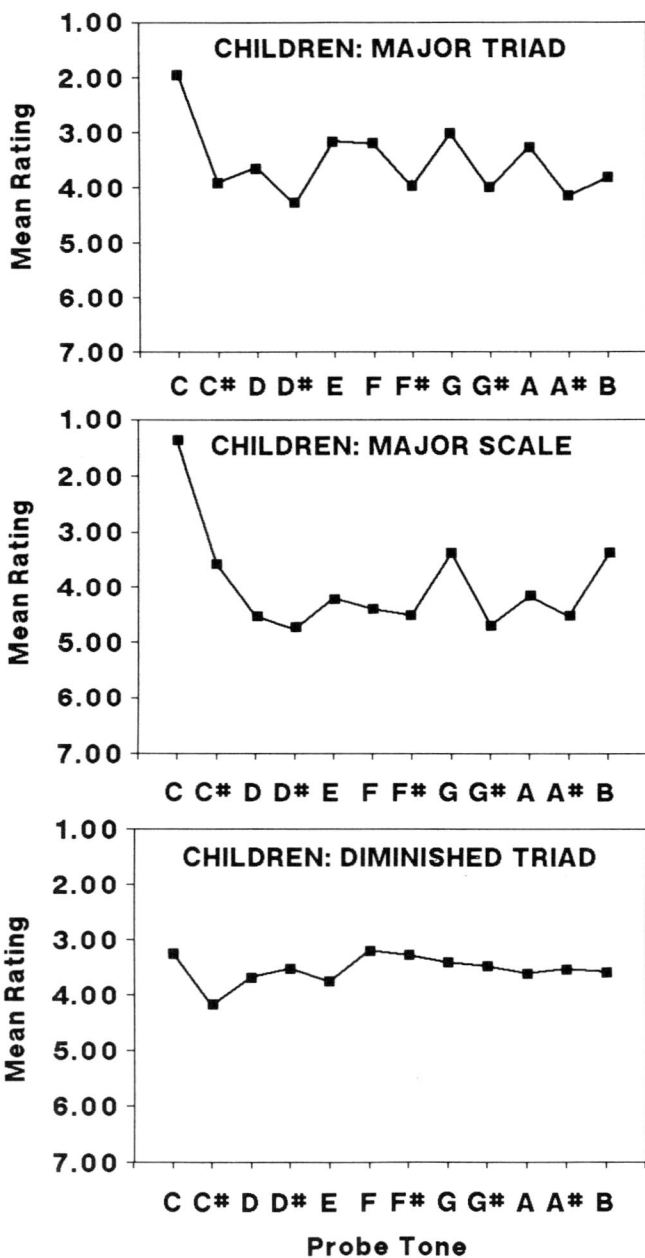

FIG. 2.5. Children's average probe-tone ratings for the major triad, major scale, and diminished triad patterns. Copyright © 1987 by the Psychonomic Society, Inc. Reprinted by permission of the publisher.

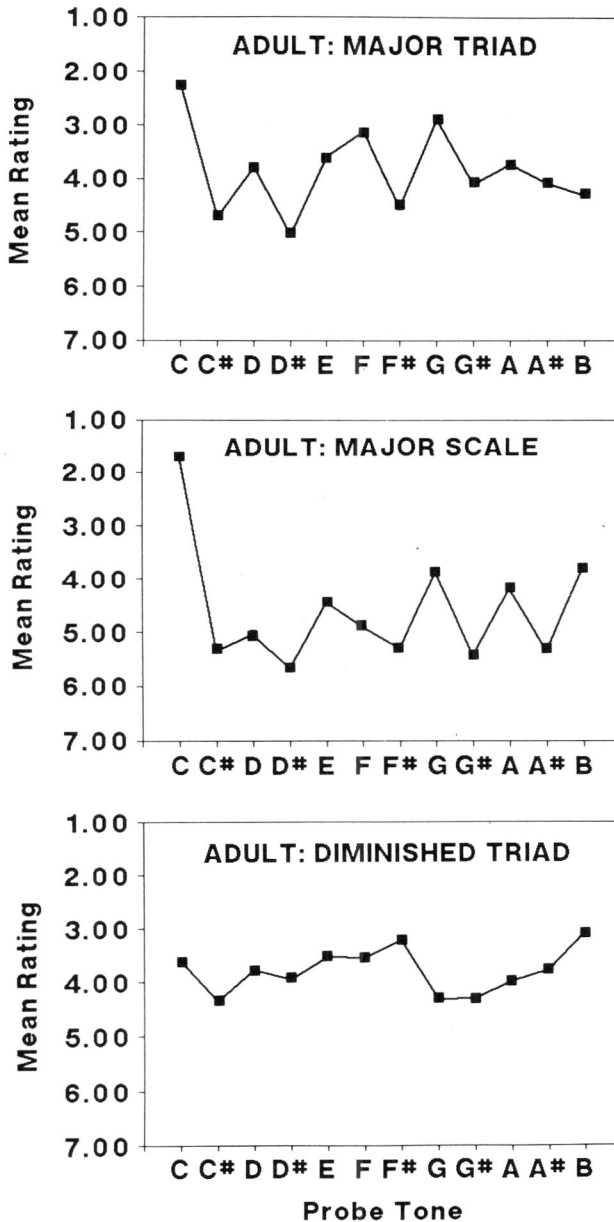

FIG. 2.6. Adults' average probe-tone ratings for the major triad, major scale, and diminished triad patterns. Copyright © 1987 by the Psychonomic Society, Inc. Reprinted by permission of the publisher.

The top panel of both Figs. 2.5 and 2.6 is the profile for the pattern based on the major triad. The children's and the adults' mean profiles are in close agreement, and in close agreement with the standardized profile for the major key derived by Krumhansl and Kessler (1982). Correlations between the obtained probe-tone ratings and the ratings for the standardized C-major profile were very high: 0.97 for the children's data, and 0.94 for the adults' data. Note that in the children's and the adults' profiles the full tonal hierarchy for the major key was recovered. The order of ratings for the probe tones was first the tonic note, followed by the other notes of the tonic triad, the other scale tones and, finally, the nonscale tones. The distinction between the other scale (nontriad) tones and nonscale tones is particularly important because neither type of tone occurs in the stimulus pattern. This distinction must be based on a strategy that engages an abstract musical knowledge.

The second panel of Figs. 2.5 and 2.6 shows the profiles for the major scale. Note here that there was a strong preference for the tonic note, but other features of the tonal hierarchy are somewhat attenuated, especially for the children. In particular, the children liked the notes C# and B as completion notes for the scale, perhaps because they are close in pitch to the tonic note.

The bottom panel of Figs. 2.5 and 2.6 shows the profiles for the diminished triad pattern (the third pattern). For the children, this pattern was meaningless. The profile is essentially flat. There were no statistically significant differences among the probe-tone ratings for this profile. Any variation in this profile must be attributed to chance. For the adults, the pattern suggested several completions, notably C, F#, and B. The probe-tone ratings for this profile did not correlate significantly with the probe-tone ratings for either the standardized profile for the key of C major or the standardized profile for the key of C minor derived by Krumhansl and Kessler (1982). (The pattern is contained in these keys, but did not appear to implicate a resolution to either.) The profile seems to be reflecting a kind of ambiguity between competing keys or tonal centers. Following a suggestion from C. L. Krumhansl (personal communication, 1987), I used the values from the standardized major-key profile to obtain a profile representing a mixture of keys. First I transposed the C-major profile to the key of B major, by shifting all the values one step to the left and wrapping the value for C around to B. A similar procedure was done to obtain a profile for F major, and the two values for each probe tone were averaged. The correlation between this mixed profile and the adult profile for the diminished triad pattern was 0.81, indicating a significant relationship. The result is suggestive of a polarization between two keys in the adults' profile, indicative of an ambiguous sense of structure.

This experiment with melodic fragments shows that the nature of the stimulus pattern is a crucial factor determining the application of tonal knowledge. The major triad appeared to be the most effective pattern of those studied, both for children and adults. Moreover, the major triad elicited the full set of musical distinctions accorded the tonal hierarchy of the major key for which it is the tonic triad. Listeners did not merely reproduce the three notes of the triad in their rating profiles.

## THE ROLE OF THE TONAL HIERARCHY
## IN MELODY COMPREHENSION

In this last section, I discuss the concept of the tonal hierarchy both with specific reference to the results of the distorted melodies test summarized, and with general reference to understanding the mental processes involved in melody recognition and comprehension.[5]

First, with respect to the distorted melodies test, and the question why we are able to recognize an error in an unfamiliar melody, a possible account is as follows: As the listener hears the unfolding sequence of notes that constitute the melody, he or she develops a sense of the key of the melody. This sense of key may arise from many cues: the scale-set from which the notes are selected, the rules by which the sequence is generated, the use of certain notes at points of rhythmic stress and at phrase endings, and so on. These cues characterize simple Western melodies of the tonal idiom, and can be detected in simple unfamiliar tunes. As part of the development of the sense of key, notes are perceived and interpreted in terms of their structural importance—tonic, dominant, and so forth. It is a two-way process, with the interpretation of notes in terms of structural importance tending to confirm the sense of key. In a sense, the listener is engaged in a strategy of hypothesis formation and testing.

On the other hand, however, the interpretation of a given note may appear to disconfirm the prevailing key. Such occurrences are used effectively in extended compositions for specific aesthetic effects. In the distorted melodies test, however, such an occurrence signals a probable error in the playing of the melody. The selection of melodies, and the instructions, encouraged listeners to expect simple, consistent, single-key melodies. The hypothesis likely included the assumption that such simple melodies are contained within a single key, and violations of the prevailing key are errors, not aesthetic deviations.

Moreover, the kind of disconfirmation referred to may be predictable in terms of the quantifiable function of tones within the tonal hierarchy. That is, the strength of the feeling that a note has been changed to an incorrect alternative

---

[5]It should be mentioned that the concept of the tonal hierarchy, and the probe-tone methodology—one of the techniques used in the empirical study of the tonal hierarchy—has recently been subject to considerable scrutiny. Many substantial issues are reviewed by Krumhansl (1990b). I have addressed some of these issues, insofar as they concern the data reported, in subsequent articles (Cuddy, in press; Cuddy & Thompson, 1992). The results of my further study have been to confirm both the essential validity of the concept and reliability of the technique. Many questions remain, but it is entirely appropriate to build from the initial definitions and constructs introduced in this chapter.

may depend on the relationship between the altered note and its original (correct) identity. For example, in Mawhinney's (1987) data, it was noted that a distortion of a melody where the tonic note was moved to an error note one semitone above the tonic (from C to C♯ with reference to Fig. 2.2) was easily recognized as incorrect. This semitone shift represents a shift from the top to the bottom of the tonal hierarchy. Melodies that had a note of intermediate importance in the tonal hierarchy, usually the third or fourth scale note, moved to a nondiatonic note, were detected with an intermediate level of accuracy. The melody with the poorest score ("When I'm 64") was in the key of C major; the alteration involved a change of the note B to the note A♯. Note that in Fig. 2.2 both B and A♯ have similar ratings in the C major profile—the shift in rating from the diatonic tone (B) to the nondiatonic tone (A♯) is not very great.

Such an analysis of this exploratory study raises a number of further questions. For example, a future study should independently manipulate the nature of the melody and the nature of the alteration. In general, a distortion in an unfamiliar melody for which the key is clearly implicated by the opening notes should be more easily recognized than a distortion in a melody for which the key is less clearly implicated. More specifically, the clarity of the implication will likely depend on the degree to which the opening notes outline the tonic triad of the key (Cohen, 1991). Here again, variability among listeners may be partially explained in terms of the degree to which their experience with the music of the tonal idiom has taught them to use appropriate cues for key detecting.

For more complex melodies, the questions become more complex. Listeners are capable of detecting key shifts in melodic excerpts, and of keeping track of the extent of key shift (Thompson & Cuddy, 1989). This finding implies that listeners can abstract and keep track of multiple tonal hierarchies. Notes may be assigned multiple levels of structural importance, and in this case, the task of detecting structural alterations in unfamiliar melodies becomes quite complicated.

With respect to general implications for melody comprehension, the general point is that the principles of tonal organization refer to processes that go beyond the first stages of acoustic processing and grouping according to acoustic principles. The principles of tonal organization assign perceptual identities to tones that they do not possess when presented in isolation. The identity of each tone derives from the relationship of the tone to an overall structural framework provided by the key. For listeners familiar with the Western tonal idiom, these relationships are abstracted quickly and without conscious effort. Nevertheless, they contribute to the perceived coherence or "meaning" of a melody, and help us detect melodic events that do not "make sense."

I emphasize the word "contribute" because, of course, knowledge of tonal hierarchies is not the only form of musical knowledge that might guide interpretation of a melody. As noted in the beginning of this chapter, the research strategy has been to isolate a particular topic for study. Connections must be drawn between the abstract form of knowledge represented by tonal hierarchies, and knowledge of the actual events that are specific or unique to a given melody. Bharucha (1984b) has aptly referred to the latter as *event hierarchies*; event hierarchies comprise rules for the succession of events, and invoke expectancies about temporal patterning. Expectancies may reflect the influence of structural importance of tones, but will reflect other influences as well. Other chapters in this volume deal with work that has been done, or needs to be done, on perceiving the temporal structure of musical events.

It was encouraging, from the point of view of musical education and practice, to find that our self-reported "tone deaf" listeners were in fact not entirely "deaf" to the tonal organization of melody. Perhaps for them the sense of tonality is capable of further development, leading to the potential for greater music appreciation. Moreover, the work that is currently ongoing in my laboratory and other laboratories, is leading to the implication that a good sense of tonality for the Western tonal idiom does not hinder our ability to pick up the tonal organization of other cultures, or the organization of pitch materials for entirely novel idioms. In learning to abstract the relations of our Western tonal system, we probably learn a general strategy of attending to cues for pitch organization. Thus, exposure to the music of our Western culture appears to enhance our comprehension of the form and coherence of music generally.

## ACKNOWLEDGMENTS

I am grateful to C. L. Krumhansl, Cornell University, for discussions, advice, and encouragement, Lise de Kok and Dan Scheidt for invaluable technical assistance, and M. G. Wiebe for editorial comments on an earlier version of the chapter. I also thank Tom Mawhinney for giving me access to his data for further analysis.

Research was supported by an operating grant from the Natural Sciences and Engineering Council of Canada and an award from the Advisory Research Committee of Queen's University.

## REFERENCES

Bharucha, J. J. (1984a). Anchoring effects in music: The resolution of dissonance. *Cognitive Psychology, 16,* 485–519.

Bharucha, J. J. (1984b). Event hierarchies, tonal hierarchies, and assimilation: A reply to Deutsch and Dowling. *Journal of Experimental Psychology: General, 113,* 421–425.

Cohen, A. J. (1991). Tonality and perception: Musical scales primed by excerpts from *The Well-Tempered Clavier* of J. S. Bach. *Psychological Research [Psychologische Forschung], 53,* 305–314.

Cuddy, L. L. (in press). Melodic patterns and tonal structure. *Psychomusicology.*

Cuddy, L. L., & Badertscher, B. (1987). Recovery of the tonal hierarchy: Some comparisons across age and levels of musical experience. *Perception and Psychophysics, 41,* 609–620.

Cuddy, L. L., Cohen, A. J., & Mewhort, D. J. K. (1981). Perception of structure in short melodic sequences. *Journal of Experimental Psychology: Human Perception and Performance, 7,* 869–883.

Cuddy, L. L., Cohen, A. J., & Miller, J. (1979). Melody recognition: The experimental application of musical rules. *Canadian Journal of Psychology, 33,* 148–157.

Cuddy, L. L., & Thompson, W. F. (1992). Asymmetry of perceived key movement in chorale sequences: Converging evidence from a probe-tone analysis. *Psychological Research [Psychologische Forschung], 54,* 51–59.

Deutsch, D. (1982). Grouping mechanisms in music. In D. Deutsch (Ed.), *The psychology of music* (pp. 99–134). New York: Academic.

Deutsch, D., & Feroe, J. (1981). The internal representation of pitch sequences in tonal music. *Psychological Review, 88,* 503–522.

Dowling, W. J. (1991). Tonal strength and melody recognition after short and long delays. *Perception and Psychophysics, 50,* 305–313.

Dowling, W. J., & Harwood, D. L. (1986). *Music cognition.* New York: Academic.

Edworthy, J. (1985). Melodic contour and musical structure. In P. Howell, I. Cross, & R. West (Eds.), *Musical structure and cognition* (pp. 169–188). London: Academic.

Ehrenfels, C. von. (1937). On Gestalt-qualities. *American Journal of Psychology, 44,* 521–524. (Original work published 1890)

Johnston, J. C. (1985). *Perceptual salience of melodic structures.* Unpublished honors thesis, Queen's University, Kingston, Ontario, Canada.

Kalmus, H., & Fry, D. B. (1980). On tune deafness (dysmelodia): Frequency, development, genetics, and musical background. *Annals of Human Genetics, 43,* 369–382.

Kennedy, M. (1980). *The concise Oxford dictionary of music* (3rd ed.). New York: Oxford University Press.

Koffka, K. (1935). *Principles of Gestalt psychology.* New York: Harcourt, Brace, & World.

Krumhansl, C. L. (1983). Perceptual structures for tonal music. *Music Perception, 1,* 28–62.

Krumhansl, C. L. (1990a). *Cognitive foundations of musical pitch.* New York: Oxford University Press.

Krumhansl, C. L. (1990b). Tonal hierarchies and rare intervals in music cognition. *Music Perception, 7,* 309–324.

Krumhansl, C. L., & Keil, F. C. (1982). Acquisition of the hierarchy of tonal functions in music. *Memory and Cognition, 10,* 243–251.

Krumhansl, C. L., & Kessler, E. J. (1982). Tracing the dynamic changes in perceived tonal organization in a spatial representation of musical keys. *Psychological Review, 89,* 334–368.

Krumhansl, C. L., & Shepard, R. N. (1979). Quantification of the hierarchy of tonal functions within a diatonic context. *Journal of Experimental Psychology: Human Perception and Performance, 5,* 579–594.

Mawhinney, T. A. (1987). *Tone-deafness and low musical abilities: An investigation of prevalence, characteristics, and tractability.* Unpublished doctoral dissertation, Queen's University, Kingston, Ontario, Canada.

Randel, D. (Ed.). (1986). *The new Harvard dictionary of music.* Cambridge, MA: Belknap.

Shepard, R. N. (1964). Circularity in judgments of relative pitch. *Journal of the Acoustical Society of America, 36,* 2346–2353.

Shepard, R. N. (1982). Structural representations of musical pitch. In D. Deutsch (Ed.), *The psychology of music* (pp. 344–390). New York: Academic.

Thompson, W. F., & Cuddy, L. L. (1989). Sensitivity to key change in chorale sequences: A comparison of single voices and four-voice harmony. *Music Perception, 7,* 151–168.

# Tonal Structure of Melodies

James C. Bartlett
*University of Texas at Dallas*

A furniture store in Dallas once used television and radio commercials in which the owner of the store—we call him Mr. Springfield—played the role of a loveable, clumsy, buffoon. In one of these commercials, which was to feature Mr. Springfield, it transpired that our hero had forgotten the commercial and gone away fishing. In another commercial, the camera zoomed in on the rattling door handle of a locked door as Mr. Springfield struggled, apparently having lost his key, on the other side. In still another commercial, this one on radio, the voice-over was accompanied by rapid banjo picking that we assumed was Mr. Springfield's. All went well until the final note, which was one half-step sharp. The announcer's voice uttered the standard last line: "Oh . . . Mr. Springfield . . ."

The banjo commercial was based on two tacit assumptions regarding tonal structure of music. The first assumption is that virtually all listeners, whether they are trained musicians or not, will have no trouble identifying Mr. Springfield's "sour" note. Given the low level of musical talent that most of us possess, and the small amount of formal musical training that most of us receive, this assumption is telling. It is a claim that knowledge of the tonal structure of melodies, a sense of the key in which melodies are played, is widely shared in our culture. We may not be able to sing "in tune," or to pick out a simple melody on the piano, but we are able to identify an atonal melody, or an out-of-key note in an otherwise tonal melody. And not only can we identify atonal melodies and out-of-key notes, we appear to identify them automatically, without anything resembling a conscious critical analysis of the music. One does not need to concentrate to hear Mr. Springfield's mistake; the wrong note has the perceptual quality of jumping out at the listener from the pattern of "right" notes. It is virtually impossible to ignore.

The second assumption underlying Mr. Springfield's banjo commercial concerns our emotional reaction to out-of-key notes. Noticing a note has been played out of key hardly engages a distanced, cool, appraisal of Mr. Springfield's musical aptitude. The note sounds bad; it actually seems to hurt one's ears. This emotional component to our sense of tonality is critically important to the power of music. It certainly helped this listener remember Mr. Springfield and his store!

## THE CONCEPT OF SCALE

That ordinary people have a sense of tonality that affects their emotional reactions to music is supported by more than Mr. Springfield's commercial. Quite a number of experiments have shown strong effects of a particular type of tonal structure, that pertaining to musical *scales*. In order to understand such experiments, let us consider the musical scale most common in western cultures. This is the diatonic major scale, the scale portrayed in the "do-re-mi" tune from *The Sound of Music*. This scale is defined by a pattern of pitch relationships, that is, a pattern of pitch distances between successive scale notes. The pattern is that of 2—2—1—2—2—2—1, where each "1" corresponds to a semitone interval (that between one note and the next note higher in pitch), and each "2" corresponds to a 2-semitone interval (that between one note and the next note *after* the next note higher in pitch). Because the diatonic scale is defined as a pattern of pitch intervals instead of as a set of particular pitch values, it can be played in higher or lower pitch ranges and maintain its essential identity (i.e., the diatonic scale can be transposed to different "keys"). To hear the diatonic major scale in the key of C, simply find a piano or some other keyboard instrument and play the white-colored notes starting from middle C to the C an octave higher. Note that the first and second intervals, as well as the fourth, fifth, and sixth intervals, occur where intermediate black-colored notes are skipped—these are the "2"-semitone intervals of the scale. The same diatonic scale can be played in any other key simply by starting on the appropriate note and playing a rising sequence of notes with the 2—2—1—2—2—2—1 pattern of intervals. However, when playing the scale in any key besides C, it will be necessary to use at least one black-colored note, and avoid at least one white-colored note, in order to preserve the major diatonic scale pattern. Those black-note substitutions are called "sharps" and "flats."

The concept of scale allows us to distinguish among melodies in terms of their scalar structure (Cross, Howell, & West, 1983; Dowling & Harwood, 1986); melodies can be said to differ in how well they conform to scalar structure. At one extreme, a highly scalar melody is one whose notes all fit the same diatonic major scale. If such a melody were played on the piano in the key of C, it would require only the white-colored notes. At the other extreme, a nonscalar or "atonal" melody fits no diatonic major scale. Playing such a melody regardless of key would require both white-colored and black-colored notes; it deviates from the scalar interval pattern. In more musical terminology, a highly scalar melody has no "accidental" alterations, that is, no sharps or flats beyond those in the key signature (and no sharps and flats at all when played in the key of C). Speaking very roughly, the more alterations a nonscalar melody has, the less scalar it is.

Of course, accidentals within a melody do not usually render this melody nonscalar. Many melodies that sound quite normal and pleasant, at least to adults, include many notes outside of their keys. For instance, Dowling (1988) examined the sheet music for 223 nursery songs, 317 adult folksongs, and 44 songs from Schubert's *Die schone Mullerin* and *Die Winterreise*. The Schubert songs, from the 1820s, are in the classical-romantic tradition of European music, but "have a folk-like, singable character, and are of the same general length and form as the songs in the other categories" (Dowling, 1988, p. 121.) Analysis of all the songs revealed a noteworthy result. Accidental alterations were present in only 7% of the nursery songs. However, alterations were present in 31% of the adult folksongs and 96% of the Schubert songs. Admittedly, some Shubert songs might sound less than perfectly scalar, or at any rate they might sound a bit "complicated," to musically untrained listeners. However, folk songs sound scalar to just about everyone, and yet almost one third of Dowling's sample of folk songs had at least one out-of-key note.

Just how nonscalar notes can coexist with scalar structure has not been thoroughly explored. However, one factor is clearly rhythmic—if the accented or strong notes of a passage all are members of the same diatonic scale, the melody sounds tonal despite a number of nonscalar notes on unaccented or "weak" beats (Cross et al., 1983). Another factor is "anchoring": Bharucha (1984) showed that if a melody contains a nonscalar note that is followed by a scalar note that is proximal in pitch, the sense of tonality tends to be well preserved. Indeed, a melody with a note that is nonscalar but anchored can be highly confusable with a melody containing no nonscalar notes at all. Try playing C—E—C—F♯—G—C on the piano or another musical instrument. Now try playing C—E—C—F—G—C. The two sound quite similar. But if you switch the positions of the fourth and fifth notes (C—E—C—G—F♯—C and C—E—C—G—F—C), the first melody sounds atonal and quite different from the second.

## SCALAR STRUCTURE AND PERCEPTION OF MELODIES

There is more to say about anchoring later. For the present, let us turn to evidence that ordinary people, even non-musicians, are sensitive to the scalar structure of melodies. It has been known for some time that scalar melodies, those melodies conforming to a diatonic major scale, are better remembered than nonscalar melodies (Francès, 1958/1988). It also has been shown that people who have heard a short musical sequence can generate notes of the appropriate musical scale (Cohen, 1978; Francès, 1958/1988). Of greater relevance here, scalar structure of melodies affects subjects' (even childrens') aesthetic reactions to these stimuli; scalar melodies sound "better." For example, Krumhansl and Keil (1982) played six-note melodies to adults as well as to children from Grades 1–6. Each six-note melody began with the notes C—E—C—G and continued with two additional notes that sometimes were scalar (within the key of C) and sometimes were nonscalar (outside the key of C). The listeners were simply asked to rate how "good" or "bad" each melody sounded on a 7-point scale. (The children chose one of seven dots ordered along a line with a smiling face at one end and a frowning face at the other.) All subjects, even the first and second graders, judged the scalar melodies as "better" than the nonscalar melodies. In a more recent study, Dowling (1988) showed that knowledge of scalar structure of melodies can be present as early as 3 years of age. Dowling developed tonal and atonal transformations of eight familiar tunes—both kinds of transformations made the tunes hard to recognize, but the atonal transformation made them also nonscalar, that is, out of conformity with any diatonic scale. Children were played each of the transformations, including both the scalar and nonscalar transformations, and were asked, in essence, whether each tune sounded "funny" or not. Although not all children could perform the task, children who were rated as being better singers—even "better singers" only 3 years old— distinguished the scalar from the nonscalar melodies at a level exceeding chance.

If children as young as 3 have a sense of scalar structure, one would expect that adults would have this sense also, even adults who lack formal musical training. Indeed, Cross et al. (1983) varied the degree of scalar structure in artificially derived melodies, and found that both musicians and nonmusicians gave generally higher "liking" ratings to the more scalar melodies that they heard. Indeed, they detected no differences between the ratings of musicians versus nonmusicians.

It might seem puzzling that children as young as 3 years old and adults with no formal musical training have a sense of scalar structure. Is it not obvious that trained musical experts know more about structural properties of music than untrained musical novices? It is obvious indeed, but it is important to consider that approximation to scalar structure—the sense of a melody's maintaining a key—is only one aspect of the listener's sense of tonality. Other aspects are acquired much later, and perhaps not at all in the absence of training. For instance, the Krumhansl and Keil (1982) study showed not only that their more scalar melodies received higher "goodness" ratings—they also showed that within the set of scalar melodies goodness ratings were higher for those that ended on the tonic (C in the key of C), or other notes of the major triad (C, E, and G in the key of C), than to those that ended with other diatonic notes (D, F, A, and B in the key of C). Thus, within the set of scalar melodies, some clearly are more tonal than others. However, this sensitivity to tonality differences within the set of scalar melodies was not present in the youngest (first- and second-grade) subjects—it appeared to emerge gradually in the years from 6 to 12.

Psychologists have a good deal to learn about different types of knowledge of tonality and their order of emergence in the course of development and formal musical training (Dowling, 1982). However, experiments like that of Krumhansl and Keil (1982), as well musicological considerations, support a distinction between melodies' *scalar structure* from what has been termed their *modal structure* (Cross, Howell, & West, 1985; Dowling & Harwood, 1986). Whereas scalar structure refers to a listener's sense of key, his or her feeling for what is "in key" versus "out of key," modal structure refers to more refined knowledge of which in-key notes are dominant or particularly stable. Studies of childrens' singing abilities, and their goodness/silliness ratings of tunes, make it clear that a sense of scalar structure, a sense of what is "in key" versus "out of key," emerges quite early and maintains itself throughout the life span even in the absence of formal musical training. In contrast to knowledge of scalar structure, knowledge of modal structure appears to develop more slowly and is more closely linked to formal musical training. The remainder of this chapter focuses on scalar structure, which appears more widely shared among persons with differing musical backgrounds and aptitudes. Our specific concern is with the deceptively simple question of *why* scalar melodies sound "stable" and "good," whereas nonscalar melodies sound "unstable" and "bad," even to those of us nonmusical persons who identify with Mr. Springfield.

## WHY SCALAR STRUCTURE AFFECTS PERCEPTION: THE IDEA OF PATTERN GOODNESS

In approaching the question of scalar structure in melodies, it helps to consider some related phenomena outside the field of music. A few decades ago the Gestalt psychologists, Wertheimer (1944), Köhler (1947), and Koffka (1935) among others, began studying the phenomenon of pattern goodness, relying primarily on visual stimuli. They marshalled many observations and clever demonstrations pointing to the general conclusion that some visual patterns make good "gestalts"—that is, "wholes" with emergent properties that cause them to be different from the sums of their parts. A few of their examples are shown in Fig. 3.1: In each of these examples, several elements of a pattern form a perceptual group—a "Gestalt"—that is perceived to be separate from another Gestalt formed from another subset of elements.

Most people today have had some exposure to concepts of Gestalt psychology—we have "Gestalt medicine" (treat the whole patient), "Gestalt psychotherapy" (ditto), and Richardson, Texas, has a "Gestalt Hair Salon" (I leave the reader to interpret that one). However, the arguments of Gestalt

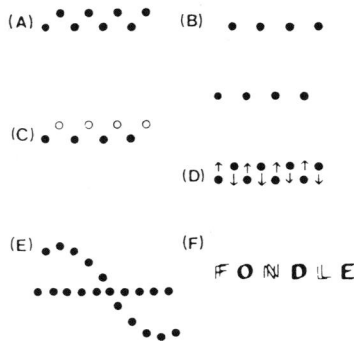

FIG. 3.1. Gestalt phenomena: Dots are perceived as forming one group that follows a zig-zagging line (a), or two separate groups (b), illustrating the Gestalt principle of proximity. Dots are perceived as forming two separate groups due to dissimilarity (c), or "common fate" revealed by similar direction and extent of movement (d). Dots are perceived as a wavy line crossing a straight line illustrating the principle of good continuation. Letters are alternately perceived as forming two groups based on similarity, or one group based on prior learning of a word (f). From Dowling and Harwood (1986).

psychology are often misconstrued. The claim was not that all collections of elements form good gestalts; rather it was that some collections form very good gestalts, others form very poor gestalts, and others fall somewhere in between. Put simply, there is a dimension of "gestaltness," or "pattern goodness," and different patterns fall at different points on this dimension.

A key claim of the Gestalt psychologists was that good patterns differ from relatively poor patterns in having greater perceptual stability. This notion of stability has always been somewhat difficult to grasp, and matters were not helped very much by the theory of stability that the Gestalt psychologists forwarded. They proposed the existence of mysterious psychic forces that act on internal impressions of patterns, gradually transforming these patterns into better and more stable forms. A good pattern would not be changed by these forces, but a poor pattern might be dramatically distorted over time. Experiments were done to test the idea, and some of the stimuli used in one such experiment (Perkins, 1932) are shown in Fig. 3.2. Subjects initially studied five visual patterns, and attempted to reproduce these forms from memory immediately, and again after delays of 1, 2, 8, 15, 29, and 48 days. There was some indication that successive reproductions moved in the direction of goodness, that is, these reproductions sometimes appeared to become gradually more symmetrical, as shown in Fig. 3.2. As symmetry is associated with the goodness of patterns, the findings suggested that indeed there may be forces that "push" internal impressions of patterns in the direction of goodness.

The implications of Perkins' (1932) study, as well as of several similar studies, have been questioned over the years. For example, interpretive issues were raised by the absence of distortions toward goodness in *recognition* memory as well as *reproduction* of forms (Riley, 1962). Recognition is generally much easier than reproduction, which depends on subjects' drawing abilities as well as their memories. However, if there truly exist psychic forces that distort impressions of patterns toward goodness, subjects should tend to recognize falsely patterns that are better than patterns they have previously seen, as well as to *reproduce* such patterns. But such biases toward goodness in recognition memory are not readily observed. Indeed, Hanawalt (1937) tested subjects first on their ability to reproduce forms and then on their ability to recognize these forms. He showed that subjects were quite capable of judging that a copy of a previously viewed form matched this form better than did their own drawing. This result is reminiscent of the everyday experience of trying to sing a melody heard earlier, only to produce a quite distorted (and inferior) rendition. Upon hearing the original a second time, it is easy to tell it is a much better match to one's prior experience than was one's own reproduction.

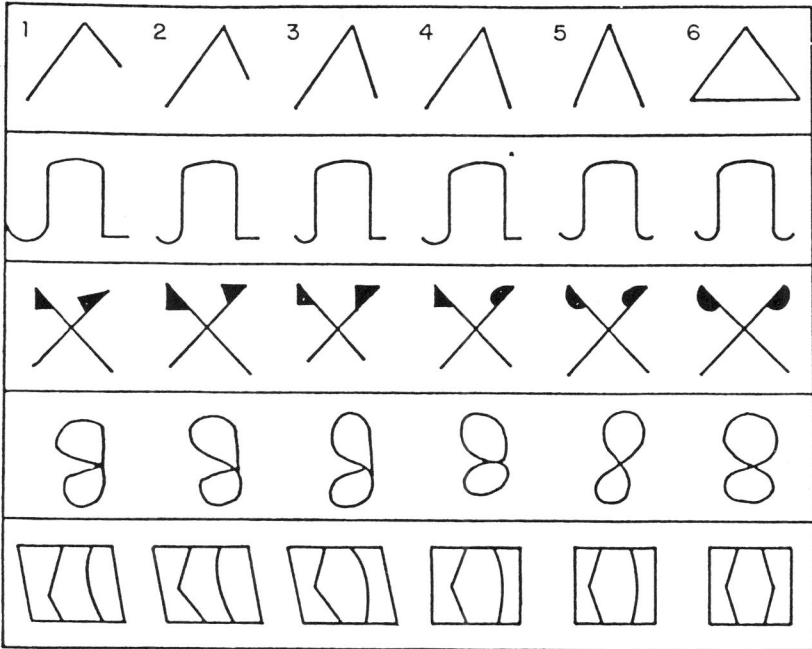

FIG. 3.2.   Examples of successive reproductions of forms in the experiment by Perkins (1932). From Riley (1962).

## PATTERN GOODNESS
## AND PERCEIVED ALTERNATIVES

Due to problems of interpreting studies on memory for forms, the Gestaltists'
hypothesis of mysterious psychic forces distorting memories toward goodness
is no longer taken seriously today. However, that goodness of patterns is an
important dimension, and that poor patterns are unstable in certain ways, has
never been disproven and indeed has been repeatedly supported in research.
Garner (1974) and his colleagues have contributed some of this research, and
Fig. 3.3 shows some of the stimuli they have used—each of these stimuli is
a pattern of five dots placed on a 3 × 3 grid.

A first important finding from Garner's research (Garner & Clement, 1963)
is that if subjects are asked to rate dot patterns for "goodness," they give much
higher ratings to some patterns than others. You could probably have guessed
that the upper-most pattern in Fig. 3.3 would be rated as "better" than the
bottom pattern, and indeed it was (the scale went from 1 for the best patterns
to 7 for the worst). Several studies showed that the "better" patterns were:
(a) more rapidly encoded or identified; (b) better remembered in recognition,
reproduction, and other memory tasks; and (c) received shorter verbal descriptions (try describing the top three patterns in Fig. 3.3 and then the bottom three).
Most important, good patterns have few perceived alternatives (Garner, 1970).
Specifically, if people are given the task of "free categorization," in which they
simply sort dot patterns into a number of piles based on similarity, they sort
the better patterns into smaller, more individualized piles (Fig. 3.3 includes the
mean size of the pile for each pattern shown). The poorer patterns are placed
in larger, "miscellaneous" piles containing other poor patterns.

That goodness of patterns is linked to number of alternatives provides a new
perspective on the instability of poor patterns. According to Garner (1970), poor
patterns are unstable precisely in the sense that they are perceived as members of relatively large sets of essentially similar alternative stimuli. Perceived
as being members of relatively large sets, poor patterns are perceived as being
changeable in a large number of ways while still remaining within these sets.
In contrast, good patterns are perceived as members of relatively small sets.
This means that they are perceived as being changeable in only a very few ways
without moving outside their sets. These ideas sound abstract, but think of the
piles into which patterns are sorted. Changing the position of a dot in a good,
"stable" pattern would likely cause it to be sorted into a different pile. In contrast, changing a dot in a poor, "unstable" pattern would likely allow it to remain in the same "miscellaneous" pile. In summary, poor patterns are perceived
as easily changeable, and this is the reason they are perceived as unstable as
compared to good patterns.

One of Garner's (1970) most important claims is that a stimulus is not perceived as an isolated entity. It is always perceived as a member of some set

| CODE | PATTERN | MEAN RATING | MEAN GROUP SIZE |
|---|---|---|---|
| 11 | ⦂ | 1.00 | 9.35 |
| 12 | ⦂ | 1.03 | 8.25 |
| 41 | ⦂ | 1.55 | 9.80 |
| 42 | ⦂ | 1.71 | 12.69 |
| 43 | ⦂ | 1.74 | 14.04 |
| 44 | ⦂ | 1.78 | 11.26 |
| 45 | ⦂ | 1.77 | 10.40 |
| 46 | ⦂ | 2.24 | 12.16 |
| 47 | ⦂ | 3.05 | 15.36 |
| 48 | ⦂ | 3.50 | 16.69 |
| 81 | ⦂ | 3.40 | 14.52 |
| 82 | ⦂ | 4.59 | 15.43 |
| 83 | ⦂ | 4.77 | 16.81 |
| 84 | ⦂ | 4.80 | 16.37 |
| 85 | ⦂ | 5.19 | 16.39 |
| 86 | ⦂ | 5.11 | 16.69 |
| 87 | ⦂ | 5.49 | 15.74 |

FIG. 3.3.   Mean ratings of pattern goodness and mean size of groupings for different dot patterns. Taken from Garner and Clement (1963).

of alternative stimuli. In most cases the alternatives are not explicitly present, but are inferred by the observer. But even if implicit, they are psychologically real. The inferred alternatives to a stimulus determine which of its features we take as unique, what sets it apart from other stimuli, and how good and stable a pattern it is (see Kahneman & Miller, 1986).

Consider meeting a person and being impressed that his face has a very large nose. This happens, according to Garner's (1970, 1974) account, because the face evokes a set of alternative faces that share many of its features but not its large nose—hence the large nose jumps out in perceptual awareness. Like

Mr. Springfield's sour note, it seems almost impossible to ignore. Of course, if we came from a country in which noses were generally large, such a face would evoke a different set of alternatives—namely, a set of faces all having large noses. Then, the nose would not jump out at all.

Garner's (1974) views on pattern goodness and perceptual stability have a highly attractive aspect—they suggest an explanation for the fundamental puzzle that repeated reproductions of previously viewed forms sometimes show distortions in the direction of pattern goodness. The original account of the distortion phenomenon was that mysterious forces inside the brain exerted a kind of pressure on memories for poor forms, such that these memories were gradually transformed into better forms. This account did not survive, but the initial phenomenon of distortions toward goodness was never seriously in question. How then might it be explained?

Garner's (1974) account starts from the plausible assumption that the sets of alternatives evoked by different patterns are not mutually exclusive. In fact, we might suppose that if poor patterns have large sets of perceived alternatives, and good patterns have relatively small sets of perceived alternatives, then there are probably cases in which the alternative set for a poor pattern *includes* that for a good pattern. The consequence is provocative: The poor pattern should be perceived as easily changeable into the better pattern; yet the good pattern should *not* be perceived as easily changeable into the poorer pattern. We should find asymmetrical relationships between good and poor patterns.

Following this suggestion, Handel and Garner (1966) convincingly demonstrated asymmetrical relatedness of good and poor patterns. Subjects were given two 3 × 3 matrices, the left-hand matrix containing a five-dot pattern, and the right-hand matrix blank. Their task was to "draw a pattern of five dots, which was suggested by, but different from, the pattern in the left-hand matrix." Their responses revealed asymmetrical relationships such as those shown in Fig. 3.4. Poorer patterns tended to evoke patterns that were similar, but better. But good patterns produced no corresponding tendency to evoke patterns that were similar, but worse. Thus, the association process tended to move away from poor patterns in the direction of better patterns. This result is reminiscent of the Gestaltist's observation that memories for forms become distorted in the direction of goodness. However, there is no need to posit mysterious psychic forces that gradually change internal impressions in the direction of goodness. Rather, the data provide evidence for two points: First, a pattern will be used as an associate to another pattern only if it is a member of the same set of perceived alternatives. Second, sets of alternatives for patterns are often nested, such that the set of alternatives for a poor pattern often includes that for a better pattern, but not vice versa. Figure 3.5 illustrates this concept of nesting.

The effect of pattern goodness on asymmetry of pattern relationships shows up when subjects rate pattern similarity. Tversky and Gati (1978) showed subjects pairs of patterns, each pair consisting of a relatively good pattern and a

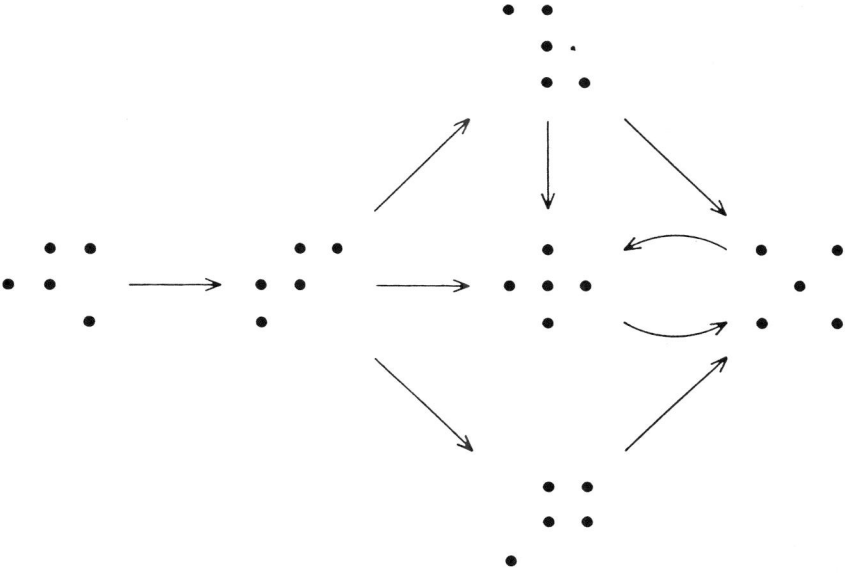

FIG. 3.4.   An example of asymmetric associations of patterns. Associations are produced unidirectionally for all patterns shown except for the " + " and the "x." From Garner (1974). Reprinted by permission.

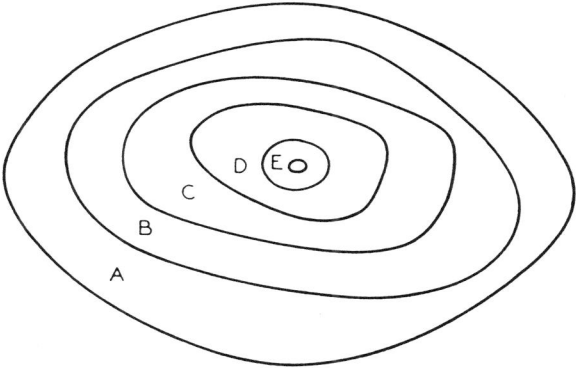

FIG. 3.5.   A conception of subsets of unequal size produced by nesting, with each subset including all smaller subsets. From Garner (1974). Reprinted by permission.

relatively poor pattern. The task was to rate the similarity of the left-hand pattern to the right-hand pattern on a 20-point scale. The finding was that similarity was higher when the left-hand pattern was the poorer of the two. Poor patterns are more similar to good patterns than good patterns are to poor patterns.

## PERCEIVED ALTERNATIVES
## AND SCALAR STRUCTURE OF MELODIES

The ideas that good patterns have few perceived alternatives, and that the alternatives for good patterns can be nested within those for poor patterns, turn out to be relevant to scalar structure of melodies. This notion rests on two important points. First, pattern goodness in the Gestalt sense was never intended to be restricted to vision. Indeed, musical stimuli, and especially melodies, have long been viewed as prime examples of gestalts. Whereas a melody consists of a sequence of notes, research (Dowling, 1972) suggests that we "hear" a melody as grouped rhythmically into phrases. Moreover, melodies are transposable: A melody retains its essential identity regardless of the pitch level (or "key") in which it is played. Anyone familiar with "Jingle Bells" or "I Did it my Way" can recognize those melodies in any of 12 different keys. This means that a melody exists apart from any particular set of pitches—it is truly a whole that differs fundamentally from the sum of its individual parts.

A second point is that differences in stability of different patterns, and asymmetrical relatedness between more and less stable patterns, are easily observed in the music domain. In one experiment, Krumhansl (1979) had musically sophisticated subjects judge the similarity of pairs of musical notes within the context of a musical key (C major). Asymmetrical similarity was clearly in evidence, as the rated similarity between a diatonic (scalar) note and a nondiatonic (nonscalar) note was higher when the nondiatonic note was presented first. In a more recent study (Krumhansl, Bharucha, & Castellano, 1982) subjects listened to pairs of seven-chord sequences, and judged whether or not a single chord had been changed. When (a) the prevailing key was C major, (b) a chord was in fact changed between the two sequences, and (c) the change was to a key (F♯) musically distant from C major, asymmetries appeared in judgments of the patterns. Mistaken judgments that the two sequences were identical were quite frequent (39%) when the unstable F♯ chord was in the first sequence, but much less frequent (8%) when it occurred in the second sequence. This pattern suggested that the similarity between the two chord sequences was greater when the sequence containing the out-of-key chord came first.

These asymmetrical similarity effects observed by Krumhansl et al. (1982) pertain as much to modal structure as they do to scalar structure, and indeed, they have been obtained primarily with musically sophisticated subjects. However, the effects extend readily to scalar structure of melodies, and in this domain they are easily observable even with musically unsophisticated subjects. If you have a piano or other musical instrument handy, play the following five-note sequence: C—D—F—E—G. Now, play a second sequence: C—D—F—Eb—G. How similar did they sound? Now play the two sequences in the opposite order: C—D—F—Eb—G, followed by C—D—F—E—G. How similar did the two melodies sound this time? You might want to repeat this little exercise with several additional melody pairs—always make one melody strongly scalar, that is, consistent with a major diatonic scale (e.g., stick to the white notes on the piano and start on middle C). And always make the second melody identical except for a one-semitone change in just one note so that this note falls outside of the key of the first melody (e.g., if the original melody uses only white notes, the change should involve adding a black note). Ideally, the second melody itself should fit no diatonic major scale (making sure the changed note is one of the black keys on the piano will usually accomplish this). You should observe that perceived similarity is generally higher when the nonscalar melody comes first. We have here a case of asymmetrical relatedness of scalar and nonscalar melodies.

Dowling and I recently investigated asymmetric similarity of scalar and nonscalar melodies (Bartlett, 1984; Bartlett & Dowling, 1988; Dowling & Bartlett, 1981), and we were able to show some quite robust effects. Originally, we attributed these effects to a process of "assimilation"—a notion close to the Gestalt concept of a mysterious psychic force pushing memory traces of stimuli toward goodness. However, we began to doubt the assimilation concept after conducting a second experiment. In this experiment, we manipulated the delay in between two melodies being compared. This delay was either 1 second or 5 seconds, and we predicted that the longer delay would allow more time for assimilation to occur and would therefore produce a strengthening of the asymmetric relatedness effect. But no such strengthening occurred.

Our doubts about an assimilation notion were reinforced by an additional experiment in which four different types of melody pairs were employed. In addition to scalar/nonscalar and nonscalar/scalar pairs, we also used scalar/scalar and nonscalar/nonscalar pairs. Examples are presented in Table 3.1, which shows that the members of all four types of pairs differed by a semitone change in just one note. That is, members of all four types of pairs differed *physically* to exactly the same degree. Despite the constancy of the one-semitone changes, rated similarity was high for both scalar/scalar and nonscalar/scalar pairs, lower for nonscalar/nonscalar pairs, and lowest for scalar/nonscalar pairs. The high similarity of scalar/scalar pairs is what is most important—there is no reason to expect assimilation of the stable, scalar, first members of such pairs. Yet, perceived similarity was high.

A more workable hypothesis for asymmetrical relatedness is that the effects of scalar structure in processing melodies are closely linked to effects of "goodness" or "well-formedness" in processing visual patterns. Following Garner's

TABLE 3.1
Examples of Melody Pairs Used by Bartlett and Dowling (1988)

| Item Type | First Melody | | | | | | | Second Melody | | | | | | |
|---|---|---|---|---|---|---|---|---|---|---|---|---|---|---|
| SS | C | B | D | G | E | A | C | C | B | D | G | F | A | C |
| NN | C | B | D# | G | E | A | C | C | B | D# | G | F | A | C |
| SN | C | B | D | G | E | A | C | C | B | D# | G | E | A | C |
| NS | C | B | D# | G | E | A | C | C | B | D | G | E | A | C |

*Note:* S = scalar, N = nonscalar.

(1970, 1974) conception that "good patterns have few alternatives," we suggest that a melody, like a simple visual pattern, is perceived as belonging to a set of alternative melodies. The smaller the set of alternative melodies, the better (more pleasant/stable) the melody is. Finally, the perceived alternatives for scalar melodies can be *nested* within those nonscalar melodies, such that the relation of nonscalar melodies to scalar melodies can be stronger than vice versa.

## THE MELODIC MAP

To understand how the nesting concept might be applied to melodies, it helps to consider spatial models of pitch (Krumhansl, 1979), especially that of Shepard (1982). Shepard's model includes five distinct dimensions of pitch that serve to explicate a large number of musical phenomena. However, two such dimensions are particularly relevant to the scalar structure of melodies—indeed, together they form a "melodic map" in which "paths" formed by melodies can be visually traced. One of the dimensions of the melodic map is pitch height, which can be experienced by going from one end of a piano keyboard to the other. The second dimension of the map is that of "key distance," defined in terms of the classic "cycle of fifths" of western music theory. This second dimension is more complex, and demands further explication.

The cycle of fifths is created by changing pitch by the musically critical interval of the fifth (or seven semitones) either up or down. Starting with any note, and proceeding consistently up or down, the cycle generates all 12 pitch classes that are used in western music, returning to the starting note. For example, starting with F and moving upwards pitch, we generate the notes C, G, D, A, E, B, F#, C#, G#, D#, A#, and, finally, F. The cycle has generated all 12 pitch classes with no repeats, a feat that can be accomplished with no other musical interval excepting that of the semitone. More important, the cycle of fifths reveals the relations among the 12 possible diatonic major scales. Any successive set of seven notes along the cycle constitutes the seven notes of a single diatonic scale. Note that the seven notes from F to B around the cycle constitute

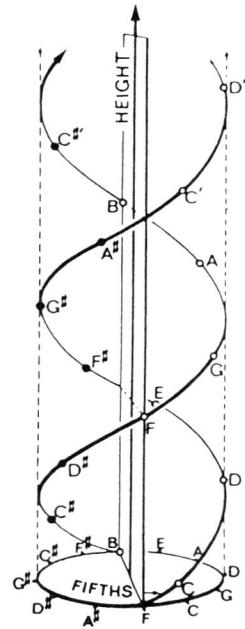

FIG. 3.6. A cylinder representing the cycle of fifths together with pitch height. From Shepard (1982).

the notes of the C major scale (no sharps or flats). Shifting one step along the cycle, the set of notes from C to F♯ constitute the notes of the closely related G major scale (one sharp). Shifting three more steps, the set of notes from A to D♯ gives us the distantly related E major scale (four sharps).

To enhance visualization of the cycle-of-fifths dimension together with the pitch height dimension, Shepard (1982) presented the cylinder that is shown in Fig. 3.6. Note that moving around the base of the cylinder takes one through the cycle of fifths, whereas moving up and down along the length of cylinder takes one up and down in pitch height. Any given note is defined by its position within the cycle of fifths as well as its pitch height.

Melodies can be visualized within this framework by cutting open the cylinder at an arbitrary point around the cycle of fifths, and flattening the space as shown in Fig. 3.7 to make a melodic map (Shepard, 1982). Although the flattening is useful, note that the A♯ on the right of the map was actually next to the F on the left before the cylinder was cut. The situation is similar to what we experience with a flat map of the world—Siberia at the right edge is actually proximal to Alaska at the left. Panel A of Fig. 3.7 displays a melody that begins and ends on C, containing neither flats nor sharps. This melody matches the key of C, which is made manifest on the map by means of a vertical line that delimits the notes of the C-major scale. All notes of the melody fall between the ordinate and this line, so that the melody occupies a restricted map region. The same

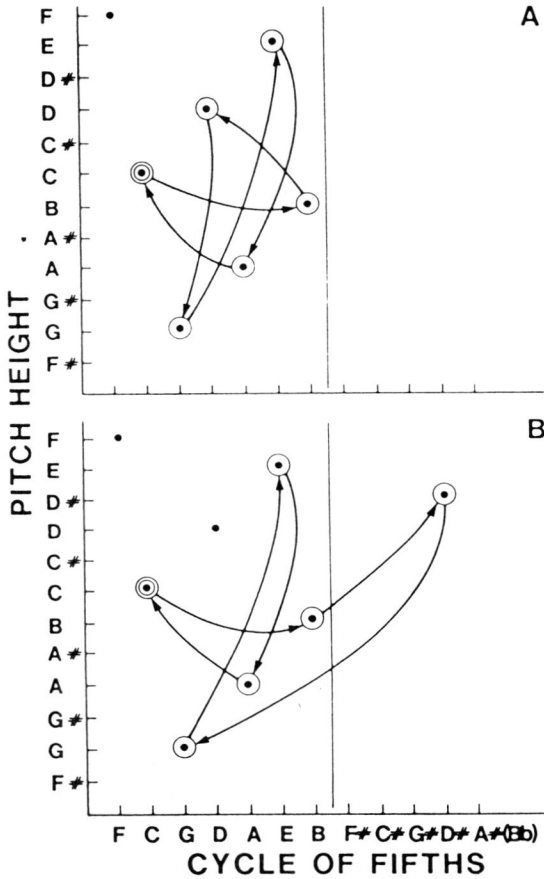

FIG. 3.7. A portion of Shepard's (1982) melodic map, unrolled onto a two-dimensional surface with the dimensions of pitch height (ordinate) and key distance around the cycle of fifths (abscissa). Filled circles represent the seven pitches of the C-major scale, and the vertical line separates scalar from nonscalar pitches. Open circles and arrows indicate (a) the scalar melody C-B-D-G-E-A-C, and (b) the nonscalar melody C-B-D#-G-E-A-C. From Bartlett and Dowling (1988).

would be true of any scalar melody, regardless of its key. In contrast, nonscalar melodies will tend to cover the full lateral extent of the map, as shown in Panel B of Fig. 3.7.

Within the framework provided by Shepard's (1982) melodic map, the idea that scalar melodies have few perceived alternatives can be put as follows: A scalar melody evokes a set of perceived alternative melodies that occupy the same restricted region on the melodic map. In contrast, weakly scalar and nonscalar melodies will tend to cover the full lateral extent of the map, and this suggests that their perceived alternatives also will cover the entire map range. Thus, the set of alternatives for a scalar melody will tend to be smaller than that for a similar nonscalar melody. Moreover, the former will be nested within the latter.

To account for the finding of asymmetrical relatedness, we assume that if a first melody evokes a set of alternatives (falling within a restricted map range), and if a subsequent melody falls outside this set of alternatives, an impression of dissimilarity results. This type of violation of an alternative set should be probable with scalar/nonscalar pairs. Because the initial melodies of scalar/nonscalar pairs have sets of alternatives constrained by their key, the second melodies in such pairs should frequently fall outside of these sets. In contrast, violations of alternative sets should be rare in the case of nonscalar/scalar pairs; the first melody in such a pair is likely to have a large set of alternatives, including not only other nonscalar melodies, but also scalar melodies. Thus, the second, scalar melody is likely to fall within the alternative set of the first.

Unlike the hypothesis of assimilation, or of psychic forces that push toward goodness, the idea that good melodies have few perceived alternatives can explain why scalar/scalar pairs are perceived as highly similar. Because the second melody in such pairs perfectly matches the key of the first, it should not violate the perceived alternative set of the first. Hence, perceived similarity should be high, despite there being no clear reason why any of the notes of the first melody should be subject to assimilation.

The intermediate similarity of nonscalar/nonscalar pairs can also be easily handled. Presumably an initial nonscalar melody can be perceived as lacking a key, or perceived as essentially consistent with a key except for one discrepant note. In the former case, a subsequently presented nonscalar melody should be perceived as highly similar—it would fall within the (large) set of alternatives evoked by the first melody. In the second case, however, a subsequently presented nonscalar melody would violate the (small) set of alternative melodies evoked by the first melody. Hence, similarity would be low. If both such cases exist on different trials, the overall result would be intermediate similarity for nonscalar/nonscalar pairs. This was, of course, the result obtained.

The melodic map framework carries several additional implications pertaining to tonal structure of melodies. One of these topics is that of anchoring, discussed previously. I noted earlier that a nonscalar note in a highly tonal melody need not always be perceived as outside of the key. Indeed, as previously mentioned, Bharucha (1984) showed that if a melody contains a nonscalar note that is followed by a scalar note that is proximal in pitch, the melody tends to be confused with a melody containing only scalar notes. Apparently, the consequence of anchoring is that out-of-key notes are perceived as if they were in key. How could this be so?

The melodic map framework provides a perspective on this question. Figure 3.8 shows that there are at least two ways of perceiving a melody containing

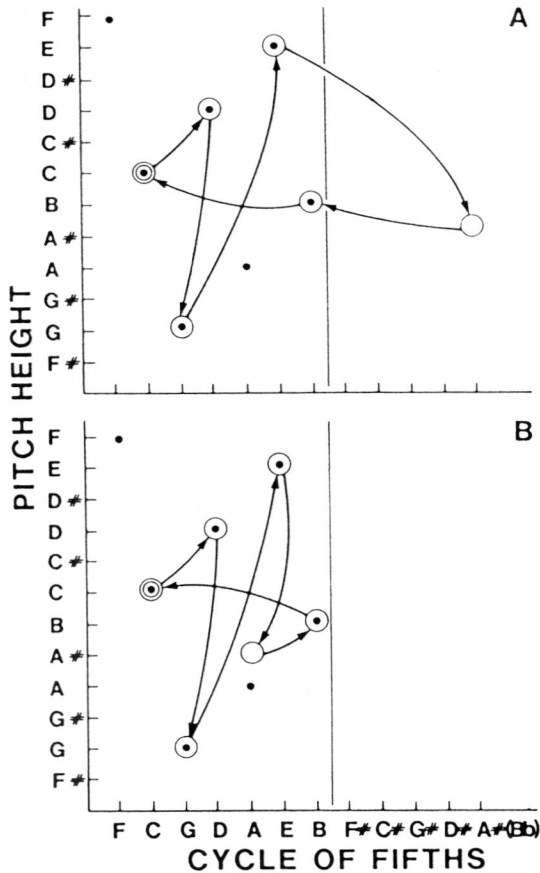

FIG. 3.8.   The melody C-D-G-E-A♯-B-C in which the A♯ is interpreted as a nonscalar pitch (a) or as a variant of a scalar pitch (b). From Bartlett and Dowling
(1988).

one nonscalar note. Panel A represents a case in which the nonscalar note is
*perceived* as nonscalar—in this case the nonscalar note disrupts the perceived
tonality of the melody, creating a large set of alternative melodies. Panel B
represents a case in which the nonscalar note is perceived as in key—note that
its pitch height is represented accurately, but that it is perceived as related to
a within-key note. In this case the nonscalar note does not disrupt the impression of tonality, so the perceived alternative set remains small. The main point
is that the melodic map framework implies that nonscalar notes are in essence
ambiguous—they can be perceived in at least two different ways. The principle
of anchoring—and quite possibly a number of other factors as well—determine
how the ambiguity is resolved.

## THE MELODIC MAP AND MELODIC CONTOUR

Another topic clarified by the melodic map framework concerns the function of melodic contour in perceiving and recognizing melodies. Defined as the sequence of ups and downs in the pitches of the melody, *contour* is known to be a highly attention-catching aspect of melodies, an aspect that even infants perceive (Trehub, Bull, & Thorpe, 1984). Moreover, research on "octave-scrambled" melodies has shown that contour plays a role in recognizing melodies. To octave-scramble a melody, one takes its notes and randomly places them in differing octaves. Such scrambling makes the melodies almost impossible to recognize (Deutsch, 1972), but recognition is improved if the scrambling is constrained such that contour is preserved (Dowling & Holombe, 1977). Despite the role of contour in aiding recognition, contour by itself is virtually useless as a cue. If one alters the pitches of a scrambled melody, preserving only melodic contour, recognition of the melody is poor (Kallman & Massaro, 1979). Moreover, recent evidence suggests that the particular contour of a melody is perceived quite accurately but is poorly retained, suffering substantial forgetting over intervals as short as 10 seconds (DeWitt & Crowder, 1986; Dowling & Bartlett, 1981). Apparently, then, contour is not sufficient to recognize melodies, but it can facilitate the use of interval information in recognizing these melodies.

The complex effects of melodic contour have been variously explained, but the melodic map framework offers a new and different perspective in which melodic contour can be defined more broadly. The standard characterization of contour assumes a unidimensional definition of pitch based only on pitch height. However, the melodic map framework implies that melodic contour might not be entirely separable from the cycle-of-fifths dimension. Two melodies with similar patterns of pitch height, but with widely differing patterns of pitch on the cycle-of-fifths dimension, might be perceived as different in contour. Indeed, Dowling and I (Bartlett & Dowling, 1988) have recently collected some data on this point. This evidence came from another experiment using scalar/scalar, scalar/nonscalar, nonscalar/scalar, and nonscalar/nonscalar pairs. A change from prior studies was that half of the pairs of melodies differed in melodic contour. In the changed-contour pairs, a high G in the first melody was replaced with a low G in the second, or vice versa, which always produced a change in the pattern of ups and downs in pitch height. Subjects responded to each melody pair with a similarity rating, as well as with a rating of confidence that the two melodies possessed the same contour, or else a different contour.

The proportions of "same-contour" judgments are shown in Table 3.2. Note first that the same-contour items received more same-contour judgments than different-contour items—thus, subjects made their contour judgments with greater-than-chance accuracy. More important, there was a general tendency for the scalar/scalar and nonscalar/scalar pairs to receive greater proportions of same-contour judgments than the scalar/nonscalar and nonscalar/nonscalar

TABLE 3.2
Average Proportions of Same-Contour Decisions in each Tonality
and Contour Condition

| Contour Condition | Scalar Structure | | | |
| --- | --- | --- | --- | --- |
| | Scalar/ Scalar | Scalar/ Nonscalar | Nonscalar/ Scalar | Nonscalar/ Nonscalar |
| Same-Contour Items | .68 | .54 | .71 | .60 |
| Different-Contour Items | .29 | .21 | .26 | .21 |

pairs. The similarity judgments showed a similar pattern. And it is noteworthy
that with both types of judgments subjects with little or no musical training
showed effects of scalar structure just as strongly as did more musically experienced subjects. Thus, the scalar relationship between the melodies of the
pairs affected judgments of whether or not contour had changed, even with subjects having quite limited formal training in music. The implication is that ordinary people perceive scalar structure, and they perceive it so naturally, so
automatically, that scalar structure can influence their judgments of contour.
This is consistent with the melodic map framework.

## SUMMARY AND IMPLICATIONS

To summarize, I have reviewed existing evidence that a sense of scalar structure, a sense of what is in key versus out of key, is strongly developed among
ordinary listeners, even those with no formal musical training, and even those
who are still quite young (say, 6 years old to be conservative). I went on to
argue that the Gestalt concept of pattern goodness, coupled with the more recent idea that good patterns have few perceived alternatives (Garner, 1970),
provides a perspective on this sense of scalar structure: Scalar melodies are
perceived as members of relatively small sets of alternative melodies, and their
sets of alternatives can be nested within the larger sets of alternatives evoked
by nonscalar melodies. I explored an implication of this line of reasoning: There
should be asymmetric similarity between scalar and nonscalar melodies; two
slightly different melodies should be perceived as more similar if the first-
presented melody is the one that is less scalar, that is, the one that evokes
the larger set of alternatives. Such asymmetric similarity has been confirmed
in research, and has been shown to generalize to judgments of contour. Specifically, a judgment that two melodies share the same contour (the same sequence
of ups and downs in pitch) is more likely if the less scalar item comes first. Finally, I pointed out that Shepard's (1982) melodic map—a spatial combination
of pitch height and the musical cycle of fifths—helps in visualizing the ideas that
melodies are perceived as members of sets of alternative melodies, that scalar

melodies have relatively small perceived alternative sets, and that the perceived alternative sets for scalar melodies can be nested within those for nonscalar melodies.

What are some implications of this line of argument and evidence? I believe one of the more interesting implications concerns popular music, and the perennial question of what makes a popular song a "hit." There doubtlessly are many factors, but two characteristics of the melodies of hit songs seem clear. First, the melodies of hit songs are almost invariably strongly scalar—one would have to search for a popular song with more than occasional accidentals (i.e., out-of-key notes) in its main melodic line. And what accidentals exist are likely to be found between beats or on nonaccented beats, and also are usually "anchored" (i.e., followed by a scalar note one-semitone removed, Bharucha, 1984), so that their nonscalar nature is not very noticeable. Second, despite this strong and apparently well-enforced restriction, hit song melodies often have the psychological property of *sounding* original or unique, that is, different from other songs. Of course, this uniqueness is partly in the ear of the listener—not all of us feel that popular songs sound unique. But it seems inescapable that many such melodies sound unique to many listeners. And this simple fact, together with the strong scalar structure in such melodies, poses something of a puzzle. The restriction of popular music to strong scalar structure coexists with an interest on the part of many listeners in unique or different-sounding melodies . . . why?

Garner's (1974) concepts of goodness and perceived alternatives suggest an answer to this question. To say that good patterns have few perceived alternatives is to say that good patterns strike the observer as unique—they strike the observer as similar to only a few other patterns. And so if scalar melodies have few perceived alternatives, as I have tried to argue throughout this chapter, they should be perceived as more unique than melodies that violate simple diatonic scales. Somewhat paradoxically, restricting the pitch classes to be used in making melodies results in sets of melodies that strike listeners as unique. Relaxing this restriction may allow for more melodies, but most of these melodies will sound non-unique, that is, they will be perceived as essentially similar to a variety of other melodies, many of which also are perceived as non-unique. Partly for this reason, they will tend to sound "bad."

# REFERENCES

Bartlett, J. C. (1984). Cognition of complex events: Visual scenes and music. In W. R. Crozier & A. J. Chapman (Eds.), *Cognitive processes in the perception of art* (pp. 225–251). Amsterdam: North Holland.

Bartlett, J. C., & Dowling, W. J. (1988). Scale structure and similarity of melodies. *Music Perception, 5,* 285–314.

Bharucha, J. J. (1984). Anchoring effects in music: The resolution of dissonance. *Cognitive Psychology, 16,* 485–518.

Cohen, A. J. (1978, April). *Inferred sets of pitches in melodic perception.* Paper presented at the meetings of the Western Psychological Association, San Francisco.

Cross, I., Howell, P., & West, R. (1983). Preferences for scale structure in melodic sequences. *Journal of Experimental Psychology: Human Perception & Performance, 9,* 444–460.

Cross, I., Howell, P., & West, R. (1985). Structural relationships in the perception of musical pitch. In P. Howell, I. Cross, & R. West (Eds.), *Musical structure and cognition* (pp. 121–142). Orlando, FL: Academic Press.

Deutsch, D. (1972). Octave generalization and tune recognition. *Perception & Psychophysics, 11,* 411–412.

DeWitt, L. A., & Crowder, R. G. (1986). Recognition of novel melodies after brief delays. *Music Perception, 3,* 259–274.

Dowling, W. J. (1972). Recognition of melodic transformations: Inversion, retrograde, and retrograde inversion. *Perception & Psychophysics, 12,* 417–421.

Dowling, W. J. (1982). Melodic information processing and its development. In D. Deutsch (Ed.), *The psychology of music* (pp. 413–429). New York: Academic Press.

Dowling, W. J. (1988). Tonal Structure and children's early learning of music. In J. Sloboda (Ed.), *Generative processes in music* (pp. 113–128). Oxford: Clarendon.

Dowling, W. J., & Bartlett, J. C. (1981). The importance of interval information in long-term memory for melodies. *Psychomusicology, 1,* 30–49.

Dowling, W. J., & Harwood, D. L. (1986). *Music cognition.* Orlando, FL: Academic Press.

Dowling, W. J., & Holombe, A. W. (1977). The perception of melodies distorted by splitting into several octaves: Effects of increasing proximity and melodic contour. *Perception & Psychophysics, 21,* 60–64.

Francès, R. (1988). *The perception of music.* Hillsdale, NJ: Lawrence Erlbaum Associates. (Original work published 1958)

Garner, W. R. (1970). Good patterns have few alternatives. *American Scientist, 58,* 34–42.

Garner, W. R. (1974). *The processing of information and structure.* Hillsdale, NJ: Lawrence Erlbaum Associates.

Garner, W. R., & Clement, D. E. (1963). Goodness of pattern and pattern uncertainty. *Journal of Verbal Learning and Verbal Behavior, 2,* 446–452.

Hanawalt, N. G. (1937). Memory trace for figures in recall and recognition. *Archives of Psychology, 216.* (pp. 1–89).

Handel, S., & Garner, W. R. (1966). The structure of visual pattern associates and pattern goodness. *Perception and Psychophysics, 1,* 33–38.

Kahneman, D., & Miller, D. T. (1986). Norm theory: Comparing reality to its alternatives. *Psychological Review, 92,* 136–153.

Kallman, H. J., & Massaro, D. W. (1979). Tone chroma is functional in melody recognition. *Perception & Psychophysics, 26,* 32–36.

Koffka, K. (1935). *Principles of gestalt psychology.* New York: Harcourt, Brace, & World.

Köhler, W. (1947). *Gestalt psychology.* New York: Liveright.

Krumhansl, C. L. (1979). The psychological representation of musical pitch in a tonal context. *Cognitive Psychology, 11,* 346–374.

Krumhansl, C. L., Bharucha, J. J., & Castellano, M. (1982). Key distance effects on perceived harmonic structure in music. *Perception & Psychophysics, 31,* 75–85.

Krumhansl, C. L., & Keil, F. C. (1982). Acquisition of the hierarchy of tonal functions in music. *Memory & Cognition, 10,* 243–251.

Perkins, F. T. (1932). Symmetry in visual recall. *American Journal of Psychology, 44,* 473–490.

Riley, D. A. (1962). Memory for form. In L. Postman (Ed.), *Psychology in the making: Histories of selected research problems* (pp. 402–465). New York: Knopf.

Shepard, R. N. (1982). Geometrical approximations to the structure of musical pitch. *Psychological Review, 89,* 305–333.

Trehub, S. E., Bull, D., & Thorpe, L. A. (1984). Infants' perception of melodies: The role of melodic contour. *Child Development, 55,* 821–830.

Tversky, A., & Gati, I. (1978). Studies of similarity. In E. Rosch & B. B. Lloyd (Eds.), *Cognition and categorization* (pp. 79–95). Hillsdale, NJ: Lawrence Erlbaum Associates.

Wertheimer, M. (1944). Gestalt theory. *Social Research, 11.*

# II

# THE INTEGRATION OF
# MELODY AND RHYTHM

W. Jay Dowling
*University of Texas at Dallas*

The rhythmic organization of a melody is, if anything, more important psychologically than is the pitch pattern. In his 1890 work, *Principles of Psychology*, William James observed that melodies can be recognized from just the rhythmic pattern alone. And as Jones observes in the following chapter, distorting the rhythm of a tune makes it difficult to recognize. In fact, changing the rhythm of a familiar tune effectively turns it into a new tune, as Monahan shows in her examples of Schubert's *Unfinished Symphony* and the theme from "Dragnet." Pitch and rhythmic patterns are not just separable aspects of a melody that can be considered in isolation. To return to one of the themes of the first section, a melody must be treated as an integral whole and not as a mere collection of elements. Going beyond the general proposition that a melody is an integral whole composed of rhythmic and pitch patterns, Jones provides concrete detail concerning ways in which those patterns integrated into a melody interact with one another. She describes patterns of melodic accent that arise from variations in pitch and duration (her "joint accent structure"), and demonstrates the psychological effects of alterations in those patterns.

Other themes running through the first section continue their development here as well. The theme of the importance of cognitive frameworks reflecting the structure of the world is important to the grasp of rhythmic organization just as it is in the perception of pitch patterns. And the theme of the fundamental importance of procedural knowledge and the relative superficiality of declarative knowledge in music cognition is echoed here in an emphasis on studying the perception of rhythms as performed, and not just as notated.

It is clear in all three of the following chapters that rhythmic organization in European music typically involves at least two psychologically important structural levels. There is a level of metric regularity—the level at which a regular beat is heard—overlaid by a complex level of rhythmic patterning. The meter provides a cognitive framework upon which to hang the more complex rhythms. The presence of such a framework improves the accuracy of time judgments by listeners, and provides for the introduction of aesthetically important tensions between regularity and variation, between stability and instability. In these ways the framework for time functions much as does the framework for pitch described in the first three chapters, a theme elaborated by Monahan.

We are reminded by Gabrielsson, however, that the experience of rhythm can arise in a wide variety of ways, including contexts to which the description from music theory of metric and rhythmic levels does not apply. Gabrielsson provides a very useful outline of stimulus features that facilitate the experience of rhythm, including the temporal grouping of pattern elements, the introduction of emphasis through accent, the introduction of regular periodicities in any aspect of the pattern, and the restriction of all of the foregoing types of events to time spans that fit within William James' psychological present.

A musician's declarative representation of a melody is typically taken to be what we see in standard musical notation. Gabrielsson reminds us that such a representation is artificial with respect to what actually occurs in musical performance. Notation partakes of the necessary artificiality of all declarative knowledge. Categorization ignores, and must ignore, subtle differences. Gabrielsson demonstrates the psychological importance of what the performer and listener know regarding rhythmic patterning in actual music. In doing that he uses a wide range of methods, including novel ways of measuring responses, analyses of temporal patterning in performances, and the construction of simulated performance patterns.

In all of these chapters there is an underlying concern to clarify the relation, central to aesthetic questions, between physical patterns of sound energy in the world and our psychological experience of them. It is clear that there are a number of levels of structure in the world, and that each of them is grasped psychologically in a different way. For each level of structure the mind and brain seek to grasp a pattern of invariant relationships that remains relatively constant over time, such as the tonal scale or the beat pattern of a waltz. We may conclude from this that music, to be accessible to human cognition, must afford the possibility of the grasping of invariants, though these invariants need not be precisely the ones on which European tonal music has traditionally relied.

Music requires an interplay over time of tensions involving stability and change, of invariant patterns and variations upon them. These chapters explore some of the ways in which that can be accomplished.

# 4

# Dynamics of Musical Patterns: How Do Melody and Rhythm Fit Together?

Mari Riess Jones
*Ohio State University*

Animals produce sounds that are patterned in time. Think of the eerie sounds of the humpback whale and the wolf's cry, or the high-pitched noises of dolphins and bats. Other sound patterns come to mind when we think about "true" songs: a sparrow's tune, a lyrical ballad, or simply human instrumental music. Each "song" has something special about the way its energy changes over time to realize the function it plays for a particular organism. In fact, the structure of sound patterns created by living things is often tailored to serve certain functions. Sometimes these functions are purely exploratory. In other cases, sound energy is designed to achieve one or several communicative goals.

Consider the exploratory sound patterns produced by bats, who are nocturnal, or those of dolphins, who live in murky waters. Both these animals use sound to locate themselves in the world relative to rocks and other obstacles. They create these patterns using special combinations of high frequency sound bursts and rhythmical timing. Thus, they scan their environment by relying on the way sound waves bounce off surfaces and return as "re-textured" energy in an echo. What is especially interesting is that the temporal structure of produced noise patterns is finely regulated so that echoes will return to the explorer's ears at "predictable" times thus enabling efficient attending. Such sound structures serve a *locative* function for these organisms.

Both bats and dolphins create other sound patterns with distinctive dynamics designed to communicate to other members of their species. Mother bats "talk" to their infants with softer and lower pitched tones, for example. Of course, when we consider sound as a communicative medium, it is clear that humans do fairly well on this score. Perhaps our relatively high level of refinement in sound patterns designed to serve *communicative* functions is related to the fact that we are not nocturnal and tend to rely more on vision and patterns in reflected light to explore our world than on sound and patterns in echoes. In any case, it is the structure and function of certain communicative sound patterns of humans that I am concerned with in this chapter. In particular, I consider musical sound patterns that are created and performed by one human being to communicate something to another.

Along with speech, music is preeminent among communicative sound patterns produced by humans. As generic categories there are significant differences between speech patterns and music, but both are very complex and in both a single pattern can serve several different functions. These sound patterns can at once inform a listener about the speaker or singer (a male or female voice), a content, the speaker's mood, and other things.

Of course, when we consider music, it is evident that there are many styles of music and contexts in which humans experience music. These range from the spontaneous (shower humming) to the banal prepared (commercial jingles) and the artfully inspired (classical tonal music). Among these various kinds of music, structural differences exist that accommodate the different communicative goals of both composer and performer. Much of music is composed with special goals and audiences in mind.

In this chapter, I focus on two very general communicative goals that I suspect obtain in many different musical genres. The first involves melodic theme recognition and the way in which a composer or performer achieves different degrees of familiarity in reactions of listeners to recurrent themes. The second involves a listener's ongoing attending and the way in which a musical artist can effect predictability, or conversely, surprise, through clever control of the listener's reactions to the dynamically unfolding musical structure.

With regard to theme recognition, many musical compositions "work" because their creators assume listeners will come to recognize an earlier melodic theme at certain points. Interestingly, timing variations that often accompany a theme play an important part in enabling the artist to introduce various subtle shadings, variations, and degrees of melodic familiarity in the listener. Good artists intuitively "know" how various relationships in music combine to produce the right psychological degree of familiarity in the listener. As a psychologist, I am intrigued by the fact that rhythm, or relations in time, appear to be an effective part of the structural tool chest composers use for provoking recognition of some melody. For me this raises psychological questions about the best way to describe functional *pattern similarities* in music.

It is also critical for the artist to know how to keep a listener's attention relatively high, or at least, to know when it is most likely to flag. This relates to the second function of music I consider, namely the musical artist's control of a listener's ongoing attentional response to a sound pattern. As with the way theme recognition works, many of the psychological principles used by inspired artists to achieve this control of listener response remain mysterious. Nevertheless, it seems clear that the way in which listeners attend and "track" information in ongoing musical patterns depends importantly on their use of certain structural constraints in music. In much of Western music there are latent principles of dynamic lawfulness that seem to insure a sort of simply timed synchronicity in listeners' attending. Not only does the discovery of these principles present a challenge, it raises fascinating psychological issues related to ways in which music achieves its communicative goals. If an artist can somehow insure that a listener will indeed pay attention to a sound pattern at certain points in time, then it's wise to insert the more important thematic information *at* those times. In a curious way, this is reminiscent of our fellow creature the bat who both "composes" and "appreciates" his own sound patterns: Bats "time" various pitches in their sound productions so that echoes will return to them at optimal times to pick up important locative information. Are there corresponding and, perhaps, simple timing patterns that permit musical artists to communicate melodic information optimally to dynamically attending listeners? I assume that there are. In fact, I describe some research that my students and I have undertaken to address this issue that relates to *dynamic pattern simplicity* in music.

The two issues I focus on in this chapter then involve *dynamic pattern similarity* and *dynamic pattern simplicity*. The explicit reference to "dynamic" pattern structure in both is intentional. I deal with patterns in and of time, and my position is that the most fruitful description of their governing structural constraints will include time relationships as integral and interacting parts of the whole pattern structure. Thus, by dynamic pattern structure, I mean a description of musical structure that includes time in a meaningful way. Specifically, I focus here on relationships between melody and rhythmic structure.

The remainder of the chapter concerns dynamic pattern structure and the psychological response to it as we currently understand it. First, I briefly introduce some descriptive terms that are specific, separately, to pitch relations in melodies and to time relations in rhythm and meter. Then I present a preliminary proposal for a description of dynamic pattern structure. Because my focus is on the integration of melody and rhythm, this description deals with interrelations of pitch and time. Finally, I show how research on melody recognition and melody reproduction has shaped the application of this description of dynamic pattern structure to issues of dynamic pattern similarity and dynamic pattern simplicity.

## SOME STRUCTURAL DESCRIPTIONS OF PITCH (MELODY) AND TIME (METER AND RHYTHM) RELATIONSHIPS IN WESTERN MUSIC

Pitch relationships contribute to a melody and time relationships contribute to meter and rhythm. Here I introduce some elementary ways of describing their respective structures in music.

## Pitch Relationships, Melodies, and Melodic Themes

Pitch is determined by tone frequency and by frequency relationships. In music, pitch transformations that carry melodic themes are logarithmically related to the frequency changes among the tones in the melody, and this logarithmic property is embodied in many of the most common musical scales of pitch (e.g., the equally tempered chromatic scale and related diatonic scales). Musical scales, along with musical grammars, reflect some of the constraints that operate to define the pitches and pitch relationships that form a particular melody. Some frequencies and frequency changes are unlikely to occur if certain scales and grammars are at work in a particular musical context, and others are more likely.

The most basic musical scale in Western music, the equally tempered chromatic scale, offers a sort of unit pitch "distance" or basic musical interval called the semitone (ST). (It is actually a constant *ratio*, but given this scale's logarithmic properties the constant ratio of two frequencies is referred to as an interval.) Notes from the chromatic scale, marked off in semitone pitch units, are shown on the ordinate of Fig. 4.1. Other pitch intervals are made up of n semitones. Thus, a perfect fifth spans seven STs and a major third has four ST intervals.

Many melodies are based on special combinations of pitch intervals, combinations that suggest what is called *tonality*. Tonality refers to the characteristic use of certain subsets of relationships within the chromatic scale, ones that imply use of a particular referent tone. Although musical scales themselves do not define tonality, tonal relationships can be partly summarized by a musical scale. For instance, a diatonic set of tonal relationships is formally one that preserves the succession of pitch interval: 2ST, 2ST, 1ST, 2ST, 2ST, 2ST, 1ST. If we also select a particular starting frequency (*referent tone* or *key-note*) then a particular major diatonic musical scale is fixed. Figure 4.1 illustrates the familiar C major scale. It is determined when the note, C, is established as the start note or key-note of this sequence of intervals. Here the sequence of pitch changes ascends (+) to reveal the C major scale as a time pattern within a pitch-space and time coordinate system. Tonal music arranges these and related pitch transformations in grammatically special ways that communicate both "keyness" and thematic information. Some problems associated with listeners' identification of musical keys are being studied by Professor David Butler, Helen Browne, and their colleagues at Ohio State University. They suggest that we learn to "listen" for critical tonal information.

This analysis suggests, then, that there are various ways in which frequency relationships can determine relevant pitch constraints that form a melodic line. At an elementary level, we can speak simply about a succession of "ups" (+, + . . .) and "downs" (−, − . . .) in pitch. Thus, in Fig. 4.1, the ascending sequence determines this melody's pitch contour. We know from the work of Jay Dowling and others that pitch contour is an important determinant in people's ability to recognize many melodies (Dowling, 1978; Dowling & Fujitani, 1971; Massaro, Kallman, & Kelly, 1980; Watkins, 1985). But it is also evident

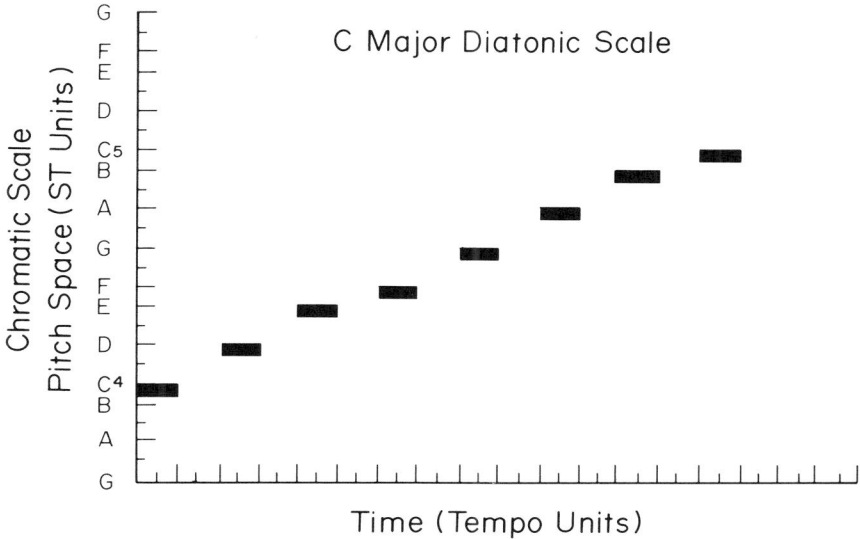

FIG. 4.1. A pitch-space and time coordinate system for presenting the dynamic structure of tunes. Steps on the ordinate reflect the chromatic scale unit of a semitone (ST). Steps on the abscissa reflect the tempo established by the value of the beat period. The space-time pattern is a diatonic C major pattern, which itself establishes tonal relationships.

that there are more melodic relationships than these at play. Musical intervals, measured in ST units, reflect other pitch relations that enter in, as in Fig. 4.1. Finally, there can be an overlay of tonal meaning, derived from a particular context, in which one pitch comes to function as a referent from which other pitches are heard. Here relative position within a diatonic set is the defining property so that relationships between the referent pitch (e.g., C) and other pitches can be cast in terms of scale steps. Thus, E and G are, respectively, two and four scale steps above the key-note in C major scale. However, the same notes bear different relationships to the key-note in another major scale; for example, F major.

All of these pitch relationships play roles in fleshing out melodic structure. If a melody consists of special arrangements of these pitch relationships, then melodic themes that recur in larger musical contexts are sound patterns that preserve these same constraints. Recent work in music perception indicates that listeners are sensitive, in various degrees, to melodic patternings that exploit each kind of pitch relationship (Dowling and Harwood, 1985).

Finally, there are nagging questions that strike to the heart of the problem of studying responses to music. In real music, patterning of these several kinds of pitch relationships frequently covaries. A change in pitch contour in a recurrent theme is often carried by the same musical interval and this, in turn, can have a special tonal significance. How do all these things add up to determine melodic theme recognition, for example? These are unsolved problems. Indeed, they become even more challenging when related timing changes are considered, as shall be seen.

## Temporal Relationships in Meter and Rhythm

Thus far, I have said relatively little about temporal relationships. These often covary with melodic patterns in complex ways. My students and I have been especially interested in some of the ways that temporal relationships covary and indeed seem to become an integral part of melodic lines, psychologically speaking. In fact, the average listener does have difficulty separating the two, as I show later.

For heuristic reasons, however, it is useful to consider some elementary aspects of rhythmic structure abstracted from pitch relationships. I use the generic term *rhythmic structure* to include three temporal aspects of music: tempo, meter, and rhythm proper.

*Tempo.*   As with pitch, it is possible to identify a functional time unit for time relationships in music. This unit is often referred to as the *beat period*. In theory, the beat period is supposed to remain roughly constant over large musical segments. The specified beat period communicates the tempo or pace of a piece to the listener. Often it is the beat period that establishes what you tap your foot to in music. I denote a beat period by a dot, as · . It has been argued that the tempo provides an important anchor in the time domain for a listener, in that it offers a temporal frame or perspective for other time periods. If we describe the pitch-time structure of a melody in a space-time coordinate system as in Fig. 4.1, then tempo units are given by prominent markings on the abscissa or time axis. Other time periods, larger and smaller, are lawfully related to this unit time period.

*Meter.*   Western music tends to be metrical, at least as notated. This means that a constant number of unit time periods (beat periods) are contained within some regularly recurring higher order time span, the measure. For instance, if you find yourself tapping to a tune in groups of four beats with the first beat seeming stronger ( / ) for some reason as in / . . . / . . . , then you are following a meter based on a multiple of two (a kind of duple meter). If the unit time period of this beat is further assigned the durational value of a quarter note ( ♩ ) in a musical score, then the meter is four-four time, meaning four quarter notes occur in a measure. Two and three quarter notes per measure denote simple duple and triple meters respectively.

It is important to understand that "the" meter is typically known by a performer, but it must be somehow communicated through the sound pattern to the listener. This means that the composer, in delineating musical structure, and the performer, in producing it, must "mark" appropriate beginnings and endings of the time periods associated with, respectively, beat periods and measures, so that a listener can detect that the time ratios of these periods are, for example, 1 to 2 (duple), or 1 to 3 (triple). This is not always easy, as the work of Dirk Jan Povel of Nijmegen University and others have shown. Good performers succeed in this communicative effort in ways we are only beginning to understand (Essens & Povel, 1985; Palmer, 1992; Povel, 1981; Sloboda, 1983).

*Rhythm proper.* *Rhythm proper* refers to durational patterns. The durations are variations of a unit time period that preserve temporal proportions implied by a given meter. Thus, if the beat period is a quarter note, ♩, and the meter dictates four quarter notes to a measure, then the rhythmic pattern of: ♪♪♩ (where ♩ = ♪ + ♪) forms a *rhythmic* figure of two shorter notes followed by a proportionately longer one. Rhythmic figures can, and often do, reinforce a melodic theme but they may also serve as invariant time patterns in their own right. Ravel's famous *Bolero*, for instance, is a classic example of a piece where primarily rhythm and tempo carry the theme.

## Summary and Comments

I have outlined elementary ways to conceive of pitch and time relationships as these contribute separately to melodies and to rhythmic structure, respectively. In each case, it was useful to identify functional relational units such as the semitone interval for pitch and the beat period for time. At a conceptual level, we might think of these units as marking off independent interval distances on separate axes in a pitch-time coordinate system. Such a portrayal has heuristic merits for outlining some of the global relationships that enter into a musical pattern. But pitch-time coordinate descriptions must be used with caution. For instance, we know that pitch relationships in music are far more complex than is captured by this unidimensional and interval-scaled description of pitch space. The research of Roger Shepard and Carol Krumhansl shows this (Shepard, 1982; Krumhansl & Shepard, 1979). And we also know that the conceptual abstraction of a fixed tempo, and hence unvarying beat period, is untenable as a precise description of the produced sound pattern. Recent analyses of the musical productions of professional musicians, discussed in this book by Alf Gabrielsson, show that interval and ratio properties of notated scores are not always precisely realized in the pitch and time relationships that turn up in the sound pattern itself. Frequencies associated with some pitch intervals are merely approximated. And tonal durations in rhythms are modulated as well, often intentionally to enhance an expressive communication. Finally, if pitch and time relationships are psychologically dependent, then the artifice of independent pitch and time units is just that: a convenient way of suggesting some relationships in the stimulus. All of this means that in outlining some properties that emerge when we consider higher order relationships *between* melody (pitch) and rhythm (time), it will be useful to describe these joint relations within pitch-time coordinate systems—but with caution!

## DYNAMIC PATTERN STRUCTURES:
## A PREVIEW OF THE FRAMEWORK
## FOR INTEGRATION OF MELODY AND RHYTHM

Perhaps the fact that melody and rhythm should be considered together as psychologically interdependent parts of musical structure is obvious to the reader. What may be less obvious are ways that we can study and describe this interdependency. There are many ways to proceed, and we need to be careful that our experiments do not wind up destroying the thing we seek to study. Sometimes, perhaps because we have failed to define our variables correctly or have ignored important covariances in structure, the functioning part of a complex stimulus is chopped up, distorted, or lost. In real music, many things covary and appear to have interactive effects that we do not entirely understand. These interdependencies, if correctly captured, may tell us interesting things about the way music achieves its communicative effects. Thus, the fact that we can so neatly abstract separate melodic and rhythmic components, as shown in the last section, should not seduce us into routinely studying them in separate experimental designs. Nor should we assume that this means that pitch and time relationships function for a listener as independent or separate psychological constructs (Jones & Boltz, 1989).

Having said this, how should we directly address the possibility that melodic and rhythmic structures are psychologically interdependent? We began to consider this problem a number of years ago and I confess we are still at it. In recent years we have focused on some ways in which pitch and time relations appear to co-constrain each other in real music and have tried to abstract out for study functioning parts of these interrelationships. For instance, not only do melodic and rhythmic figures covary and reinforce one another, but also certain contextually defined pitch changes within a melodic line can delimit or strengthen one or another time span within the meter. Relatively large pitch intervals, for instance, can outline (i.e., "mark") significant durations in the rhythmic structure, such as measure spans. On the other hand, meter and rhythm, by definition, fix the relative times of various pitch changes in the melody. These kinds of co-constraints of pitch and time seemed to suggest several ways we could go beyond the separate abstractions of melodic (pitch) and rhythmic (time) structures and more directly address the interplay of melody with rhythm in a pitch-time musical sequence.

However, hindsight is always clearer than foresight. Good ways to actually manipulate the interplay of melody and rhythm were not immediately obvious to us. Consequently, we simply began to explore it experimentally in a straightforward way using standard psychological tasks for studying melody recognition or immediate recall. Listeners heard many melodies and had to respond to each tune in some way to indicate what they remembered about it. Sometimes we used listeners who had little musical training and other times we used very skilled musicians. Typically the melodies themselves differed in systematic ways and we placed them in various rhythms (and meters) as well. Thus some sound patterns might differ from each only with respect to melody and others only with respect to rhythm; still others differed in both melody and rhythm. However, in spite of the fact that this meant that we had carefully included joint variations of melody and rhythm in our experimental designs, our attempts to make sense of listeners' responses in these first few studies were frustrating. We came to realize that this was because we had, after all, not yet formulated a sufficiently clear idea of how the pitch and time co-constraints really worked. We needed to be quite explicit about why certain combinations of melody and rhythm should create patterns that seemed similar to each other and, as a consequence, confuseable to listeners; and we also needed to be specific about which melody–rhythm combinations should be simplest for listeners and so easy to follow ("track") in time. After some thought, we developed a reasonable framework that allowed us to directly address these two issues that concern, respectively, dynamic pattern similarity and dynamic pattern simplicity. The framework, which I preview in this section, is by no means complete. However, it represents a plausible and useful initial description of certain interdependencies of melody and rhythm, and I rely on it here to explain some of our research.

## Basic Ideas: Joint Accent Structure and Temporal Phasing

To illustrate the basic ideas behind this framework, consider melodic and rhythmic structures, but now from a perspective of their joint contributions to an integrated and dynamic description of a musical sound pattern. First consider melody. Let us conceive of melodic structure in terms of its potential for delimiting time periods within a sequence. There are several plausible ways in which pitch relationships, as defined thus far, can do this. That is, anything that "marks" beginnings and endings of coherent pitch groups, such as relatively large pitch intervals, must mark also the durations of these groups. We know relatively little at this point about how and how effectively the different pitch relations discussed earlier actually do this, but it is clear that things related to pitch contour, pitch intervals, or tonality have some potential to mark time periods. Next consider rhythm. The time relationships within a recurrent rhythmic figure can also delimit time periods in the larger sequence. For instance, lengthened (L) notes in the time pattern SSLSSL . . . . can function in this way. The point is that both melody and rhythm offer up "markers" for time periods within the same sound pattern. These markers represent prominent attention-getting relational changes and they can be assumed to be synonymous with the musical term "accent." Therefore, we can state the general idea succinctly. The key to this analysis of the interplay of melody and rhythm involves the way in which accents from pitch and time patterns combine into a common dynamic structure called a *Joint Accent Structure*.

Musical accents may be of various sorts, but all tend to define for a listener beginnings and endings of more or less important time spans within the same overall sound pattern. Things in a melody that mark the beginnings and endings of coherent pitch groups will, of course, also mark durations of these groups. Similarly, notes in a durational sequence that define beginnings or endings of a rhythmic figure at once also carve out higher order time spans. Both of these accent types have a common role in delimiting time spans. Consequently, any given combination of melody and rhythm can be conceived in terms of properties associated with the resultant joint set of accents and their time spans. In considering these properties, I use the terms *Joint Accent Structure* and *Temporal Phasing*.

Briefly, Joint Accent Structure refers to the particular combination of accents and their temporal patternings that result when melodic and rhythmic structure join. We have gradually refined this idea in order to investigate ways in which certain musical properties determine pattern similarity in melody recognition and pattern simplicity in melody reproduction. Temporal Phasing refers to relative time properties associated with separate melody and rhythm components of Joint Accent Structure. Phasing is of interest because it seems to yield an easy way to assess some dynamic properties of the Joint Accent Structure. I elaborate on these ideas in the context of research on dynamic pattern similarity and dynamic pattern simplicity.

## The Role of Melodic and Temporal Accents

Before we turn to this research, it is wise to be more specific about the nature of melodic and rhythmic accents. I consider each in turn.

If now we return to melodic structure with the idea of identifying melodic accents within a melody, it becomes apparent that there are various ways a given melodic line offers melodic accents. I denote melodic accents generally by the symbol m. Here I mention three kinds of m accents.

The first type of m accent involves pitch contour. Pitch contour yields *contour-based melodic accents* (m) as shown in Panel A of Fig. 4.2. Successive pitch trajectories segment a melody meaningfully, and beginnings or endings of these rising or falling trajectories can function as melodic accents. These correspond to locally higher and lower pitches associated with contour changes. They are potentially important melodic markers for durational spans.

## (a)
### melodic <u>contour</u> accents

## (b)
### melodic <u>pitch interval</u> accents

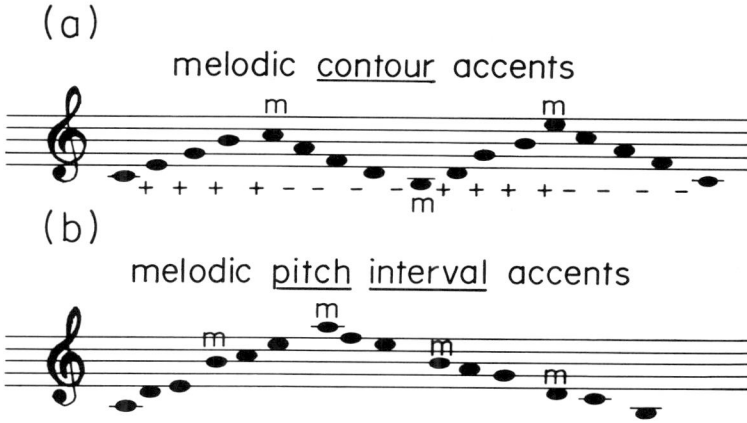

FIG. 4.2.  Two kinds of melodic accent: In panel A are Contour accents, designated by m, which fall on locally higher and lower pitches; in Panel B are Pitch interval accents, also designated by m, which fall on the pitch following a locally larger pitch interval.

Another way melodic structure groups and differentiates a pitch series involves temporal ordering of pitch intervals of different sizes. Relatively small pitch intervals (one or two ST) are common in Western music, and so when a relatively large pitch change (e.g., four or five ST) is introduced, it is noticeable. Therefore, relatively large pitch intervals, defined by certain pairs of tones, may produce melodic accents. Panel B of Fig. 4.2 illustrates these. *Pitch interval melodic accents* (m) here are assumed to fall on the second tone of a pair, namely the one which completes the unusual pitch change.

Finally, neither contour change nor pitch interval change depend on the established musical key to have their effect. But, a third kind of melodic accenting does. This sort of accenting arises from pitch changes that imply tonality. In contrast to contour and interval accents, which depend on local surprise or "differentness" for contextual saliency, *tonal melodic accents* (m) can also come from confirmation of a contextually governed expectation. The occurrence of a resolving key-note at a phrase ending is an example of a tonal end accent that is often accompanied by a sense of completion or finality. Tonal accenting necessarily depends upon listeners' culturally acquired attunements to tonal grammars (Narmour, 1990; 1992).

Accents offered by a durational pattern, namely by rhythm proper, are *temporal accents* and are denoted by t. Temporal accents, like melodic ones, come from deviations within a serial context. In this case, context and deviation are durational: Any very long or short note relative to, say, the established period of a beat may yield a t accent. Also pauses, which are measured in beat periods, may create t accents. Often pause-based accents follow the silent period (or rest), but this is a complicated matter. As Paul Fraisse (1964) and Steven

Handel (1989) have shown, t accents depend upon the whole durational pattern. A sequence of short (S) notes, such as SSS pause SSS pause . . ., often determines a t accent on the note *following* the pause. Thus if these notes require a beat (·) and the pause takes two beats, then the accent sequence is t · · · t · · · ·, and so on. (I assume that initial pattern tones always receive accents.) However, if the rhythm is SSL pause SSL pause . . ., then the primary t accent is likely to fall on the lengthened note *prior* to the pause. In musical notation, if the short note is scored as a quarter note (♩) (requiring one beat) and the longer one twice its duration (♩), then the accent sequence becomes: t . t . . . . . t . . ., and so on. (I assume that the t accent falls on the first of the two beats of the longer tone.)

This analysis sets the stage for previewing the notion of Joint Accent Structure. To keep matters simple, imagine that the six-tone melodic sequence of Fig. 4.3 (i.e., CDEABC′) is presented to a listener (in a C major context). In addition to an opening m accent, the pronounced pitch interval from note E to note A in this melody also produces an m accent on note A. Now, in theory this melodic string can be presented to a listener in different rhythms. Two rhythms appear in Fig. 4.3. In Example 1 (Panel A), the rhythm is ♩♩♩.♩♩♩, and so on. Here a one-beat rest creates two three-tone groups, and t accents fall on the first and fourth tone. Thus, the second t accent falls on note A and it coincides with the m accent. Finally, let us combine three separate melodic and temporal beat patterns to yield a Joint Accent Structure as shown in Example 1. I assume that *coupled* or coincident accents (m *plus* t) yield stronger accents than single accents (m *or* t), and recent research supports this assumption (Ralston, 1992). Thus, in integrating melody and rhythm we can ask how melodic and temporal accent structure combine to strengthen a common or joint accent structure. We are also interested in how resultant accent couplings of various strengths define or mark different higher order time spans within the whole tune. Notice that coupling of m and t accents yield relatively strong markers of constant time spans (of four beats) throughout this tune. In Fig. 4.3, joint accent strength is suggested by a values (a, a′, a″, etc.) in the final row where more primes imply stronger accents.

This same melody is combined with a different rhythm, namely ♩♩♩♩♩♩ . . ., in Example 2 (Fig. 4.3b). This rhythm differs from that of Example 1 in terms of the location of its t accent, which now falls on the lengthened final note of each three-tone melodic group. As a result m and t accents do not coincide. This weakens accent strengths in the joint accent pattern (relative to Example 1). Notice, however, that lawful temporal relationships remain. This lawfulness is related to the fact that t accents fall halfway between m accents in the joint sequence. I return to this issue later.

This, I hope, conveys the gist of the ideas with which we have been working.

# (a) Example 1: Rhythm is sss pause sss...

| Notes: | C | D | E | | A | B | C′ | |
|---|---|---|---|---|---|---|---|---|
| Beats: | • | • | • | • | • | • | • | • |
| | 1 | 2 | 3 | 4 | 5 | 6 | 7 | 8 |
| Melodic Accents: | m | • | • | • | m | • | • | • |
| Temporal Accents: | t | • | • | • | t | • | • | • |
| Joint Accent Structure: | a‴ | a′ | a′ | a | a‴ | a′ | a′ | a |

# (b) Example 2: Rhythm is ssLssL...

| Notes: | C | D | E | | A | B | C′ | |
|---|---|---|---|---|---|---|---|---|
| Beats: | • | • | ∧ | | • | • | ∧ | |
| | 1 | 2 | 3 | 4 | 5 | 6 | 7 | 8 |
| Melodic Accents: | m | • | • | • | m | • | • | • |
| Temporal Accents: | t | • | t | • | • | • | t | • |
| Joint Accent Structure: | a‴ | a′ | a″ | a | a″ | a′ | a″ | a |

FIG. 4.3. The same melody is shown in two different rhythms. In Panel A, Example 1 involves an SSS pause SSS... rhythm producing a t accent after each pause. In Panel B, Example 2 involves an SSSLSSL... rhythm producing a t accent on L notes. Example 1 produces the more strongly outlined Joint Accent Structure as m and t accents which are coupled yield stronger combined accents (i.e., a″).

## SOME APPLICATIONS OF DYNAMIC
## PATTERN STRUCTURES

In this section, I consider how the ideas of Joint Accent structure and Temporal Phasing introduce ways to study effects of dynamic pattern similarity in melody recognition and effects of dynamic pattern simplicity in immediate melody reproduction tasks.

### Dynamic Pattern Similarity in Melody Recognition,
### Or "I'd Swear I've Heard That Tune Before . . ."

We have all experienced the feeling that a song or a melodic theme is oddly familiar but perhaps it doesn't sound quite as we remembered it. Yet we might guess that it *really is* the same song or theme. My students and I have been exploring a general hypothesis about what affects our degree of certainty in such situations. Clearly, this must be related to certain similarities between what we have heard at one point in time and at another. But which similarities? Functional similarities for a listener will depend on both what captures the listener's attention in the first place and how this is reinstated later during some recognition test. I claim that the acts of both attending and remembering have dynamic qualities. Given this perspective, it made sense to formulate a general hypothesis that the functional *dynamic pattern similarity* of two different tunes for listeners is directly related to relational commonalities in their Joint Accent Structures.

This section considers research addressed to a specific version of this hypothesis involving the way average listeners attend to music. It focuses on the function of contour accents and their relation to temporal accents. Specifically, we proposed that the joint relation of contour-m accents and t accent specifies a tune's *dynamic shape* and that this global property is important in melody recognition. Dynamic shape refers to that part of the joint accent structure that involves the relative timing of the *pitch contour* m accents with respect to t accents. It focuses on timing of a melody's "ups" and "downs" in pitch. Thus, dynamic shape is not simply pitch contour. We already know from the work of Jay Dowling and others cited earlier that people do confuse two different melodies with the same pitch contours. But we wanted to extend these ideas to include the relative timing of pitch trajectories that make up pattern contour, so we formalized the idea of dynamic shape in order to capture salient, intonational-like aspects of a tune's pitch contour in time.

Our hunch was that average listeners tend to remember musical themes in a rhythmical way that dynamic shape might tap into. To test this we asked whether people would falsely recognize unfamiliar tunes with the same dynamic shapes as familiar ones. In recent studies we familiarized people with different tunes called *target tunes*. The target tunes differed from one another with respect to melodic interval structure and pitch contour as well as rhythm. Later on listeners heard these same target tunes in a recognition memory test and had to decide whether they had heard them before. The tricky part of this was as follows: The melody of a given target tune could appear now either with its original rhythm or with the rhythm of another target tune. And, in addition, decoy melodies were presented at recognition time in both original and different rhythms. These decoys were novel melodies with the same notes as target tunes. Their interesting feature was that half of them precisely mimicked the dynamic shape of some target tune.

We were interested in two questions concerning dynamic pattern similarity and melody recognition. First, we wondered how well people could recognize simply the melody of an original target when the dynamic similarity of the tune as a whole was changed by a rhythmic shift. Secondly, we sought to discover the degree to which *similarities* in *dynamic shape* contribute to recognition confusions. Specifically, how often would people be fooled by novel melodies that mimicked the dynamic shapes of targets?

To introduce some detail, I focus on a recent study completed in our laboratories in which average listeners were initially familiarized with three target melodies of the same musical key. An example target tune in C major is outlined in a pitch-space and time coordinate system in Fig. 4.4a. The three targets differed primarily with respect to the central notes (as indicated) where both pitch contour and interval structure distinguishes the three. We wanted to insure that target tunes differed explicitly in dynamic shape as well as in other features. Therefore, correlated with their several melodic differences were timing variations in the form of three different rhythmic figures: SSL pause..., SLS pause..., and LSS pause..., (where L and pause duration were identical and twice S). The example target combination, shown in Fig. 4.4a, relies on LSS . . LSS . . in the familiarization phase. The main constraint here on pairing melodies with rhythms was that the resultant target tune should have a prominently outlined dynamic shape in which the number of *coincidences* of contour-based m accents with rhythm-based t accents was maximized. Coupled accents are circled in Fig. 4.4. The idea was to create tunes with distinctive dynamic shapes given by strong accents.

Listeners heard these target tunes in an initial familiarization phase and they were told to *ignore* the rhythm and to selectively attend strictly to the pitch sequence. After this phase they performed an unrelated task for about 15 minutes and then received an unexpected melody recognition test. They weren't told initially about the delayed recognition test because we thought this would make the situation more realistic and also discourage people from rehearsing.

During recognition, people heard both old target tunes (from the familiarization phase) and decoy tunes (which were new). Whenever a target melody occurred, its structure in terms of pitch intervals, contour, and tonal relations remained the same as before, but it appeared in a new key so that the specific tones differed. The significant feature was that the rhythmic accompaniment

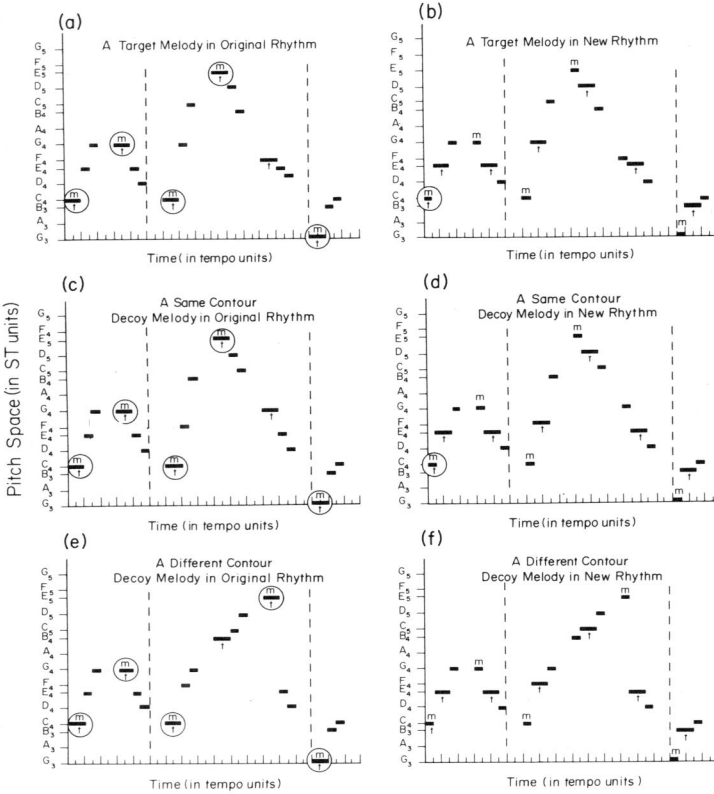

FIG. 4.4.   Example melodies used to study dynamic pattern similarity in melody recognition. A target melody is shown in original and new rhythms (Panels A, B). A decoy melody with pitch contours of the target (Same Contour) is also shown in corresponding rhythms (Panels C, D). A decoy melody with a Different Contour is shown in corresponding rhythms (Panels E, F).

of a target pitch sequence could either be the same as before (i.e., the original rhythm) or different (a new rhythm). Consequently, a target melody, when presented for recognition, could occur either within the same Joint Accent Structure as before, or within a new one resulting from the new rhythm. So, for example, the target melody shown in Fig. 4.4a with SSL appears in recognition either with this rhythm or with SLS (Fig. 4.4b). The decoys are also interesting. They were designed to gauge whether these listeners could be fooled by novel tunes with the same dynamic shape as targets. Some decoy melodies had their central notes rearranged (see dashed lines) so as to preserve only the pitch contour of a given target (Same Contour Decoys, Fig. 4.4, c,d), whereas others had these notes with the same contour accents shifted to create contours different from a given target (Different Contour Decoys, Fig. 4.4, e,f). Decoys also appeared in two different rhythms. A given decoy sometimes appeared in target's original rhythm but equally often it could appear in the rhythm of another target (i.e., a new rhythm). The design for this study is suggested by Fig. 4.4a through f, in which an example tune from each of the six conditions is shown. Note that some decoys (Same Contour Decoy plus original rhythm) followed precisely the dynamic shapes of certain targets, given jointly by m and t accents, whereas others followed only a target's t accent pattern (Different Contour Decoy plus original rhythm) or only its contour (m) accents (Same Contour Decoy plus new rhythm). Finally, some decoys followed neither m or t accent patterns (Different Contour Decoy plus new rhythm).

In recognition, people had to decide whether a presented pitch sequence was familiar ("OLD") or not ("NEW") based on earlier familiarizations. Again they were told to ignore the rhythm. In assessing performance we were interested in why people might judge an old target tune to be familiar, that is, respond "OLD" to an "OLD" melody. Could a shift in timing properties throw them off? And with respect to dynamic shape, we were interested in how often people would give a false recognition response of "OLD" to a new (decoy) melody having the target's original dynamic shape (i.e., same Contour plus original rhythm). Would they be fooled by certain decoys? These issues concern what functions for an average listener as "differentness" and "similarity" in music. We hypothesized that similarities are related to the relative timing of contour and temporal accents. Further, if initial familiarization encouraged these listeners to attend in a dynamically global way to distinctive shapes of targets, then we expected that any change in similarity, measured by relative accent timings, would reduce a listener's chance of judging either a target or a decoy melody to be "OLD."

In short, we predicted that the probability of recognizing the target melody in a new key should be lower when it also appears in a new rhythm than when it appears with its original rhythm. Secondly, we predicted that if these listeners rely heavily on dynamic shape to recognize melodies, then the probability of misjudging those decoys that simulate the dynamic shape of real targets should be relatively high.

Although these predictions seemed straightforward to us, they had not been previously evaluated. In fact, they are not the only possible predictions, given current thinking. For instance, if people treat melody and rhythm as independent components of a tune, then perhaps they *can* independently attend to melodic structure and ignore rhythm as instructed. If so, then the prediction is that rhythmic changes should not affect melody recognition. Or, to take another example, some coding accounts imply that if rhythm has a general effect on melody recognition, it stems from the rhythm's pause structure: Pauses enforce melodic codes of certain tone groups. However, in these particular rhythms we insured that the pause-based grouping potential was *identical* for all rhythms.

Therefore, even this account predicts that rhythmic changes should not affect recognition of either targets or decoys because their melodic codes will be unaffected in this case.

The results of this study, which replicated earlier ones (e.g., Jones, Summerell, & Marshburn, 1987) are in Fig. 4.5. The probability of an "OLD" recognition response given the melodic structure of a pattern (Target, Same Contour Decoy, or Different Contour Decoy) is plotted as a function of the rhythm presented in recognition (original and new).

In terms of our questions, the data clearly suggest the influence of dynamic pattern similarity on melody recognition. People had significant difficulty recognizing a key-transposed target melody in a new rhythm even when they were told to ignore the rhythm. Apparently they cannot easily do this because the probability of correctly identifying the melody drops to near 60% in the new rhythm. Melody and rhythm do seem to be psychologically inseparable. With regard to the second question, people were also significantly misled by decoys with the same dynamic shape as target tunes: The probability of saying (incorrectly) "OLD" to decoy melodies with the same contour and rhythm as the target is fairly high. These findings have recently been extended by Jones and Ralston (1991). They suggest that functional similarity for musically unsophisticated listeners has a dynamic component. A wholistic property, dynamic shape partly determines how people remember tunes.

In summary, one means of describing the interplay of melody and rhythm involves the Joint Accent Structure. If the accent and timing relationships that characterize Joint Accent Structure are taken as a basis for manipulating dynamic pattern similarity, then this explains why people tend to judge a familiar melody to be unfamiliar when it appears in a new rhythm. Its dynamic similarity to the old tune has changed. Likewise, if we manipulate only the contour and temporal accents in a Joint Accent Structure, then the dynamic shape of a novel melody can be made to mimic that of a familiar tune and, in recognition, listeners are fooled by this. This suggests that people attend to and remember the dynamic shape of a tune (within some key). Composers seem to know these facts about human nature quite well. Rules of dynamic pattern similarities are tacitly used by artists as tricks-of-trade to create in listeners different degrees of recognition for recurrent melodic themes.

## Dynamic Pattern Simplicity in Reproducing Melodies, Or "It's Just a Simple Little Melody . . ."

Pattern similarity refers to ways things are alike regardless of how simple or complex they are. A second issue concerns musical pattern simplicity. However, I maintain that simplicity, too, must be dynamically conceived, for it pertains to the way in which melody and rhythm combine. An advantage of the idea of Joint Accent Structure is that it permits us to address not only functional

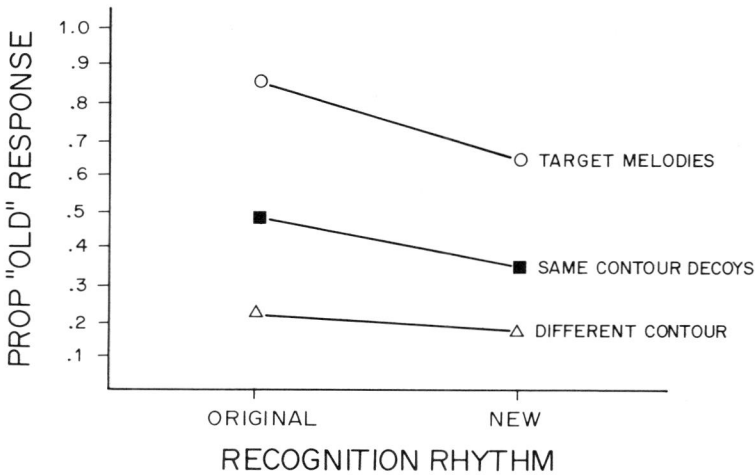

FIG. 4.5.    Proportion of "OLD" recognition responses (after 11 familiarization trials with each target tune) to target melodies and to Same Contour Decoys and Different Contour Decoys as a function of rhythm. Note that an "OLD" response is correct for targets (Hit) but erroneous for decoys (False Alarm).

similarities among dynamic patterns but also their simplicity properties. This section considers *dynamic pattern simplicity*. By definition, simpler tunes should be those easier for people to reproduce. Especially if pattern simplicity is gauged in situations where people can "use" a tune's structure to remember it later, simpler sequences should encourage more efficient use. I assume that dynamically simple patterns are more easily "tracked" during attending and hence more accurately reproduced during remembering. Effectively, I assume that the psychological activities of attending and remembering are linked and that both are dynamic in nature. A further link is between attending and musical pattern structure. Marilyn Boltz and I formalized the latter link by relying on the construct of Joint Accent Structure (Boltz & Jones, 1986). We suggested that some combinations of m and t accents in patterns produce greater symmetry in the time relations associated with a Joint Accent Structure. These should be more effective in guiding dynamic attending. That is, melody and rhythm combinations that yield greater temporal regularity in their Joint Accent Structure should be simpler.

Of course, the big question is "What combinations of melody and rhythm can be predicted to yield these nice time properties (and, parenthetically, how do we measure nice)?" Our research has led us to think about dynamic simplicity criteria not only in terms of Joint Accent Structure, but also in terms of Temporal Phasing of m and t accents. Yet, as this question suggests, both constructs require refinements. I mention two refinements, one involving accent strength and time hierarchies, and the other involving time ratios in Temporal Phasing.

*Accent Strength and Time Hierarchies.* Lawfulness in time relationships can be more directly addressed if we consider different time levels that
are "marked" by accents in the Joint Accent Structure. To illustrate, imagine
that a melody, as a sequence of pitch relationships, displays a relatively large
pitch interval after every fourth tone, one that sort of catches the attention.
According to the prior rationale, then every fifth note can function as a melodic
accent, m. Thus for a 16-beat (·) melody with a tone sequence of this sort, the
m accent sequence is as shown in Table 4.1. As before, we may "add in" some
rhythmic structure with temporal accents. Let the durational pattern of an ac-
companying rhythm be one where a prominent pause or silence occurs after
every seven beats. As shown, t accents then follow on every eighth beat. Thus,
the m accent period is four beats, and the t period is eight beats. Considering
m and t accents together, the Joint Accent Structure is shown in Table 4.1.

Now consider possible differences in accent strength. To illustrate, let accent strength vary from 0 to n as indexed by the number, n, of primes associated with a. Then the strongest accents will occur with coupled m and t accents.
These are denoted by a ''' with a strength metric of three (i.e., three primes).
Singly occurring accents, m or t, are less prominent markers of time periods
and are denoted by a '' with a strength metric of two. Onsets of ordinary tones
create still weaker accents, namely a ' with a strength of one; and finally simple
beats, which happen in silences or longer notes, are unaccented with no primes
for a and hence have a strength of 0 (see also Fig. 4.3).

Accent strength differences allow us to amplify some hierarchical time properties. The hierarchical nature of accent-based time spans in a Joint Accent Structure is also evident in Table 4.1. If we consider simply time spans marked by
the stronger accents (e.g., a'''—a'''), then temporal regularity is realized in
a fixed number of beat spans throughout for that level (i.e., eight beats). Smaller
(nested) time spans (e.g., a''—a') are marked by correspondingly weaker

TABLE 4.1
A Simple Melody-Rhythm Combination with No-Phase Shift of Accents
(m-accent period is four beats, t-accent period is eight beats)

| Beats | 1 | 2 | 3 | 4 | 5 | 6 | 7 | 8 | 9 | 10 | 11 | 12 | 13 | 14 | 15 | 16 |
|---|---|---|---|---|---|---|---|---|---|---|---|---|---|---|---|---|
| Melodic Accents | m | . | . | . | m | . | . | . | m | . | . | . | m | . | . | . |
| Temporal Accents | t | . | . | . | . | . | . | . | t | . | . | . | . | . | . | . |
| Joint Accents Structure | $a'''$ | . | . | . | $a''$ | . | . | . | $a'''$ | . | . | . | $a''$ | . | . | . |

$TR_{t/m} = 8/4 = 2$     Hierarchical Time Spans*: span:     Lengths in beats
                                              a'''—a''': 8
                                              a''—a'':  4, 4, 4

*Assume that stronger (e.g., a''') accents can also initiate and close time spans of adjacent
weaker (e.g., a') accents. Thus a'''—a'' is summarized as a''—a''.

accents but these are regular, too (i.e., four spans each of four beats). The idea of the inverse relationship between accent strength and time period was first proposed by Jim Martin in 1972 and it has been adapted and modified by others, including myself. One modification I have suggested involves summarizing covarying structural changes in a musical pattern in terms of accent strengths that relate to the number of coupled accents. Another adaptation involves the time spans themselves and their ratio relationships; I consider this next.

***Time Ratios and Temporal Phasing.***     One property of time hierarchies I have been interested in involves time ratios (Jones, 1976, 1981). I think these can summarize how effectively the hierarchy's time symmetries, namely its temporal regularities, can be used by a rhythmically sensitive attender. Functionally speaking, dynamic pattern simplicity can be related to time hierarchies and their ratio properties. In this section, I'll illustrate two kinds of time ratios.

Consider first the higher order, $a'''$ to $a'''$, time spans in Table 4.1. These neatly divide the pattern's total duration, and are, in turn, divided in the same way by lower order time spans ($a'''$ to $a''$ spans). One way to formalize these temporal relations is in terms of time ratios, TR, for example:

$$ TR = \frac{a''' - a'''}{a''' - a''} \frac{8 \text{ beats}}{4 \text{ beats}} = 2 $$

This integer ratio is invariant over the whole time pattern. Clearly, this is because t to t spans are always eight beats in duration, whereas the m to m spans always cover four beats. That is, the ratio invariant time property of a Joint Accent Structure stems from the time relation between invariant periods, respectively, of m and t accents. Thus, this time ratio is based directly on time relations *between* the two accents, $TR_{t/m}$, is:

$$ TR_{t/m} = \frac{t - t}{m - m} \frac{8 \text{ beats}}{4 \text{ beats}} = 2 $$

Because t and m accents everywhere have the same period and because the pattern begins with a coincidence (m with t), the m and t relations in the $TR_{t/m}$ specify temporal lawfulness in the Joint Accent Structure.

This time ratio can take several forms, but all reflect the idea that phasing of melodic and temporal accent periods indexes simplicity of accent-time hierarchies. To see this, we can play with temporal phasing of m and t accents. For example, we can change t accents by changing the rhythm and holding melody constant or vice versa. In theory there are many ways to do this and I leave most to the reader's imagination.

Instead, let me concentrate on a manipulation that we have recently studied. It involves temporal manipulations of either the m or t beat pattern that (a) preserves both of the individual accent m, t periods but (b) modifies time hierarchy relationships so as to affect pattern simplicity via phasing relationships.

Here, a relevant manipulation involves a rhythm change that shifts only t accents, relative to m accents. An example of this occurred with the rhythm changes reported in the last section on pattern simplicity. That is, the same melody appeared in different rhythms but all rhythms had identical t accent periods (e.g., see Fig. 4.4). Phase shifts that changed dynamic similarity by decoupling contour and temporal accents were achieved by modifying only the length of the *first* t accent period.

Other examples of phase-shifting are shown in Tables 4.1 and 4.2. In Table 4.1 is the melody previously described in a rhythm that introduced a constant eight-beat t accent period with no phase shift. This combination gave TR = $TR_{t/m}$ of 2. Now, holding melody constant, if this rhythm is changed so that the eight-beat t accent sequence is initially phase-shifted to various degrees, then different temporal phase relations of m and t appear. These are shown in Table 4.2. Table 4.2 illustrates initial phase shifts of the eight-beat t period that are one, two, three, and four beats long.

What does a phase-shift do to the time symmetry of a hierarchy built on the Joint Accent Structure? Time spans of the accent-time hierarchies associated with all phase-shifts can be seen in Tables 4.1 and 4.2. Notice two aspects of these hierarchies: (a) When t accents are shifted by a time interval greater than zero (No Phase-Shift), but less than the four-beat m accent period (i.e., by one, two, or three beats), then hierarchical time spans are less clearly outlined (than for shifts of zero and four beats). This is because fewer strong, coupled, accents appear; and (b) The higher order time periods, although outlined by weaker accents, are more uniform in the hierarchy resulting from a two-beat phase-shift than in hierarchies of one- or three-beat phase-shifts. That is, the former has only periods of two and four, whereas in the latter periods of three, one, and four appear (see Table 4.2).

One way of assessing dynamic pattern simplicity associated with temporal phasings relies on time ratios. But here a new time ratio is needed. Note that all Phase-Shifted patterns yield a basic $TR_{t/m}$, of 2.00. However, they differ with respect to the *initial* periods of m and t accents. For instance, if the larger *initial* accent period, the m period now, is divided by the *initial* t accent period (one, two, three or four beats) then a Shift $TR_{m/t}$ ratio can be defined. For initial phase-shifts of one, two, three, four beats, this Shift $TR_{m/t}$ metric takes on values of 4, 2, 1.33, and 1, respectively. Whole integer and small integer values of the Shift $TR_{m/t}$ appear to be correlated with simpler time hierarchies, and so this sort of Temporal Phasing metric further clarifies dynamic simplicity properties. More symmetrical time hierarchies are those with Temporal Phase ratios (Shift TRs) based on small integer values.

Marilyn Boltz and I found general support for a time ratio metric in performances of musically sophisticated listeners who had to reproduce melodies (Boltz & Jones, 1986). We manipulated both m and t accent sequences using simple melodies, where m accents came from both pitch contour change and interval

# TABLE 4.2
## Four Different Phase-Shifts of Rhythmic Accents

*(m-accent period is four beats, t-accent period is eight beats)*

### 1. One Beat

| | 1 | 2 | 3 | 4 | 5 | 6 | 7 | 8 | 9 | 10 | 11 | 12 | 13 | 14 | 15 | 16 |
|---|---|---|---|---|---|---|---|---|---|---|---|---|---|---|---|---|
| Beats | 1 | 2 | 3 | 4 | 5 | 6 | 7 | 8 | 9 | 10 | 11 | 12 | 13 | 14 | 15 | 16 |
| Melodic Accents | m | · | · | · | m | · | · | · | m | · | · | · | m | · | · | · |
| Temporal Accents | t | t | · | · | · | · | · | · | · | t | · | · | · | · | · | · |
| Joint Accent Structure | a''' | a'' | · | · | a'' | · | · | · | a'' | a'' | · | · | a'' | · | · | · |

$TR_{t/m} = 8/4 = 2$

$\text{Shift } TR_{m/1} = 4/1 = 4$

Hierarchical Time Spans: (in beats)  a''—a'': 1, 3, 4, 1, 3

### 2. Two Beats

| | 1 | 2 | 3 | 4 | 5 | 6 | 7 | 8 | 9 | 10 | 11 | 12 | 13 | 14 | 15 | 16 |
|---|---|---|---|---|---|---|---|---|---|---|---|---|---|---|---|---|
| Beats | 1 | 2 | 3 | 4 | 5 | 6 | 7 | 8 | 9 | 10 | 11 | 12 | 13 | 14 | 15 | 16 |
| Melodic Accents | m | · | · | · | m | · | · | · | m | · | · | · | m | · | · | · |
| Temporal Accents | t | · | t | · | · | · | · | · | · | · | t | · | · | · | · | · |
| Joint Accent Structure | a''' | · | a'' | · | a'' | · | · | · | a'' | · | a'' | · | a'' | · | · | · |

$TR_{t/m} = 8/4 = 2$

$\text{Shift } TR_{m/2} = 4/2 = 2$

Hierarchical Time Spans: (in beats)  a''—a'': 2, 2, 4, 2, 2

### 3. Three Beats

| | 1 | 2 | 3 | 4 | 5 | 6 | 7 | 8 | 9 | 10 | 11 | 12 | 13 | 14 | 15 | 16 |
|---|---|---|---|---|---|---|---|---|---|---|---|---|---|---|---|---|
| Beats | 1 | 2 | 3 | 4 | 5 | 6 | 7 | 8 | 9 | 10 | 11 | 12 | 13 | 14 | 15 | 16 |
| Melodic Accents | m | · | · | · | m | · | · | · | m | · | · | · | m | · | · | · |
| Temporal Accents | t | · | · | t | · | · | · | · | · | · | · | t | · | · | · | · |
| Joint Accent Structure | a''' | · | · | a'' | a'' | · | · | · | a'' | · | · | a'' | a'' | · | · | · |

$TR_{t/m} = 8/4 = 2$

$\text{Shift } TR_{m/3} = 4/3 = 1.33$

Hierarchical Time Spans: (in beats)  a''—a'': 3, 1, 4, 3, 1

### 4. Four Beats

| | 1 | 2 | 3 | 4 | 5 | 6 | 7 | 8 | 9 | 10 | 11 | 12 | 13 | 14 | 15 | 16 |
|---|---|---|---|---|---|---|---|---|---|---|---|---|---|---|---|---|
| Beats | 1 | 2 | 3 | 4 | 5 | 6 | 7 | 8 | 9 | 10 | 11 | 12 | 13 | 14 | 15 | 16 |
| Melodic Accents | m | · | · | · | m | · | · | · | m | · | · | · | m | · | · | · |
| Temporal Accents | t | · | · | · | t | · | · | · | · | · | · | · | t | · | · | · |
| Joint Accent Structure | a''' | · | · | · | a''' | · | · | · | a'' | · | · | · | a''' | · | · | · |

$TR_{t/m} = 8/4 = 2$

$\text{Shift } TR_{m/4} = 4/4 = 1$

Hierarchical Time Spans*: (in beats)  a'''—a''': 4, 8  a''—a'': 4, 4

*Assume that stronger (e.g., a''') accents can also initiate and close time spans of adjacent weaker (e.g., a'') accents. Thus a'''—a'' is summarized both as a''—a''.

differences, and simple rhythms, where t accents were determined by pauses. Of interest, from the point of view of temporal phasing, were several conditions wherein m and t accents, both with constant periods, either were not phase-shifted, or were phase-shifted. Other, more complicated variations of accent timing relations were also introduced in these studies so that the ratio metric used was a more elaborate one. However, the main point is this: The easiest tunes to reproduce were those with simple $TR_{t/m}$ ratios, which involved no phase-shifts. Next were those with both simple $TR_{t/m}$ ratios and simple Shift $TR_{m/t}$ ratio values. In general, a time–ratio metric sensitive to both m and t time periods and to their various phase relations nicely predicted performance. We considered this promising support for the idea that dynamic pattern simplicity is tied to symmetry in time hierarchies of the Joint Accent Structure, and that it can be estimated from time ratios related to accent periodicities and their phase relationships.

In summary, time hierarchies of Joint Accent Structures suggest new ways to approach dynamic simplicity in musical patterns. This approach assumes that simplicity of patterns arises from interdependencies of melody and rhythm. It works because listeners are sensitive to higher order relative time properties in music, ones that can be described in terms of several ratio properties (e.g. complex versus simple time ratios). Undoubtedly, musical artists rely upon this intuitive knowledge about the way people "track" and anticipate things in time in order to control a listener's attending. Among other things, it enables composers and performers to communicate important new musical ideas and to insert meaningful surprises at the "right" time.

## CONCLUSION

In summary, I have tried to suggest some new ways of experimenting with the complex problem of integrated musical structure. My bias has been evident. I assume that the most meaningful way to conceive of the functional structure in musical patterns is to directly attack interrelationships of melody and rhythm. In this chapter I indicated that concepts such as Joint Accent Structure and Temporal phasing can be profitably used to design and analyze experiments about dynamic pattern similarity and dynamic pattern simplicity. Both issues are fundamentally related to ways musical artists rely on principles of dynamic lawfulness to communicate melodic themes, while at the same time controlling the listener's attending.

## ACKNOWLEDGMENTS

This chapter was based on a talk presented by the author at the meeting of the American Association for Advancement Science in May 1986. Research was sponsored in part by a National Science Foundation (BNS-8204811) to the author.

The chapter was revised and expanded while the author was a fellow at the Netherlands Institute for Advanced Study (1986–1987).

## REFERENCES

Boltz, M., & Jones, M. R. (1986). Does rule recursion make melodies easier to reproduce? If not, what does? *Cognitive Psychology, 18*, 389–431.
Dowling, W. J. (1978). Scale and contour: Two components of a theory of memory for melodies. *Psychological Review, 85*, 341–354.
Dowling, W. J., & Fujitani, D. S. (1971). Contour, interval, and pitch recognition in memory for melodies. *Journal of the Acoustical Society of America, 49*, 524–531.
Dowling, W. J., & Harwood, D. L. (1985). *Music cognition.* New York: Academic Press.
Essens, P. J., & Povel, D. J. (1985). Metrical and nonmetrical representations of temporal patterns. *Perception & Psychophysics, 37*, 1–7.
Fraisse, P. (1964). *The psychology of time.* London: Eyre & Spottiwoode.
Handel, S. (1989). *Listening: An introduction to the perception of auditory events.* Cambridge, MA: MIT Press.
Jones, M. R. (1976). Time, our lost dimension. *Psychological Review, 83*, 323–335.
Jones, M. R. (1981). Only time can tell: On the topology of mental space and time. *Critical Inquiry, 7*, 557–576.
Jones, M. R., & Boltz, M. (1989). Dynamic attending and responses to time. *Psychological Review, 96*, 459–491.
Jones, M. R., & Ralston, J. T. (1991). Some influences of accent structure on melody recognition. *Memory & Cognition, 19*, 8–20.
Jones, M. R., Summerell, L., & Marshburn, E. (1987). Recognizing melodies: A dynamic interpretation. *Quarterly Journal of Experimental Psychology, 39*, 89–121.
Krumhansl, C. L., & Shepard, R. N. (1979). Quantification of the hierarchy of tonal functions within a diatonic context. *Journal of Experimental Psychology: Human Perception and Performance, 5*, 579–594.
Martin, J. (1972). Rhythmic (hierarchical) versus serial structure in speech and other behavior. *Psychological Review, 79*, 487–509.
Massaro, D. W., Kallman, H. J., & Kelly, J. L. (1980). The role of tone height, melodic contour, and tone chroma in melody recognition. *Journal of Experimental Psychology: Human Learning and Memory, 6*, 77–90.
Narmour, E. (1990). *The analysis and cognition of basic melodic structures: The implication-realization model.* Chicago: University of Chicago Press.
Narmour, E. (1992). The influence of embodied registral motion on the perception of higher-level melodic implication. In M. R. Jones & S. Holleran (Eds.), *Cognitive bases of musical communication* (pp. 69–90). Washington, D.C.: American Psychological Association.
Palmer, C. (1992). The role of interpretive preferences in music performance. In M. R. Jones & S. Holleran (Eds.), *Cognitive bases of musical communication* (pp. 247–262). Washington, D.C.: American Psychological Association.
Povel, D. J. (1981). Internal representations of simple temporal patterns. *Journal of Experimental Psychology: Human Perception and Performance, 7*, 3–18.
Ralston, J. T. (1992). *Listening and responding to music: Exploring the influence of melodic accents, temporal accents, and task.* Unpublished doctoral dissertation, The Ohio State University, Columbus.
Shepard, R. N. (1982). Structural representations of musical pitch. In D. Deutsch (Ed.), *The psychology of music* (pp. 343–390). New York: Academic Press.

Sloboda, J. A. (1983). The communication of musical metre in piano performance. *Quarterly Journal of Experimental Psychology, 35*(A), 377–390.

Watkins, A. J. (1985). Scale, key, and contour in the discrimination of tuned and mistuned approximations to melody. *Perception & Psychophysics, 37,* 275–285.

# The Complexities of Rhythm

Alf Gabrielsson
*Uppsala University, Sweden*

Most people seem to have an intuitive notion of what is meant by rhythm in music. It is often the rhythm that provides the basic structure as well as the dominant emotional character of a piece of music—be it a short tune, a dance, a jazz improvisation, or a symphonic work. It establishes a regular pulse, in relation to which the musical events develop in ever-changing combinations, from the most simple and safe (sometimes even tedious) to the extremely complex and tense. You may feel it in your body as an impetus to move—and in fact you often do: tapping your foot, clapping your hands, shaking your head, maybe even dancing. But rhythm is not always an "energizer." On the contrary, it can as well be used to calm down and relax, as in lullabies. Whatever the case, rhythm and motion are inextricably joined to each other, as are motion and emotion.

But is it really correct to ascribe all these effects solely to rhythm? Music is said to be composed of many different elements besides rhythm, such as melody, harmony, and timbre. Of course, in most of our Western music all these components work together and interact in more or less complicated ways. There is always timbre of some kind, associated with the musical instruments or voices that are used. There is practically always melody and rhythm, and there may be harmony, as when a tune is accompanied by underlying chords, or when several independent parts combine in polyphonic music such as a fugue by J. S. Bach. It is hard to avoid the impression though that rhythm is somehow basic in the musical process. Music takes place in time, and the temporal organization of the sound events achieved through rhythm simply *must* be of fundamental importance. In fact there is no melody without rhythm; melody thus presupposes rhythm. But rhythm does not presuppose melody; you can clap or drum a rhythm without any trace of melodic content. The usual distinction between melody and rhythm is then not always relevant, because those two concepts often fuse in the musical reality. Harmony too is dependent on rhythm for similar reasons. Whether there are chords or tone combinations resulting from different voices in polyphonic music, they proceed and change according to the rhythmic organization, a process sometimes called "harmonic rhythm."

Despite these facts, and although we usually have a "self-evident" experience of rhythm, it has proved notoriously difficult to agree upon a proper definition of rhythm. The attempts at definitions may be counted in hundreds (Fraisse, 1982, 1987; Gabrielsson, 1986). Furthermore, rhythm is used as a concept in many contexts other than music and dance, for example, rhythm in poetry, speech, architecture, drama, film, athletics, body movements, biological processes (heart rhythm, brain rhythms), and so on. This diversity is another testimony of the importance of rhythm. At the same time, however, it makes the task of definition even more difficult. These other fields are left outside the present discussion except for such body movements that have a natural connection to music.

In the following we adopt a working definition of musical or auditory rhythm as being "a response to music or sound sequences of certain characteristics, comprising experiential as well as behavioral aspects." By analyzing and investigating these aspects of the rhythm response (mainly the experiential), and by studying the characteristics of music or sound sequences that elicit rhythm responses of various kinds, one should at least come somewhat closer to an understanding of this elusive phenomenon—but it seems wise to keep the aspirations at a low level. Maybe even part of the fascination we feel concerning rhythm (and music) is due to this elusiveness, that the phenomenon defies our usual analytic tools and keeps showing other sides of itself when we think we have caught some of them into our dissecting net.

Before that perhaps some qualifying statements are in order. A music expert may find some of the foregoing statements about the relationships between various musical elements simplistic and incomplete. He or she may also point out that there is in fact also music without rhythm, not the least in avant-garde music from our own century, and would perhaps ask to what degree the discussion is applicable to music outside the areas of Western art music and popular music focused here. At this point we can only agree and answer that rhythm is a very large subject, and this chapter is bound to be short. Hopefully the following pages will tell a story with many more nuances and inspire one to further reading of other, more comprehensive texts.

## Rhythm versus Non-Rhythm

A natural first step in the attempts at defining rhythm would be to make it clear what the difference is between rhythm and non-rhythm. In the literature you will then usually find one or more of the following characteristics, which are said to delimit rhythm from non-rhythm.

*Grouping.* The experience of rhythm means some kind of experienced grouping of the sound events. In other words, you perceive the rhythm as a pattern, as a whole, not as a series of isolated events. This is a good example of a gestalt, the key concept in the Gestalt psychology launched in Germany in the 1910s and now generally accepted in psychology. It is easy to demonstrate this principle of grouping. If somebody claps or plays a rhythm and asks you to reproduce it, you can usually do this without any conscious reflection regarding how many claps there were or how they were organized—you just clap the *pattern.* (There are limits to this, of course. If the rhythm is too complex to be grasped at once, some analysis of the difficult points may help. Once they are mastered, you may return to the spontaneous, nonreflecting mode of working.)

It was shown already in the early experimental psychology around 1900 that this tendency to grouping is so strong that even if you use a completely uniform sequence of sounds (all sounds are exactly alike and come at an absolutely regular rate, e.g., a series of identical clicks), people will tend to hear these sounds in groups of two, three, or four or even larger units. How many members are grouped together depends on the rate: the faster the rate, the more members in the perceived group, and vice versa. As there is no physical basis in the stimulus to suggest a grouping, this kind of grouping was named "subjective rhythmization." (But according to our definition of rhythm given earlier, rhythm may always be considered as "subjective" in the sense that it is some kind of a response.)

Sometimes one can read reports in which it is claimed that the rhythm factor has been eliminated or controlled by making all tones in a melody equally long and equally loud. In view of the foregoing this is of course not very convincing; grouping may appear despite these equalities. Furthermore, the sequence of pitches in the melody may in itself also suggest a grouping. To keep melody and rhythm strictly apart seems fruitless.

*Accent.* The experience of rhythm is further characterized by experienced accenting on one or more members of the pattern. In the simplest case of a group with only two events, the accent may occur on the first of them (ONE—two, ONE—two, etc.) or the second (one—TWO, one—TWO). With three members the most common case is probably ONE—two—three (e.g., oom-pah-pah), but one—TWO—three or one—two—THREE may occur as well. There can also be more than only two levels or degrees of accent (that is, accented and unaccented); for instance, that the first event is accented, the second unaccented, and the third somehow in between. With a group of four members the number of alternatives increases further, and four different levels of accent (prominence) may be used; as, for instance, ONE—two—THREE—four. These examples are but a few common cases to suggest the variety of alternatives and possibilities available in real music.

The behavioral response to accents is often easily observed: People clap their hands or stamp their feet in accordance with the pattern of accents, or sometimes in opposition to it; there are numerous ways of having fun with rhythm. The musician has many means to achieve the intended accents. He or she may increase the duration of the tone, increase its intensity, give it a slightly deviating pitch, a sharp attack, and so forth, depending on what type of instrument used and, of course, on the musical context. Sometimes the context is such that the musician would rather do the opposite to achieve the desired accent, that is, *shorten* the tone, *decrease* its intensity or the like. The thing is that the accented tone somehow should stand out from the others. Perceived accent may thus be a function of many different physical factors.

*Regularity.* Implicit in the preceding two characteristics of rhythm is some kind of perceived regularity. The groups repeat themselves, and the accented members recur regularly. Of course, there is a certain tolerance concerning this regularity, and we see later that in performance of real music there may be considerable deviations from regularity. There is also another basic experience of regularity, namely that of a regular *pulse* or *beat*, that goes through the whole piece we are listening to (or at least for long parts of it). The rate of this pulse defines what is usually called the *tempo* of the piece and is often indicated by a note value and a number in the beginning, for instance, $\quarternote = 100$, which means that the rate should be 100 quarter notes per minute. In actual musical practice there may be considerable variations around this tempo, and how fast we feel that the music moves is also affected by many other factors (to be mentioned in a later context). Nevertheless to grasp the pulse is basic to the experience of rhythm. It gives information not only about the tempo but also provides the framework necessary for realizing the *meter* of the piece (the number of beats per measure) and various subdivisions of the beat (Longuet-Higgins, 1976; Longuet-Higgins & Lee, 1984; Povel, 1981; Povel & Essens, 1985).

When we listen to music, we often follow the beat by overt movements, such as tapping the feet or fingers in synchrony with the beat. The meter and the associated accents may be reflected as well; for instance, in quadruple meter you give an extra push to every fourth beat. This is the type of information that a conductor brings to his orchestra or choir; the beat and the meter must be made clear (as well as a lot of other things, of course). Sometimes one can feel the pulse at two different rates, one of them at, say, twice the rate of the other, and perhaps you use one foot to follow the slower one and the other foot (or the hand) to accompany the faster one. Whatever the case, a feeling of regularity is established, a safe ground in the ongoing musical flow.

***The Psychological Present.*** A fourth condition for rhythm is that the phenomena described so far take place within a relatively short amount of time, what the philosopher and psychologist William James once called "the specious present." By that he meant the extent of the duration within which you can experience a sequence of events, for example, a rhythm pattern, as simultaneously present in consciousness. It was later called "the psychological present" and is related to the concept of short-term memory in contemporary psychology. This duration is short, in most cases only a few seconds. In fact, the ability to experience a rhythm pattern or a melody as a whole has been used as a criterion for measurement of the psychological present. The meaning of this condition for rhythm is easily demonstrated. Clap any rhythm pattern you like. Then make it successively slower and slower, and it won't take long until you discover that it gets very difficult to clap it any longer; the pattern dissolves, leaving only a number of isolated events. You may make a conscious mental effort to still keep them together, but in that case there is a *conceived* (cognitively constructed) rhythm rather than a spontaneously perceived one.

The same reasoning holds for melody. The phrases in a melody are typically very short, only a few seconds. See how long they are if you sing the first two phrases of "Happy Birthday to You." It is no problem to keep each of them or perhaps both in consciousness at the same time. But you can hardly pretend to have the whole tune present at once in consciousness, not even for this well-known piece. And it would be even more difficult to pretend this for an unfamiliar tune.

There is an interesting class of examples in the history of music, where melodies are used in a way that they can hardly be directly perceived. During the Baroque era many works for organ were written as artful elaborations of a hymn. The hymn itself, called the *cantus firmus*, appeared in one of the parts at a very slow pace, surrounded by much faster moving and elaborated parts. (See Fig. 5.1 for an example). A listener ignorant of this construction will naturally have his or her attention directed toward the faster parts, which allow the perception of various melodic-rhythmic patterns, whereas the listener won't at all detect the underlying *cantus firmus*, because it exceeds the limit of the psychological present to a high degree. In the present example, the listener will instead experience the single tones of the *cantus firmus* as providing a harmonic foundation for the upper parts (which it in fact *also* is).

***Summary.*** We may conclude that the experience of rhythm includes some kind of grouping, accents, and regularity within the limits of the psychological present. We would thus experience non-rhythm if these conditions are not met, that is, if there were no perceived grouping, accent or regularity, or exceeding the temporal limits for what we can perceive as belonging together at once. This seems reasonable, although it cannot be the whole story. Of course, there are sometimes also borderline cases, in which there is an unstable or inter-

FIG. 5.1.   The beginning of Johann Pachelbel's (1653–1706) organ chorale "Vom Himmel hoch, da komm ich her." The *cantus firmus* appears in the lowest (pedal) part. (From "Choralvorspiele alter Meister," edited by Karl Straube, Edition Peters No. 3048.)

mittent feeling of rhythm. Furthermore, individual differences in earlier experiences of a certain type of rhythm or music can be a decisive factor and explain why some people perceive rhythm while others do not, even when they are listening to the same music.

## Description of Musical Rhythms

Having delimited rhythm from non-rhythm, we now proceed to another problem, one that is central in any discussion of musical rhythm: how to find an adequate descriptive system or classification of musical rhythms.

Such a system presupposes a number of appropriate criteria for the division of rhythms into different categories. A fundamental difficulty is, of course, the enormous multitude of rhythms. We may in fact consider the population of rhythms in music as infinitely large, even if we restrict ourselves to rhythms in Western classical and popular music. Many writers have tried to establish an ordered system out of this confusing multitude. Nobody has succeeded, and it seems doubtful that anybody will ever succeed, if the goal is to create the "final" definitive and exhaustive system.

In textbooks on music theory one can usually find a number of proposed criteria. One common and self-evident criterion is that rhythms differ with regard to meter, that is, the number of beats per measure, such as duple meter or triple meter, both of which are called *simple meters*, the former even, the latter uneven. Compound meters are multiples of those, for example, quadruple meter (2 × 2) or sixtuple meter (2 × 3). These meters are also said to be regular, whereas irregular meters are characterized by unequally long groups, such as quintuple meter (either 2 + 3 or 3 + 2) or seventuple meter (3 + 4 or 4 + 3). Another criterion concerns the position or distribution of accents in the groups, as already briefly described in the preceding section. Still another criterion deals with the subdivision, if any, of the beat, for example, into two equal units, three equal units, combinations of unequal units, and so on.

These criteria are usually reflected in the conventional musical notation. Some examples of that are given in Fig. 5.2, in which the beat is designated by a quarter note (♩). The meter is given in the beginning, for example, 2/4, that is, two quarter notes per measure. The subdivision of a beat is also evident from the notation. There are in most cases no special designations for accents, but it is an implicit rule that the first note after the barline (the line separating measures) should have the strongest accent, unless anything else is indicated. This means, for instance, that the lowest pattern in Fig. 5.2 will have its strongest accent on its third note (that immediately after the barline), which is also evident from the text below it. The two preceding eighth notes constitute a so-called upbeat.

Another proposal is that musical rhythms could be classified in analogy with units commonly used in prosody, such as iamb (usually designated as ˘ ‐, where ‐ means accented and ˘ unaccented), anapest (˘ ˘ ‐), trochee (‐ ˘), dactyl (‐ ˘ ˘), and amphibrach (˘ ‐ ˘). The most elaborated version of this idea appears in a well-known book, *The Rhythmic Structure of Music* by Cooper and Meyer (1960; for a discussion, see Gabrielsson, 1986).

The criteria proposed in the foregoing approaches are undoubtedly important and easily applied in many contexts. They refer to what may be called the *structural aspects* of rhythms, and they are typically illustrated by examples given in musical notation as those in Fig. 5.2 (there are many more, much more varied).

FIG. 5.2. Upper: Two measures in 2/4, 3/4, and 4/4 meter. Middle: Examples of various subdivision of beats: Lower: Example of an upbeat.

It is well-known, however, that the musical notation is unable to adequately represent all those rhythmic varieties that we meet in real music (as well as other features e.g., dynamic nuances, details in pitch intonation). The notation is a kind of abstraction or rationalization, and every performing musician has to learn a set of implicit rules *outside* the notation in order to create live music. (It is a common misbelief among people not acquainted with music that the musical score gives a "true" representation of how the music sounds and/or should be performed.) These rules are different for different types of music and are learned through listening and imitating. To take but one example: It is known that the accompaniment in a Viennese waltz, which is *notated* as three equally long beats in 3/4 meter, is in fact *performed* so that the first beat is shortened and the second lengthened—in other words, the second beat comes "too early," which gives a special and characteristic rhythm to this kind of music.

A too heavy reliance on rhythms *as notated* is therefore to be avoided. There are actually rhythms that cannot be adequately represented in the common notation, and much "rhythmic" music such as jazz or folk music, never appears in notation at all. We would rather study rhythms as they are *experienced*. This is not to deny the importance of such criteria as meter, accents, and the like, only to suggest that they must be supplemented with many other factors in order to cover the varieties of rhythmic experience.

A related objection refers to the emphasis on *structural* aspects of rhythms in using this kind of criteria. Imagine that you are listening to a rhythm performed by, say, a jazz drummer. Unless you are a very music-analytical person, your spontaneous response is hardly that, for instance, "This is quadruple meter, extra accents on the second and fourth beats, and varying subdivisions from beat to beat." Rather, it could perhaps be something like "This is really an exciting rhythm, he makes it swing incredibly, I can't resist it, come let us dance" (or maybe you prefer some less demanding movements). That is, the spontaneous response is directed toward the expressive character of the rhythm rather than to its structure (which you perhaps figure out later). However, you will find very little, if anything, written about the expressive aspects in comparison with the space devoted to structural aspects. It seems that important parts of the rhythm experience are being neglected in writing and research.

There may be many reasons for this. Expressive–emotional phenomena are by their very nature elusive to analysis; they are certainly there but somehow intangible, at least by traditional methods. And in the musical notation, unlike the situation concerning structural aspects, there are no standardized or detailed designations for expressive aspects other than suggestive prescriptions, such as the Italian *vivace, furioso, dolce, giocoso, mesto, energico, risoluto*, and so on, or their translations into other languages.

## Experiments with Multivariate Techniques

In order to try a different approach to the problems discussed here, the author some time ago conducted a series of experiments on the experience of musical rhythms (Gabrielsson, 1973a, 1973b, 1973c; see also Gabrielsson, 1986). It started from the assumption that experience of musical rhythm is *multi-dimensional*, that is, composed by a number of dimensions, which might be found out by means of so-called multivariate techniques in psychology, for example, multidimensional scaling and factor analysis. A further premise was that the stimuli should really be sounding rhythms, not imagined or notated rhythms.

To obtain at least a certain representation of the population of musical rhythms, three categories of stimuli were used: (a) Monophonic rhythm patterns of varying types, see Fig. 5.3 for an example. They were performed by an advanced percussionist on the drum and tape recorded; each pattern was repeated four or five times in immediate succession; (b) Polyphonic rhythm patterns, recorded from an electronic "rhythm box" that simulates the performance on various instruments in the drum set for dances such as foxtrot, samba, rhumba, beguine, "swing," and many others; (c) Pieces of real dance music taken from phonograph records. There were 20 dances, such as foxtrot, slowfox, "swing," rock 'n' roll, several Latin American dances, three types of waltzes, and some Swedish dances.

A large number of listeners judged various subsets of these three kinds of stimuli in about 20 experiments. The judgments were either similarity ratings or adjective ratings. In the former case, the rhythm patterns in the respective experiment were presented pairwise, and for each pair the listeners rated the experienced similarity between the two rhythms in question on a scale from 100 = perfect similarity down to 0 = "minimum" similarity. In the latter case, each rhythm stimulus was presented one at a time, and the listeners judged it on a large number of adjective scales, selected by means of pilot studies, each scale extending from 9 (maximum) to 0 (minimum). Both methods aim at revealing some fundamental dimensions in the listeners' experience of the rhythm.

***Multidimensional Scaling.*** The similarity ratings are part of what is called *multidimensional scaling* (Schiffman, Reynolds, & Young, 1981). The underlying model is a geometrical one. The stimuli are represented by points in an *n*-dimensional space, and the distance between any two stimuli (points) is related to the perceived similarity: the closer they are, the more similar they appear, and vice versa. Starting from the empirical similarity data, a solution is sought by trying with different numbers of dimensions in the space that give the best correspondence (using certain criteria) between the similarity data on the one hand and the distances between the stimuli in the space on the other hand. The dimensions in the space correspond to the experiential dimensions used by the

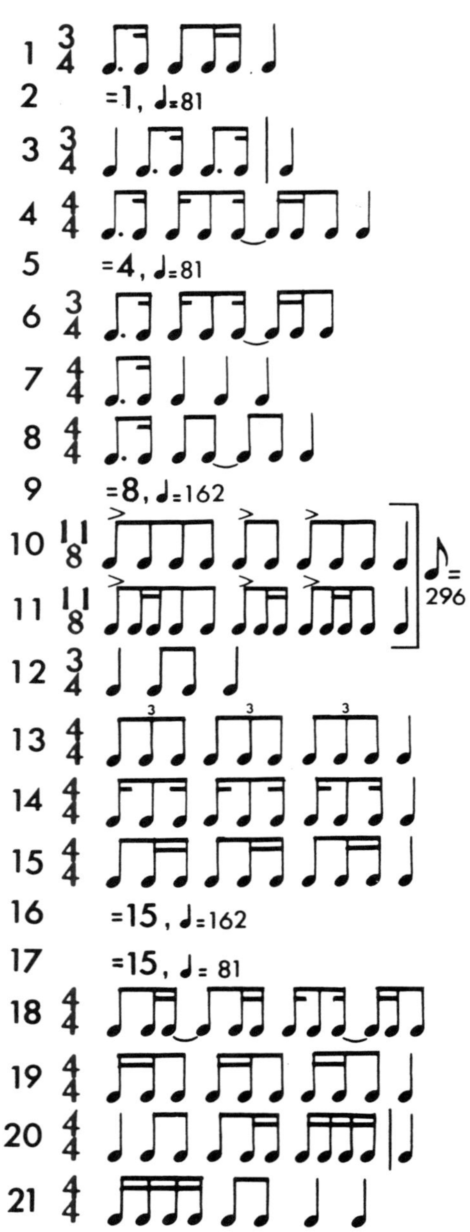

FIG. 5.3. Examples of monophonic rhythm patterns used in one experiment (Gabrielsson, 1973b). Tempo: 108 quarter notes per minute, if not otherwise stated. (Reproduced with permission from Scandinavian Journal of Psychology, 1973, *14*, 255).

listeners in doing their similarity judgments and have to be given a psychological interpretation. This can be done studying the projections of the stimuli on
the respective axes and using other information as well.

Two examples are given in Fig. 5.4. The first case represents a kind of test
of the model. Six rhythm patterns were selected in a way that one could expect
a solution in three dimensions, corresponding to meter, tempo, and position
of the subdivided beat. This also occurred, as seen in the upper part of the figure.
The first dimension reflects the position of the subdivided beat by contrasting
stimuli 1, 3, and 5 (with the subdivided beat on the second beat of the measure)

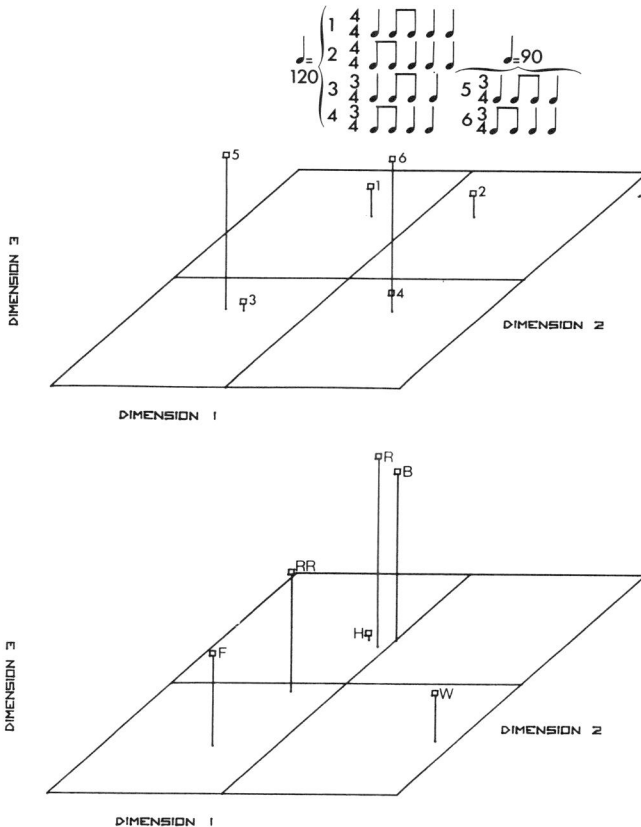

FIG. 5.4.  Upper: Configuration of six monophonic rhythm patterns in a three-
dimensional space (Gabrielsson, 1973a, 1974; reproduced with permission from
Scandinavian Journal of Psychology, 1974, *15*, 75). Lower: Configuration of six
polyphonic dance rhythms in a three-dimensional space. F = Foxtrot, W = Waltz,
H = Habanera, RR = Rock 'n' roll, R = Rhumba, B = Beguine. (Gabrielsson,
1973a, 1974; reproduced with permission from Scandinavian Journal of Psychology, 1974, *15*, 76)

against stimuli 2, 4, and 6 (with the subdivided beat on the first beat). The second dimension represents meter: stimuli 1-2 in 4/4 meter versus stimuli 3-6 in 3/4 meter. The third dimension (height) is related to tempo: stimuli 1-4 at a tempo of 120 quarter notes per minute versus stimuli 5-6 at 90.

The lower part of Fig. 5.4 refers to an experiment with six polyphonic rhythm patterns, for which the dimensionality was not self-evident. In the first dimension the waltz was separated from all the others. As the waltz was the only one in triple meter, this dimension reflected meter. In the second dimension, waltz and foxtrot, for which the sound events occurred solely on the beats, were contrasted against rhumba and beguine, having various subdivisions of the beats; the interpretation was "differences in basic pattern." For partly related reasons the third dimension was interpreted as perceived uniformity versus variation. The details must of course be studied in the original report (Gabrielsson, 1973a).

*Factor Analysis.* The results of the adjective ratings were analyzed by factor analysis (Gorsuch, 1983). The number of adjective scales was 60-90 in different experiments, and factor analysis was applied in order to reduce this large number of adjectives into a considerably smaller number of "fundamental factors." The basic idea of factor analysis—which was originally developed to study the structure of intelligence—is that intercorrelations among observed variables indicate the existence of common underlying, "fundamental," factors. The idea is illustrated in Fig. 5.5, in which the observed variables A-K (corresponding to adjectives here) are reduced to three fundamental factors. If variables A, B, C, and E are intercorrelated, this is accounted for by their sharing of a common factor (here Factor I). The intercorrelations between variables C, D, F, G, H, and I are accounted for in terms of another factor common for these variables (Factor II) and so on. Some variables, for example, C and F here, may refer to two (or more) factors; that is, they are not as pure representatives of a single factor as, say, variable A or B in the present figure. The factors themselves are usually assumed to be uncorrelated (or almost so).

The *statistical* part of a factor analysis thus means that a number of fundamental factors is inferred from the intercorrelations (usually product moment correlations) among the observed variables. The *psychological* part of the analysis then means to give an interpretation of the inferred factors. This is made by studying which of the variables that gets the highest loadings in the respective factor. These loadings can vary from $+1.00$ to $-1.00$ and are a measure of how representative (typical) a variable is for a certain factor. One thus looks for, in the factor loadings matrix, the highest loadings within each factor. The adjectives having these highest loadings are the best descriptors of the meaning of the factor. For example, in one factor, the adjectives with the highest positive loadings were *vital, lively, agile,* and *rapid,* and those with the highest negative loadings were *dull, heavy, crawling, restrained,* and *stopping.* The factor could

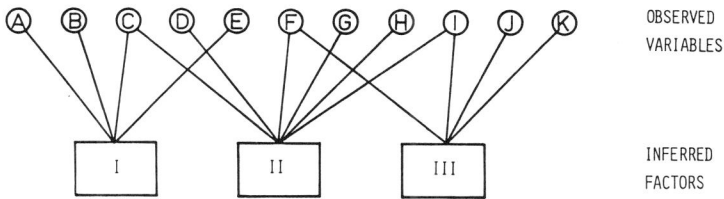

FIG. 5.5.   The basic idea of factor analysis: Intercorrelations among observed variables indicate common underlying factors.

then be interpreted as reflecting "vitality versus dullness" of the rhythms. In another factor the adjectives *excited, intense, violent,* and *powerful* were put against *calm, restrained,* and *soft,* suggesting an interpretation in terms of "excitement versus calmness."

In this way the large number of adjectives used could be reduced to a considerably smaller number of fundamental dimensions. This technique as well as the multidimensional scaling is, however, sensitive to the specific context of stimuli, rating scales, and listeners in each single experiment. Therefore a number of experiments was made with varying stimuli, judgment methods, and listeners in order to see which dimensions recurred in different contexts, and which seemed to be specific for each context. Furthermore we also used free verbal descriptions of the rhythms by the listeners, which proved to be very valuable for the interpretation of the results.

## Results

The combined results from the many experiments indicated at least 15 dimensions in the experience of musical rhythms. Furthermore, they easily lent themselves to a grouping into three categories, that is, dimensions related to *structural* aspects, *motional* aspects, and *emotional* aspects.

*Structural Aspects.*   One set of dimensions reflected the experienced structure of the rhythms and mainly agreed with proposals made in music theory as discussed earlier. These dimensions comprised *meter,* position and strength of *accents,* type and prominence of *basic pattern,* different kinds of *subdivisions within beats,* further *uniformity versus variation,* and *simplicity versus complexity.*

Perhaps the last-mentioned dimensions represent the most immediate experience of structure, at least for nonanalytical listeners, that is, if the rhythm is simple or (more or less) complex, uniform or varied. Of course, the other dimensions are more or less immediately responded to as well (also in overt movements), but to identify more precisely *which* meter (duple, triple, quad-

ruple, etc.), *which* pattern of accents, *which* subdivisions, and the like, requires
further cognitive processing of the type used in much musical ear-training. People
not directly engaged in music theory and performance may not be especially
eager to do such analyses, nor are many musicians throughout the world who
work with not notation-bound music, as in much jazz and folk music. But who
would say that their experience and performance of rhythm is ''worse'' because
of that? Witnessing the fantastic performances of many such musicians, one would
rather believe that too much analysis may be detrimental.

An important class of rhythms not included in our investigations are polyrhythms, that is, two or more rhythm patterns going on at the same time with
equal length of the patterns but with different number of beats within them.
The patterns thus begin and end at the same time, but one pattern may have,
for instance, only two beats in the same time as another has five (a 2 × 5 polyrhythm). In a case with three simultaneous patterns they may have, say, three,
five, and seven beats, respectively, in the same time (3 × 5 × 7 polyrhythm).
Although each of the patterns is simple in itself, the combination of all of them
often offers a confusing but exciting and hard-to-analyze experience. Polyrhythms
are not too common in Western music but frequent in other music cultures (e.g.,
in Africa). Experiments on the perception of polyrhythms are still few and suggest an intricate dependence on many various factors (Handel, 1984; Handel
& Lawson, 1983).

***Motional and Emotional Aspects.***   Emphasis on the connection between
rhythm and movement goes back to ancient Greece. This emphasis emerges
in the more plausible among the very general contemporary theories that point
to pendular movements of our limbs (as in walking) as a possible origin of rhythm.
However, even if we do not move at all (at least not overtly) during listening
we can still experience a specific motion character of the rhythm, which we
characterize as, say, walking, jumping, rocking, swinging, and so on.

A number of dimensions in the present investigations obviously referred to
the experienced motion characters of the rhythms. Among them was first of
all *tempo*; that is, the perceived rate of the beat, as discussed earlier. A related
dimension could be labeled *overall rapidity*, that is, the experienced rapidity as
a function not only of the beat rate but also of other factors, for example, the
number of sound events per unit of time (of course, the more events, the faster
it seems to go) and various melodic and harmonic factors. The relationships between tempo and overall rapidity are complex and yet very little investigated.
It is possible, for instance, to experience a slow tempo and a rapid movement
*within* the slow tempo at the same time—as when the left hand part in a piano
piece provides a slow tempo, while the right hand excels in rapid passages
(Gabrielsson, 1986, 1988).

Besides these dimensions there were a lot of other experienced motion
characters, such as *walking, dancing, jumping, rocking, swinging, graceful,* and

*driving forward.* Some people may find such concepts trivial and/or diffuse, but we have, in fact, no better terminology for this kind of very "direct" experiences, which by the way are also often reflected in overt movements by the listeners. What else does dance music, march music, and the like provide, if not special motion characters that invite us, sometimes even force us, to move in the intended ways? A good example is "swing," a key concept for practically all jazz music, meaning a special motional–emotional character that simply *must* be present in the music.

The investigation of dimensions like these faces many difficulties. They are not especially apt to cognitive verbal analysis, which would also be too slow and interfere with the listening. It seems in fact hard to find any suitable method. A recent proposal that holds some promise is the sentograph developed by Clynes (1977). It is a device for measuring the finger pressure exerted by a subject on a small, circular "knob" situated on top of a box. Clynes used it to study how people express, in the literal sense of the word, various emotions such as joy, love, hate, and anger, and claimed that there is a characteristic pressure pattern for each emotion. Clynes and Walker (1982) used the same device for investigating the motion character of various pieces of ethnic and rock music. The subjects in our own pilot studies, adults as well as children, find it very natural and fun to accompany the music with finger pressure on the sentograph. The instructions may vary depending on the purposes; for example, to simply "press in a way that fits the music" or "express how you feel the pulse in the music." It does not interfere with the listening, and one can respond immediately to what happens in the music. The appearance of the pressure pattern depends on the music as well as on the instruction, and it remains to be seen if there will be inter-individually consistent patterns for the various pieces used as stimuli. As a simple example, look at Fig. 5.6, which shows the vertical pressure pattern for a military march and for a jazz ballad as expressed by one experienced listener. Even without hearing the music itself you can easily

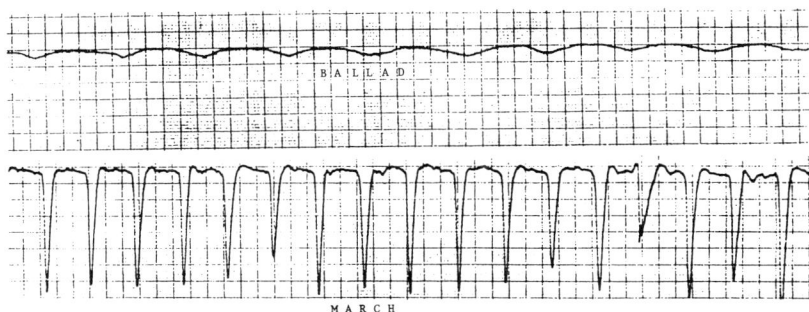

FIG. 5.6. Vertical pressure patterns exerted by a subject on the sentograph when listening to a military march and to a slow jazz ballad.

identify the march, with its distinct and powerful vertical pushes and the softly undulating pattern for the slow jazz ballad.

This example also highlights the intimate connection between motion and emotion. The experienced motion character, as manifested in the pressure pattern, has an emotional counterpart: a feeling of power and force, maybe aggressiveness, for the march, and of softness, relaxation, and dreaming for the ballad. Everyday experience also tells us about the bonds between motion and emotion: One jumps for joy, sinks down in despair, trembles from fear, and so forth. The pressure pattern exerted by the finger on the sentograph is in a sense a condensed version of expressive body movement, such as in gestures and various other forms of "body language." With regard to music listening it would be tempting to use several sentographs, for example, below the feet, to get a more complete representation of the movements. The general problem is still of course to know how to interpret the pressure patterns in terms of experienced emotion.

Returning now to the results of the multivariate techniques, the dimensions connected with emotional aspects of the rhythm experience were expressed as *"vitality versus dullness," "excitement versus calmness," "rigidity versus flexibility,"* and *"solemnity versus playfulness."* Although their meanings may seem rather self-evident, such verbal labels are but crude descriptions of multifaceted and shifting emotional expression. Much of what we experience and recognize in music even seems inaccessible to language, there are no words for it. This is a perennial problem when writing about music, and about other arts as well. We should acknowledge the limitations of language and look for other, nonverbal methods as alternatives or supplements. The limitation is perhaps especially felt when trying to describe the ongoing *processes* in music experience. Rhythm and music are never static. They are based on changes in time, often at a rapid rate, and most attempts to give them an immediate and complete representation in words seem doomed to failure. The development of methods suitable for study of processes in music experience is still in its infancy but is of utmost importance for further progress in music psychology.

*Summary.*   Musical rhythms can obviously be described or classified according to a large number of experiential dimensions, some of which refer to structural aspects and others which refer to motional and emotional aspects. The latter aspects should be given more attention in research than hitherto in order to avoid one-sided emphasis on structural features. This raises important methodological problems for future investigations.

## Performance of Musical Rhythm

The last question to be discussed concerns the performance of musical rhythm. How do musicians play or sing in order to convey the proper rhythmic character of the music to the listener? A musically naive person might assume that the musician should simply play what the musical score tells him to do. However, as indicated earlier, the musical notation is in many ways incomplete, and the musician has to learn a set of implicit rules in order to achieve a performance that appears genuine and convincing. He learns these rules through listening to his teachers and fellow musicians and incorporates them into his own playing, often or perhaps mostly at a rather unconscious level. Sometimes he also adds his own "rules," that is, other features in the performance that he finds useful for expressive or other purposes. He may even go as far as creating a highly idiosyncratic style of performance, which becomes easily identifiable. In music for which there is no notation at all, such as much jazz and folk music, the range for developing individual performance styles is very wide indeed.

The implicit rules are different for different kinds of music and may refer to various musical elements, such as timbre, intonation, rhythm, and harmony, often in complex combinations. With regard to rhythm, our present subject, the most prominent factor is various aspects of *timing* in the performance. Three such aspects are briefly discussed in the following: tempo, articulation, and deviations from mechanical regularity.

***Tempo.*** Tempo was defined earlier as the rate of the pulse or beat. In musical scores the tempo is either indicated by an exact prescription, for example, $\quarternote = 100$, that is, 100 quarter notes per minute, or by a more general advice, such as *allegro* (fast), *moderato* (moderate), *adagio* (slow), and many others. Sometimes there is no indication of tempo at all, and it is presumed that the character of the music and the musician's own experience of this music will result in a proper tempo. Of course, acoustical conditions also exert an influence. In a large hall it may be necessary to decrease the tempo, and in a small room, to increase it.

However, even if two musicians or two music ensembles use the same musical score and have the same acoustical conditions, they will rarely perform at the same tempo. Sometimes the difference is small or moderate, but sometimes it is striking indeed. In fact, when we compare two or more performances of the same piece of music, the difference in tempo is usually among the first to be noticed. And this difference means much for the listener's experience of the music. Although generalizations should always be considered with caution, it seems fair to say that a higher tempo usually provides more of, say, vitality, excitement, happiness, perhaps restlessness, whereas a slower tempo would go in the opposite directions.

Not only are there differences in tempo among different performances, but there is also considerable variation of tempo during the performance itself. Keeping the tempo absolutely constant throughout the piece gives the impression of a machine, as is in fact the case with music boxes or many electronic rhythm machines that are used in disco music and the like. In most live performances there are more or less pronounced variations of tempo, even in music where one might expect a constant tempo, for example, in dance music. An extreme case in this respect is Viennese waltzes, in which there are marked accelerations and retardations to the extent that a notated measure may at times be performed at twice the speed of another measure (Bengtsson & Gabrielsson, 1983). A typical pattern is a slow start of the phrase, followed by acceleration until the middle part of the phrase or later, and then a retardation toward the end. This may be considered characteristic for most Western classical music. An example is given in Fig. 5.7, which refers to a performance of the theme in Mozart's "Piano Sonata in A Major." It comprises eight measures, divided into two phrases, measures 1–4 and 5–8. The figure shows the duration of successive half-measures expressed in percentage of the average duration of all 16 half-measures. In the first phrase the initial half-measures are somewhat longer than the average (=slow start), the following are much shorter (=acceleration), and the final half-measure much longer (=retardation). Essentially the same pattern appears in the second phrase, but with much more pronounced retardation.

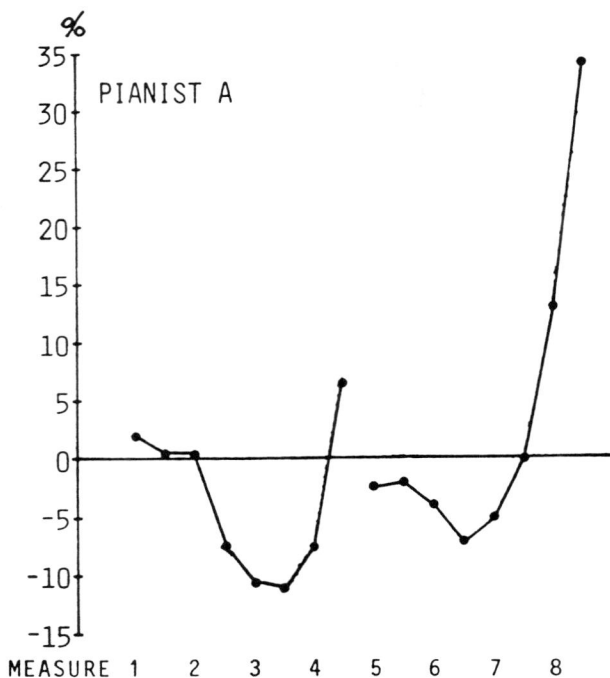

FIG. 5.7. Variation of tempo in a performance of the theme in Mozart's "Piano Sonata in A Major" (K. 331, see notation in Fig. 5.11). The figure shows the duration of successive half-measures in percentage of the average half-measure duration. (Adapted from Gabrielsson, 1987b.) Reproduced with permission from The Royal Swedish Academy of Music, Stockholm.

Much of this variation in tempo may not be consciously perceived, but it still affects our experience of the musical flow in more or less subtle ways. A skilled performer makes use of tempo variations for many purposes. The retardation toward the end can clarify the structure of a piece in a hierarchical manner: a certain retardation toward the end of a phrase, more pronounced retardation toward the end of a period (as in Fig. 5.7), and most pronounced of all at the very end of the piece. But the variations are as importantly used for expressive purposes, for example, to give a feeling of tension or relaxation, hesitation, expectation, surprise, and so forth. Varying the rate of the musical flow gives the performer numerous and delicate means to affect the listener's experiences in ways that are still poorly understood.

**Articulation.**    Articulation refers to the relative length of the sounding part of a tone in a succession of tones. If the tones are performed tightly together with no perceptible break between them, this is called *legato* performance. The opposite is *staccato*, in which the sounding part is short (as when you pluck a string) and followed by "silence" until the next tone. There are of course various degrees of *legato* and *staccato*, and a midway level between them is usually called *portato* performance.

Articulation is an extremely important device for the performing musician. It is used in a variety of ways to provide the proper character of motives, rhythms, melodies, phrases, and so forth; feeling for the possibilities and effects of articulation is certainly an important part of musicianship. Although a *physical* description of articulation is made in terms of the relative length of sound and silence, the spontaneous *experience* of various articulations is much more adequately described in terms of special motion characters. For instance, using *legato* performance may give the impression of smooth, continuous motion, whereas *staccato* may appear like bouncing, jumping, hitting, and so on, including all emotional connotations of such movements. These proposals are only hints out of a huge variety of alternatives, which change from case to case depending on the musical context.

To make a detailed account of all these alternatives would be difficult indeed. Furthermore, there is little research on these questions. However, it is not difficult at all to demonstrate the effects of different articulations in selected cases. For instance, synthesized examples with different articulations of a Swedish folk tune were given on a phonograph record (Bengtsson & Gabrielsson, 1983), along with different versions of a common accompaniment in triple meter, such as in waltzes. The latter example was constructed as illustrated in Fig. 5.8. The usual notation appears uppermost. Eight synthesized versions are made of the four measures. In all eight versions, the first beat was shortened and the second lengthened, as can be seen by comparing the width of the beats. This was made to imitate the usual performance of Viennese waltzes, in which the second beat comes "too early" (that is, too early in comparison with a strict

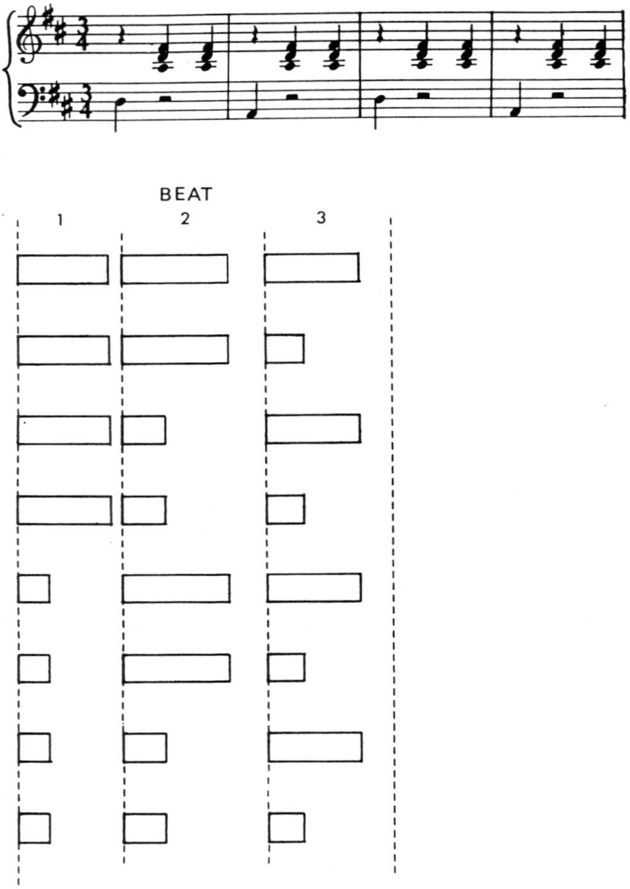

FIG. 5.8.   Different articulations of a common accompaniment in triple meter.
See further explanation in text. (Adapted from Bengtsson & Gabrielsson, 1983.)
Reproduced with permission from The Royal Swedish Academy of Music,
Stockholm.

mechanical performance). The eight versions differ with regard to the articulation
within the three beats. Only two levels were used, corresponding approximately
to *legato* (indicated by long rectangles) and *staccato* (short ones). With two levels in each of three beats, there are eight possible combinations as listed in the
figure. In the first version there is (almost) *legato* in all three beats of the measure, in the second version the first two beats are played *legato* and the third
*staccato*, and so on, until finally the eighth version with *staccato* throughout.

It is of course desirable to hear those versions directly from the phonograph
record. However, it may be possible to imagine what the different versions sound
like or to perform them on the piano. The triple meter structure is apparent

in all versions, but the various articulations give distinctly different motion characters to all of them. None of them is quite as good as a waltz accompaniment in real music; version No. 4 is perhaps closest (Nos. 3 or 8 can sometimes do as well), whereas Nos. 1 and 5, with their long after-beats on the second and third beats, sound quite impossible and usually elicit laughter from the listeners. The whole example may be thought of as eight different performances of the same notation by manipulating only one factor. It is instructive to see how much already this single manipulation means to the experience, and to imagine what could happen if it were combined with a variation of other factors, for example, dynamic differences among the beats.

### Deviations from Mechanical Regularity.

Performances proceeding in absolutely constant tempo and with exact ratios like 2:1, 3:1, and so on between tones of different note values sound mechanical and boring. When people hear such performances, for example, from music boxes and rhythm machines, they also usually realize that they are generated by machines. Live human performances are practically always characterized by deviations from such mechanical regularity. This was already illustrated with regard to tempo. However, the deviations occur at many different levels: at the sound event level (that is, for each single note), at the beat level, half-measure level, measure level, and so on. Furthermore, the pattern of deviations is often different for different types of music as well as for different performers (Bengtsson & Gabrielsson, 1980; Gabrielsson, Bengtsson, & Gabrielsson, 1983).

Although the existence of such deviations has long since been known in general musical practice, more precise knowledge about the pattern and extent of deviations has not been gained until very recently and is still limited. This is very much due to lack of accurate technical equipment for measurements of the complex flow of events in a musical performance. Impressive pioneering work on these problems was made by Carl Seashore and his co-workers at the University of Iowa in the 1930s (reviewed in Gabrielsson, 1985), but after that very little happened until around 1970, when new facilities for measurements were available. Among them was equipment for recording of monophonic performances developed in Uppsala, Sweden, that has proved to be very useful. It provides accurate measurement of the continuous variations in fundamental frequency and amplitude and can be used with any musical instrument, including the singing voice. The short example given in Fig. 5.9 is a recording of a male singer performing the first phrase of a Swedish tune. The upper curve refers to the fundamental frequency (pitch), the lower curve to the amplitude (loudness). A lot of detailed information can be extracted from those curves regarding the singer's pitch intonation and vibrato (the "waves" in the upper curve), his way of modulating the amplitude within each tone, and of course about the timing of all events.

In Exeter, England, a grand piano was equipped with photocell sensors and

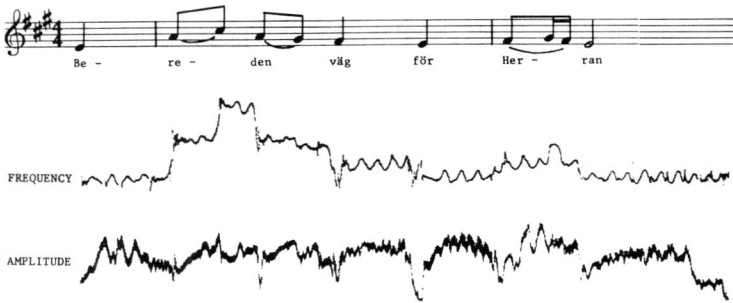

FIG. 5.9.  Recording of a male singer by equipment for registration of monophonic sound sequences. The upper curve displays the variations in fundamental frequency (pitch) and the lower variations in amplitude (loudness); calibration scales are omitted here. The melodic line is easily seen in the pitch curve. The notes in the notation are placed so as to coincide with the onsets of the corresponding tones in the pitch curve.

electronic circuitry, permitting very accurate recordings of timing and intensity of every key-press. Shaffer (1981) and Shaffer and Todd (1987) had a number of advanced pianists perform various pieces on this grand piano. The timing profiles in the performances show marked deviations from mechanical regularity and can be meaningfully related to the structure of the different pieces. High intra-individual consistency in repeated performances is demonstrated, as well as inter-individual differences in performances of the same piece. Clarke (1985) used the same grand piano to study a performance of Erik Satie's "Gnossienne No. 5," a piece that has an unusually wide variety of different subdivisions within the beat and thus provides ample opportunities for studies of the microstructure in timing.

Whereas this technique relies on measurement of the mechanical action in the piano itself, it is also possible to analyze *acoustical* recordings of piano music (or other "complex" music) with accuracy. One way of doing this is to take a performance from a phonograph record or a tape and store it in the memory of a computer for processing. For instance, a phonograph recording of the theme in the earlier mentioned Mozart "Piano Sonata in A Major" can be fed into a sampling system. If the sampling rate is, say, 50 kHz, it is thus possible to analyze both timing, down to an accuracy of 1/50,000 second, and the intensity and spectral composition of each such segment. This extreme accuracy is of course rarely needed, but the technique as such provides excellent opportunities for studying details in the performance, for listening to any selected part of it, however short it is, and even for changing the performance by taking away some portion(s) or adding something in order to see how such manipulations affect the listener's impression of the performance. An example of a recording appears in Fig. 5.10.

In a recent study using this technique (Gabrielsson, 1987), a comparative analysis was made of five pianists' performance of the Mozart theme. The results for two of them are given in Fig. 5.11. This figure shows how much the duration of each single tone deviates from what it would have been in a completely mechanical performance. The mechanical performance is represented by the horizontal line at zero (0). A position above this line means that the corresponding tone is lengthened, a position below, that it is shortened. The degree of lengthening or shortening is expressed in percentage of the duration that the corresponding tone would have in a mechanical performance. The profile for Pianist B shows large deviations; that for Pianist D has much smaller, but still considerable, deviations. The solid profile refers to the first performance, the dotted to the immediate repetition. These two profiles are very similar, sometimes identical, for each of the pianists, indicating a high degree of precision

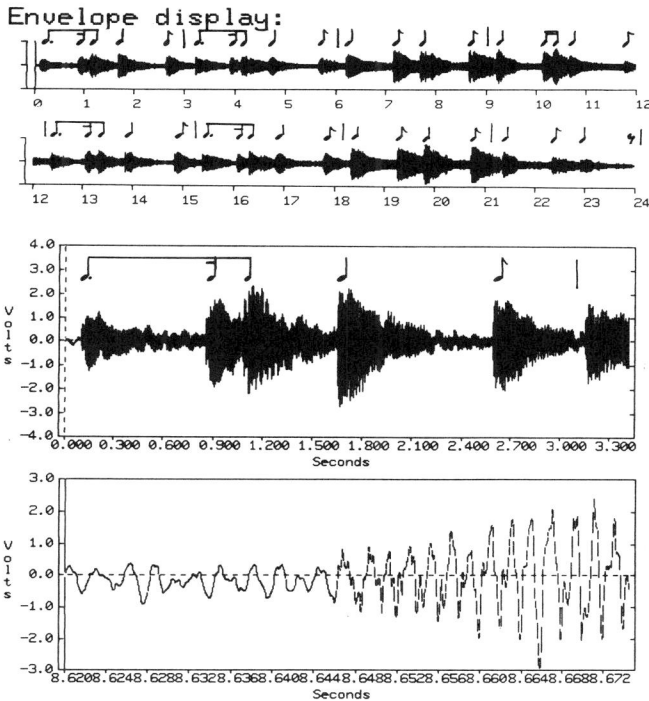

FIG. 5.10.   A recording of a performance of the theme in Mozart's "Piano Sonata in A Major" (K. 331) by means of a sampling system. Upper: Amplitude envelope for all eight measures (notation added above). Middle: Amplitude envelope for the first measure. Lower: Detailed display of an onset (starting in the middle). The steps along the horizontal axis are four milliseconds. (Gabrielsson, 1987b). Reproduced with permission from the Royal Swedish Academy of Music, Stockholm.

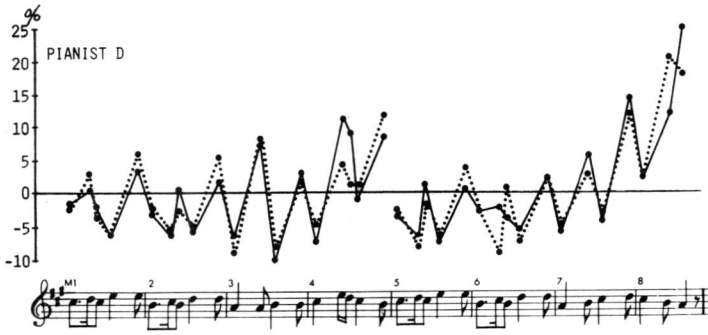

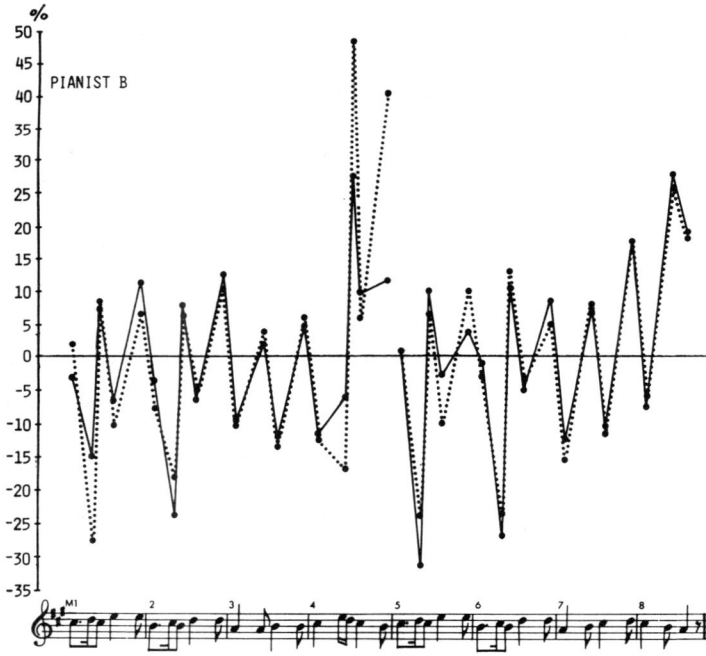

FIG. 5.11. Deviations from mechanical regularity in two pianists' performances of the theme in Mozart's "Piano Sonata in A Major" (K. 331). The solid profile refers to the first performance, the dotted profile to the repetition. See further explanation in text. (Gabrielsson, 1987b.) Reproduced with permission from the Royal Swedish Academy of Music, Stockholm.

in planning and execution. The dominating zigzag profile for both pianists is mainly due to the fact that the quarter notes are shortened, and the eighth notes are lengthened in the ♩ ♪ sequences in measures 2–3 and 6–7. In fact, the ratio between those two note values in the performance never approaches the 2:1 ratio; it is rather around 1.7:1. In both performances there is, further, a clear lengthening (that is, retardation) toward the end of the two phrases in the theme (in measures 4 and 8; cf. in Fig. 5.7).

Analogous profiles were also made concerning the deviations in intensity (loudness) from an average level. The two profiles (first performance and repetition) were very similar for each pianist, and Pianist B showed larger deviations than Pianist D, although the difference between them was not as pronounced as it was regarding timing. For the listener there is a very obvious difference between the two pianists' performances, and much of it can be attributed to the differences in timing seen in Fig. 5.11.

Even from the few examples given here it is evident that the description of musical performances is an extremely complex task. Some common tendencies can be found (Gabrielsson, 1988), for example, regarding retardations as means for phrasing, but much remains to be done in order to get a better understanding of the functions of timing in musical performance. Of course, it is not enough to make measurements of performances; these measurements must also be related to the listener's experience of the performance, that is, to the various structural and motional–emotional aspects of rhythm and music experience. After all, these are the things that the musician tries to affect through his planning and execution of hundreds or thousands of features in the performance.

Another approach is proposed by Clynes (1987). He suggested that there is a characteristic "inner pulse" for each composer, for example, Haydn, Mozart, Beethoven, or Schubert. The pulse is said to affect the musical microstructure in specific ways, including various aspects of timing and amplitude (loudness). These principles are used, together with another principle called "Predictive Amplitude Shaping," to create synthesized versions of pieces by the composers mentioned and others. It is then possible, for instance, to generate a piece by Beethoven as "performed" with the Beethoven pulse, or with a Mozart pulse, or a Haydn pulse, and to see if listeners will note the differences and prefer the "correct" version. The principles used by Clynes are admittedly based on his own listening and judgment, but empirical tests with other listeners are being conducted (Repp, 1989). Sundberg, Askenfelt, and Frydén (1983) and Sundberg (1988), also use a "Synthesis-by-Rule" approach, that is, generating synthesized versions of various pieces according to a set of hypotheses essentially based on the experience and judgment by one of the authors. Several rules concern timing in performance as it is assumed to be influenced by various factors, and examples are generated that represent performances according to the proposed rules as well as without application of the rules. Listening tests can then be made to investigate whether the differences are detectable and which version is preferred (Thompson, Sundberg, Friberg, & Frydén, 1989).

*Summary.*  To convey the intended and proper rhythmic character of the music, the performer uses the possibilities provided by different aspects of timing, such as variations of tempo and articulation and deviations from mechanical regularity. In this process he or she follows principles or rules that are mainly implicit and more or less specific for various kinds of music. To clarify the meaning of these principles is an important task for research, and the selected examples can be seen as contributions to this work.

## Conclusion

Three questions have been addressed in this chapter:

1. What are the characteristics of rhythm as opposed to non-rhythm?
2. What criteria can be used for adequate description or classification of musical rhythms, especially with regard to how they are experienced?
3. How do musicians perform music in order to provide the intended and proper rhythmic character?

The answers given to these questions are in many respects still incomplete and tentative. This is due both to the complexity of the phenomena in question and to the lack of suitable methods for investigation of crucial questions. However, the research on musical rhythm and related problems has increased considerably during the last decades, which is a promising sign for the future. We can expect further development of many projects and ideas that were discussed in this chapter. Although omissions and simplifications are unavoidable in a short chapter like this, it has hopefully provided some flavor of the exciting phenomenon of rhythm and its field of research. The selected references may help you to explore it further.

## ACKNOWLEDGMENTS

The author wants to express his deep gratitude to professor Ingmar Bengtsson for many years of pleasant and fruitful cooperation, sadly interrupted by his death in 1989. The research was supported by The Bank of Sweden Tercentenary Foundation, The Swedish Council for Research in the Humanities and Social Sciences, and Knut and Alice Wallenberg's Foundation.

# REFERENCES

Bengtsson, I., & Gabrielsson, A. (1980). Methods for analyzing performance of musical rhythm. *Scandinavian Journal of Psychology, 21,* 257–268.
Bengtsson, I., & Gabrielsson, A. (1983). Analysis and synthesis of musical rhythm. In J. Sundberg (Ed.), *Studies of music performance* (pp. 27–60). Publications issued by the Royal Swedish Academy of Music No. 39, Stockholm, Sweden.
Clarke, E. F. (1985). Some aspects of rhythm and expression in Erik Satie's "Gnossienne No. 5." *Music Perception, 2,* 299–328.
Clynes, M. (1977). *Sentics, the touch of emotions.* New York: Anchor Press/Doubleday.
Clynes, M. (1987). What can a musician learn about music performance from newly discovered microstructure principles (PM and PAS)? In A. Gabrielsson (Ed.), *Action and perception in rhythm and music* (pp. 201–233). Publications issued by the Royal Swedish Academy of Music No. 55, Stockholm, Sweden.
Clynes, M., & Walker, J. (1982). Neurobiologic functions of rhythm, time, and pulse in music. In M. Clynes (Ed.), *Music, mind, and brain. The neuropsychology of music* (pp. 171–216). New York: Plenum Press.
Cooper, G. W., & Meyer, L. B. (1960). *The rhythmic structure of music.* Chicago: University of Chicago Press.
Fraisse, P. (1982). Rhythm and tempo. In D. Deutsch (Ed.), *The psychology of music* (pp. 149–180). New York: Academic Press.
Fraisse, P. (1987). A historical approach to rhythm as perception. In A. Gabrielsson (Ed.), *Action and perception in rhythm and music* (pp. 7–18). Publications issued by the Royal Swedish Academy of Music No. 55, Stockholm, Sweden.
Gabrielsson, A. (1973a). Similarity ratings and dimension analyses of auditory rhythm patterns. I and II. *Scandinavian Journal of Psychology, 14,* 138–160, 161–176.
Gabrielsson, A. (1973b). Adjective ratings and dimension analyses of auditory rhythm patterns. *Scandinavian Journal of Psychology, 14,* 244–260.
Gabrielsson, A. (1973c). Studies in rhythm. *Acta Universitatis Upsaliensis: Abstracts of Uppsala Dissertations from the Faculty of Social Sciences,* No. 7.
Gabrielsson, A. (1974). An empirical comparison between some models for multidimensional scaling. *Scandinavian Journal of Psychology, 15,* 73–80.
Gabrielsson, A. (1985). Interplay between analysis and synthesis in studies of music performance and music experience. *Music Perception, 3,* 59–86.
Gabrielsson, A. (1986). Rhythm in music. In J. R. Evans & M. Clynes (Eds.), *Rhythm in psychological, linguistic, and musical processes* (pp. 131–167). Springfield, IL: Thomas.
Gabrielsson, A. (Ed.). (1987a). *Action and perception in rhythm and music.* Publications issued by the Royal Swedish Academy of Music No. 55, Stockholm, Sweden.
Gabrielsson, A. (1987b). Once again: The theme from Mozart's "Piano Sonata in A Major" (K. 331). A comparison of five performances. In A. Gabrielsson (Ed.), *Action and perception in rhythm and music* (pp. 81–103). Publications issued by the Royal Swedish Academy of Music No. 55, Stockholm, Sweden.
Gabrielsson, A. (1988). Timing in music performance and its relations to music experience. In J. A. Sloboda (Ed.), *Generative processes in music* (pp. 27–51). Oxford: Clarendon Press.
Gabrielsson, A., Bengtsson, I., & Gabrielsson, B. (1983). Performance of musical rhythm in 3/4 and 6/8 meter. *Scandinavian Journal of Psychology, 24,* 193–213.
Gorsuch, R. L. (1983). *Factor analysis* (2nd ed.). Hillsdale, NJ: Lawrence Erlbaum Associates.
Handel, S. (1984). Using polyrhythms to study rhythm. *Music Perception, 1,* 465–484.
Handel, S., & Lawson, G. R. (1983). The contextual nature of rhythmic interpretation. *Perception & Psychophysics, 34,* 103–120.

Longuet-Higgins, H. C. (1976). Perception of melodies. *Nature, 263,* 646–653.

Longuet-Higgins, H. C., & Lee, C. S. (1984). The rhythmic interpretation of music. *Music Perception, 1,* 424–441.

Povel, D. J. (1981). Internal representation of simple temporal patterns. *Journal of Experimental Psychology: Human Perception and Performance, 7,* 3–18.

Povel, D. J., & Essens, P. (1985). Perception of temporal patterns. *Music Perception, 2,* 411–440.

Repp, B. H. (1989). Expressive microstructure in music: A preliminary perceptual assessment of four composers' pulses. *Music Perception, 6,* 243–274.

Schiffman, S., Reynolds, M. L., & Young, F. W. (1981). *Introduction to multidimensional scaling. Theory, methods, and applications.* New York: Academic Press.

Shaffer, L. H. (1981). Performances of Chopin, Bach, and Bartók: Studies in motor programming. *Cognitive Psychology, 13,* 326–376.

Shaffer, L. H., & Todd, N. P. (1987). The interpretive component in musical performance. In A. Gabrielsson (Ed.), *Action and perception in rhythm and music* (pp. 139–152). Publications issued by the Royal Swedish Academy of Music No. 55, Stockholm, Sweden.

Sundberg, J. (1988). Computer synthesis of music performance. In J. A. Sloboda (Ed.), *Generative processes in music* (pp. 52–69). Oxford: Clarendon Press.

Sundberg, J., Askenfelt, A., & Frydén, L. (1983). Musical performance: A synthesis-by-rule approach. *Computer Music Journal, 7,* 37–43.

Thompson, W. F., Sundberg, J., Friberg, A., & Frydén, L. (1989). The use of rules for expression in the performance of melodies. *Psychology of Music, 17,* 63–82.

# 6

## Parallels Between Pitch and Time and How They Go Together

Caroline B. Monahan
*University of Oklahoma*

This chapter has two major themes: First, I develop the notion that there are strong parallels between the domains of musical pitch and duration; and second, I explore the question, "How do pitch and time go together in order to make 'good' music?" Turning to the first theme, we find that the idea of a parallel between pitch and duration goes back at least 2,300 years to Aristoxenes of Tarente (as translated by Laloy, 1904), who characterized musical rhythm as

> une série de durées comme la gamme est une série d'intervalles. . . Le rhythmicien doit s'attacher à établir les lois de la succession rhythmique comme l'harmonicien les lois de la succession mélodique. (p. 294)

> [is a series of durations as the scale is a series of intervals. . . The rhythmician must devote himself to establishing the laws of rhythmic succession just as the harmonist must devote himself to establishing the laws of melodic (interval) succession.]

It might seem odd to suggest commonalities in the structural bases for two such "obviously different" domains of perceptual experience. But here we deal with separate ranges of high and low frequency, or more simply, of fast and slow events. On one side of the boundary are fast events that become fused in perception, and on the other side are slow events that are perceived as successive. Hirsh (1959) and Julesz and Hirsh (1972) have distinguished between fast, microtime events such as frequencies that have psychological correlates in pitch perception, versus slow events such as temporal intervals that correspond psychologically to the perception of meter and rhythm. With Warren (1982) they viewed the perception of pitch and rhythm experience as opposite ends of a continuum of sensitivity to auditory periodicity. This suggests that it should be fruitful for researchers to look for commonalities as well as differences in their physical and perceptual organization.

The primary physical dimensions underlying the two perceptual domains, frequency for pitch and event time for perceived duration, can both be measured on ratio scales. These are continuous scales that have order, and equal-interval values that can be added, subtracted, multiplied, and divided. Pitch and perceived duration are measurements of these physical dimensions. Whereas instruments like oscilloscopes or sound spectrographs measure physical events along absolute scales such as frequency in Hz (Hertz), human listeners usually measure the same events *relative* to one another on logarithmic pitch scales comprised of semitones. Similarly, musicians usually measure musical time not in seconds or milliseconds but in terms of a time scale whose units are proportionally related to one another (e.g., half-note, quarter-note, etc.). Clearly, oscilloscopes and humans are different measuring instruments. The categories and scales that humans employ to measure and remember musical events are not necessarily related in a simple fashion to the frequency and time scales of an oscilloscope. Although this view does not assign primacy to machine measurement, one of our primary tasks as scientists of music is to explore and describe the relationships between human perception and machine "perception."

The second theme of this chapter is "How do pitch and duration go together in order to make 'good' music?" The word "good" here is intended in the psychological sense of "good" form or "good" gestalt. A pattern has good form to the extent that it matches listeners' and performers' perceptual and motor capabilities. I base this discussion on three metrical structures (Yeston, 1976) that categorize the organization of accents and temporal grouping. Accents can arise from patterns at various levels in the musical structure. In addition to producing an accent by stressing the intensity of a note, the musician can rely on a regular pattern of beats to provide accents, as well as on the grouping of notes in pitch and time (to which I return later). The three organizing structures for such accents are: the rhythmic consonance of hierarchically regular structures that characterizes much of Western music, and what I call (following Yeston) *out-of-phase consonance*, and *rhythmic dissonance*. The latter two involve the conflict between one or more sources of accenting. Music in the Western tradition is typically rhythmically consonant in avoiding conflict between sources of accenting so that notes tend to occur at regular time intervals. Music in other parts of the world often exploits rhythmic dissonance, thereby adding interest to their music, and this represents a different aesthetic from the Western tradition.

## PARALLELS AND DIFFERENCES BETWEEN PITCH AND RHYTHM DOMAINS

### Frequency and Interval (Period) are Equivalent Functions in Both Pitch and Rhythm Domains

The first major structural parallel between the domains of pitch and rhythm is that in both a description in terms of frequency (the number of events per time unit) is equivalent to a description in terms of period (the time taken by an event). Table 6.1 illustrates this parallel by comparing arbitrarily chosen pitches and temporal note values both in terms of frequency and period.

In comparing the ranges of iterance for the domains of musical pitch and musical time, we express the former in Hz (cycles/sec or cps), and the latter in events/sec (eps). One advantage of these physical measures is that they permit comparison of the two domains in terms of octaves (equal logarithmic frequency steps in which each higher step is in a 2:1 ratio with the preceding step). Table 6.1 also shows some of these comparisons.

### Iterance Ranges in Pitch and Time Domains (from Wide to Narrow) with Correlated Perceptual Phenomena

***Ranges for the Perception of Musical Pitch and Temporal Events.*** Frequencies in the range of 20 Hz to 5000 Hz, a distance of about eight octaves, elicit the perception of musical pitch. The piano has a range of slightly more than seven octaves (27.5 Hz to 4186 Hz), but most musical instruments have much smaller frequency ranges. The lowest pitch that can be sung by a human is about 82 Hz (E2) and the highest about 1175 Hz (D6)—a range of about four octaves; within that span, the fundamental frequency of the voice of most individuals has a range of only about 1.5 to 2 octaves (Lindsay & Norman, 1977). Turning to typical ranges of tone frequencies, we find that most European folk melodies lie within a span of a single octave. One notable exception is "The Star Spangled Banner," whose pitches span 1.5 octaves. Such a wide range makes this melody notoriously difficult for untrained singers. Thus we have a four to eight octave range of frequencies, of which one octave can be easily sung by an untrained person.

The range of temporal frequencies in music is from somewhat higher than 10 events/sec to about .5 events/sec (600 to 30 beats/min or note values of about .1 to 2 sec), a range of about 4.5 octaves (see Table 6.1). Events occurring at frequencies higher than 10 events/sec tend to lose their individuality as events (notes) and at frequencies lower than .5 events/sec (30 beats/min) tend to sound isolated and lose temporal coherence. If we look at typical ranges, Povel (1981) suggested that the typical range over which listeners can tap out

TABLE 6.1

Ranges of Frequency and Period Corresponding to the Perception
of Musical Pitch and Musical Time

| *Musical Pitch* | | | | |
|---|---|---|---|---|
| *Frequency (Hz or cps)* | *Period[1] (sec)* | *Range of Human Voice* | | *Range of a Melody* |
| 5000 Hz | .00020 | | | |
| A7 3520 | .00028 | | | |
| A6 1760 | .00057 | | | |
| | | --1046 Hz | | |
| A5 880 | .00114 | Soprano | | |
| A4 440 | .00227 | Alto | ------ | Typical range of a melody = 1 octave |
| A3 220 | .00455 | Baritone | ------ | |
| A2 110 | .00909 | Bass | | |
| | | ---80 Hz | | |
| A1 55 | .01818 | | | |
| A0 27.5 | .03636 | | | |
| 20 Hz | .05000 | | | |

| *Musical Time (Infrapitch)* | | *Range of Active Timekeeping* | | |
|---|---|---|---|---|
| ♪[2] 11.00 eps | .0909 | | | |
| ♪ 5.50 | .1818 | | | |
| ♪ 2.75 | .3636 | 2.5 'Octave' | | |
| | | Range of | ------ Short | |
| ♩ 1.37 | .7272 | "beats" or meters | | Ratio Long:Short |
| | | .25 to | ------ Long | typically 2:1 |
| ♩ 0.68 | 1.45440 | 1.5 sec | | |
| ◦ 0.34 eps | 2.9088 | | | |

[1]Period in the pitch domain refers to seconds/cycle and in the musical time domain refers to seconds/event.

[2]This is suggested temporal notation. Notated duration values (half-note, quarter-note, etc.) are a scale of proportions that may be arbitrarily placed in the musical temporal range. Typically, the half-, quarter- or eighth-note is given the "official beat" rate of active timekeeping.

124

a beat is in the middle 2.3 octaves of that 4.5 octave range (see Table 6.1), going from about 4 to .67 events/sec (equivalently, 240 to 40 beats/min or note values of .25 to 1.5 sec). Most pieces of music have events that occur at faster and slower rates than the beat rate of active timekeeping, because beats are typically subdivided into shorter events in the ratios of 2:1 or 3:1. Thus the range of musical events is about 4.5 octaves, of which the average listener finds the middle 2.3 octaves easy to use as beat rates.

*The Effects of Contour and the Relative Size of Pitch and Temporal Intervals: Accenting and Grouping.*   In both pitch and time domains, *tones that are isolated from other tones sound accented or important.* The energies of tones that are close together in either frequency or time interact and tend to mask one another. When a tone is far enough away from other tones in either domain it becomes individually salient.

1.  Accenting and pitch. Pitch-pattern coherence seems to require that most pitch intervals in a melody be four semitones or less. Pitch skips in melodies tend to be quite small relative to the range of musical pitches: The most common interval between successive tones in melodies is two semitones (a whole tone) and the next most common is one semitone, and pitch skips of more than five semitones (about a 4:3 frequency ratio) are quite uncommon in the world's music (Dowling, 1968; Dowling & Harwood, 1986). The distribution of the sizes of pitch intervals corresponds closely to several other auditory phenomena, notably (a) the trill threshold (Heise & Miller, 1951, Miller & Heise, 1950), (b) rhythmic fission or auditory streaming (Bregman & Campbell, 1971; Dowling, 1968, 1973; van Noorden, 1975), (c) various "critical band" phenomena (Scharf, 1970), and (d) the perception of pitch-level and pitch-contour accent (Monahan & Carterette, 1985; Monahan, Kendall, & Carterette, 1987; Thomassen, 1982). It is the last of these that primarily concerns rhythmic organization.

At musical tempos, tones that skip four semitones sound accented and especially so if the tone marks a point of inflection in the pitch contour (Thomassen, 1982; see Example 6.1). Furthermore, Grant (1987) has shown that a rise of four semitones in the fundamental voice frequency ($F_0$) is sufficient to cause a change in the perceived accent of a syllable in a sentence. If alternating tones (played at 8–10 tones/sec) are more than four to five semitones apart they will cease to form a trill and will form two streams. The listener can attend to the tones of one stream or the other but not both at the same time. This phenomenon is known as *rhythmic fission* or *auditory stream segregation* and was favored by Baroque composers because it permitted one instrument (often the violin) to sound like two. Thomassen (1982), Monahan and Carterette (1985), and Monahan et al. (1987) have pointed out that tones that begin different auditory streams at tempos of 8–10 notes/sec tend at slower tempos to sound accented and thus begin new pitch groupings. At musical tempos, the fifth tone in each

```
                    A.                B.                C.

                          o o o o   o o o o                      o
4 semitone skip
                    o o o o                   o o o o   o o o o   o o o o

Pitch contour       = = = + = = =   = = = - = = =      = = = + - = = =

Pitch-level accent        <               <                <
```

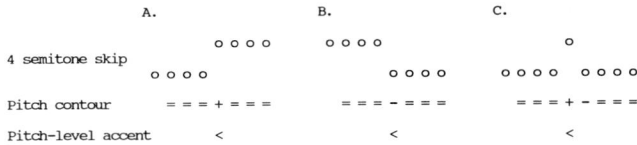

Example 6.1.   Three cases of pitch-level accenting and associated pitch contours.

of the patterns of Example 6.1 tends both to ''stick out'' and to start a new group or phrase. Thus, both relatively large upward ( + ) and downward ( − ) pitch skips, as well as pitch inflections ( + − or − + ) are associated with the accenting and grouping of the tones. Monahan and Carterette (1985) and Monahan et al. (1987) termed this type of accenting *pitch-level accenting* and have distinguished it from other sources of salience in music.

2. Accenting and timing. The perception of accent and grouping can also depend solely on changes in timing. Povel and Okkerman (1981) reported that identical tones in sequences sound accented when they begin a long interval, as well as when they end a long interval and begin a series of three or more intervals (see Example 6.2, where slashes represent tone onsets). To explain these perceptions of *natural temporal accent*, Povel and Okkerman argued that tones beginning longer intervals are ''released from backward masking'' whereas tones ending longer intervals and beginning a group of three or more intervals are ''released from forward masking.'' They suggested that the assessment of the relative strength or salience of a tone takes time and processing is interrupted when a new tone begins—so tones beginning longer intervals are relatively isolated from the interference of the following tone(s) and hence sound accented. As to the second sort of accent, they suggested that tones interfere with one another if the time from the offset of one to the onset of the next is 250 ms or less. So, tones that end a long interval and begin a series of three or more intervals are relatively isolated from the interference of the preceding tone(s) and may sound accented for that reason.

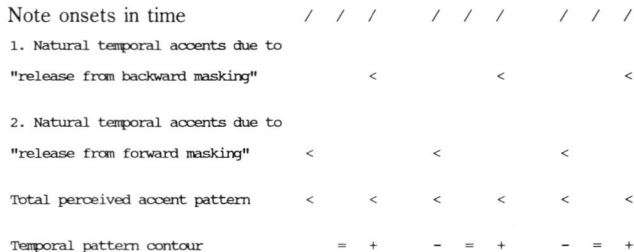

```
Note onsets in time              / / /   / / /   / / /
1. Natural temporal accents due to
"release from backward masking"        <       <       <

2. Natural temporal accents due to
"release from forward masking"   <       <       <

Total perceived accent pattern   <   <   <   <   <   <

Temporal pattern contour         = +   - = +   - = +
```

Example 6.2.   Natural temporal accenting and associated temporal contour.

Strings of shorter intervals are perceived to begin repeating rhythmic patterns whereas longer intervals tend to end them. These are respectively known as the "run" and "gap" principles (Garner, 1974). Vos (1977) has shown that the performer has enormous latitude in creating rhythmic grouping by varying both the size of temporal intervals and the manner (legato-staccato) of filling them with sound. (See Monahan et al., 1987, for a review.)

Example 6.2 includes the notion of a *temporal pattern contour*. The reader should note that not only pitch patterns but time patterns as well have shape and contour. Temporal intervals may be longer ($+$), shorter ($-$), or the same length ($=$) as the preceding temporal interval just as pitches may be higher ($+$), lower ($-$), or the same as ($=$) the preceding pitch. The perceptual effect of relatively large skips and contour inflections in both realms is to generate a sense of salience for particular tones in a pattern as well as to provide grouping of tones. Tones that are salient in each domain fail to follow the Gestalt principles of "proximity" or "good continuation."

***The Ranges of Discriminability and Similar Redundancy of Scale Units in Pitch and Temporal Domains.*** Western pitch scales are constructed from semitones and whole tones. The distance of a semitone is much larger than the least discriminable or *just noticeable difference* (jnd) between pitches. The size of the jnd depends on frequency: Trained listeners can distinguish between a 100 Hz tone and a 103 Hz tone (a jnd of 3%). As frequency rises, the jnd gets smaller, leveling off at 0.3% for frequencies of 1000 Hz and above (Zwislocki, 1965). In the middle of the range of human voices (about 330 Hz), the jnd is about 1%—so listeners can detect that 333 Hz is different from 330 Hz. Yet every ascending semitone is about 5.95% higher (more precisely, 5.9463094% higher) in frequency than the preceding semitone step. Thus a semitone in the midrange contains about 5.8 jnds and a whole tone contains about 11.6 jnds.

Pitch scales are *redundant* in the sense that they contain intervals that are far bigger than a jnd. Each scale step category subsumes a wide range of frequencies that need not be discriminated from one another in a melody. Because of the changing size of the jnd over the frequency range, the semitone scale is somewhat more redundant for high frequencies than for low.

Likewise in the temporal domain a time scale whose units are usually in the proportion of 2:1 or 3:1 has a great deal of built-in redundancy. Across the temporal range of music, listeners can discriminate differences of about 7% to 12% in duration (Bharucha & Pryor, 1986; Hirsh, Monahan, Grant, & Singh, 1990; Monahan & Hirsh, 1989). Typical beats are two or three times as long as their even subdivisions. The typical uneven division of beats is in the ratio of 2:1 (triple meter) or 3:1 (duple meter; see Clarke, 1985, 1987). Thus the difference between the lengths of any two values related as 2:1 (for example, a quarter-note and an eighth-note) represents a difference of about 7 jnds. The difference for proportions of 3:1 (dotted quarter-note and eighth-note) is about 11.5 jnds. These jnds for the two most common time intervals represent very nearly the same amount of redundancy as for the two most common pitch intervals.

This suggests that the need for a certain degree of perceptual redundancy plays a part in determining that octaves (in the pitch domain) may be divided into five to seven intervals, whereas beats are typically divided into fewer parts with ratios such as 2:1 or 3:1.

## A Major Difference Between Pitch and Time Domains: The Nature of Basic Perceptual Scales

*Pitch.* The relationship between pitch and frequency is basically logarithmic (Dowling & Harwood, 1986). What the listener hears as intervals of constant size (an octave, e.g.) correspond to constant frequency ratios (as the 2:1 ratios between As at 880 Hz and 440 Hz, or Cs at 524 Hz and 262 Hz). The experience of the listener hearing changes in the frequency of tones is one of *addition or subtraction* of pitch units. That scale is well represented by logarithmically equal units whose values can be added or subtracted, such as the chromatic scale of semitones.

*Time.* In contrast to the pitch domain, proportional relationships are important in the time domain. As Hutchinson and Knopoff (1987) pointed out, *the underlying psychological scale for musical time is linear.* The listener counts and divides the fixed time unit of the *beat.* Temporal values longer than the beat are counted in beat units. The musician is generally aware of the multiplication or division of beat values by (at least) factors of two, three, or four. There is no similar awareness of proportion in the pitch realm. C4 does not seem to be "twice as high" as C3, nor is the singer of the pitch interval C4–G4 aware that the ratio of frequencies one to another is 2:3. These differences have led several authors to suppose that different physiological mechanisms underlie the perception of pitch and time (Hutchinson & Knopoff, 1987). Kubovy (1981) suggested that the pitch aspect is mediated in listeners by "a device that loses temporal information in the process of coding it (as the tonotopic organization of the auditory cortex would suggest)," and the time aspect "by a device designated to preserve temporal information as event information" (p. 83).

## Relative Values and the Parallel of Transposition to Tempo Change

*Relative Values.* Pitch and temporal structures are preserved over a wide range of frequencies and tempos. For most people, the pitches and timing of notes in melodies are established relative to the pitch and duration of other notes;

only by assignment to particular frequencies or tempos are they given absolute values. Pitch and time are described most naturally in relative rather than absolute terms. For instance, if you asked several different people to hum "Three Blind Mice," each would be likely to start at a different frequency, and to hum the song at a different tempo. The tune would still be "Three Blind Mice" as long as relative information among the notes was preserved. For pitch, the information that must be preserved is the pitch contour and the relative sizes of pitch intervals; for temporal events, the necessary information is the temporal contour (the sequence of longer, shorter, and same-length information) as well as relative durational differences (Monahan, 1984 Expt. 1; Monahan & Carterette, 1987). As long as these relative values are approximately maintained, the absolute values of frequency and time don't matter within broad limits.

***Pitch Transposition and Tempo Change.*** In terms of structure, *transposition and tempo change are perfectly analogous operations* that preserve relative note-to-note information (Hutchinson & Knopoff, 1987; Monahan, 1984). Table 6.1 captures this parallelism. *A "movable beat" system for preserving relative sizes among note duration values is the temporal equivalent of a movable "do" pitch-scale system* (see following discussion of pitch scales) *for preserving relative pitch interval sizes.*

***The Operations of Transposition and Tempo Change Have Different Psychological Correlates.*** Because the internal scale for pitch is logarithmic, transposition of a melody in pitch is experienced as the addition or subtraction of equal intervals from each pitch of the original melody. On the other hand, because the internal scale for musical time is linear, *changing tempo is experienced as an increase or decrease in the beat frequency* (i.e., the multiplication or division of the interbeat intervals by a constant value). This, of course, means that the relative size differences among note lengths that were present in the original temporal pattern will be preserved.

## The Division of the Octave and Pitch Scales

As described in earlier chapters, the musical scale for pitch is divided into discrete scale steps, and the interval pattern of those scale steps is repeated throughout each octave in the range of musical pitch. Western equal-temperament divides the octave into 12 logarithmically equal semitones. Out of those 12 steps, 7 are selected as a diatonic scale, leaving five notes in each key that are foreign to the tonality. The relationship of within-key pitches to out-of-key pitches is well described by the circle of fifths, on which regions belonging to a particular key can be drawn. These considerations mean that pitch must be multidimensional, as Krumhansl (1990) has emphasized. Each pitch has a "chroma," "pitch class," or "tonal function" within a key, a "pitch height" or "octave level," and an assignment to a key region on the circle of fifths. Shepard (1982a, 1982b) has captured these properties of pitch in elegant geometrical representations, and provided auditory illustrations of their psychological reality.

## Musical Time: Meter and the Subdivision of Time Periods

In recent years many papers have been devoted to the description of time in a musical context (Clarke, 1985; Dowling & Harwood, 1986; Handel & Lawson, 1983; Handel & Oshinsky, 1981; Longuet-Higgins & Lee, 1982; Monahan & Carterette, 1985; Monahan et al., 1987; Povel, 1981, 1984; Povel & Essens, 1985; Steedman, 1977; Yeston, 1976). All of these authors assumed that, at the psychological level, time in music is hierarchically layered as a rate within a rate. That is, musical time may be described as a slower periodic rate, metric, "clock," or beat (all of these terms are equivalent), nested within the rhythmic surface that comprises a faster uniform pulse, temporal grain, or string of equal intervals (some of which are marked by note onsets and some of which are not).

The clock or beat framework may be evoked in the listener by local accent patterns of the rhythmic surface (see preceding). The listener may be thought of as generating a "beat" that makes some points of the rhythmic surface seem regularly more salient or accented than others. The ability to maintain an internal clock—to "feel the beat"—especially when there are no objective stimuli on the rhythmic surface, depends on musical training (Povel & Essens, 1985).

Yeston (1976) insisted that abstract (slower-paced) metric levels shape the rhythmic surface of music. In his view, the time signature is no more than a "graphic technique" that indicates to the performer the metric level chosen by the composer to provide the primary accent structure at the surface level. Thus, the time signature 3/4 indicates three groups of two eighth-notes per bar, and 6/8 indicates two groups of three eighth-notes as shown in Example 6.3. In practice, in 3/4 time the player emphasizes notes 1, 3, and 5, and in 6/8 the player emphasizes notes 1 and 4.

The question of division of time periods such as the measure and the beat may be thought of as similar to the division of the octave into the pitch intervals of the scale. The major difference is that the octave has a fixed size, but the time period to be divided varies with tradition and with the motor and perceptual limitations of performers and listeners. I survey some of the kinds of time division found in music around the world.

***Time Division for Relatively Untrained Western Listeners/Performers.***  Povel (1981) based hypotheses about rhythm perception on the accuracy and consistency of reproductions of repeating rhythmic patterns by subjects who were relatively untrained in music. He asked subjects to reproduce (by tapping)

higher level

3/4                                6/8

surface level

Accenting            >   >   >            >      >
(dynamic, temporal,
articulatory, and
timbral changes)

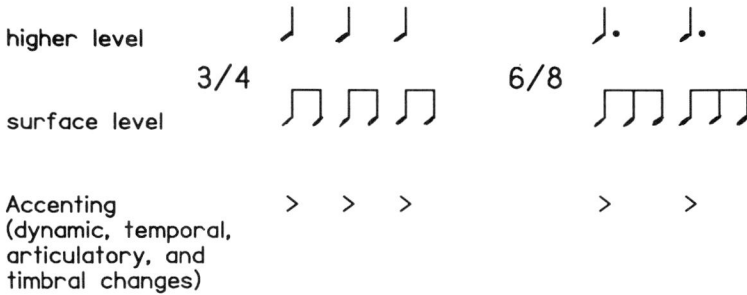

Example 6.3.  Patterns "in six" are typically divided into three groups of two (3/4 time) or two groups of three (6/8 time).

different series of two alternating interval durations that were presented aurally. The only ratio of T1 to T2 (where T1 is short and T2 is long) that subjects reproduced accurately was 1:2; other ratios tended to "drift" toward 1:2 or 1:1 ratios. Ratios of 1:3 were performed accurately in the context where there were four repeating intervals 1:1:1:3 (1113), for example 250-250-250-750 ms. (Like Yeston, I describe rhythmic patterns in terms of their attack points; that is, as intervals between note onsets, which are integral multiples of the grain, or shortest interval in the pattern.) Similarly, 1:4 ratios were performed accurately in the context 1:1:1:1:4, (11114), for example, 250-250-250-250-1000 ms. These sequences can be thought of as bars having two beat intervals: The first beat is filled with subdivisions that occur at a rate three (or four) times the beat rate, whereas the second beat interval is empty. Povel proposed that listeners first attempt to find a regular rate of note onsets in a range from 4 to .67 events/sec (240 to 40 beats/min); the equal intervals marked by these regular onsets are "beats." Only then do listeners differentiate beats into subdivisions. Beats may be undivided, have equal divisions, or be divided in the ratio of 1:2.

Western classical music from the 18th to the early 20th century clearly reflects the event-range and beat-division described by Povel. Fraisse (1982) surveyed more than 50 pieces of music from this era and found that, as a rule, most temporal values fell into two categories: long time values and short time values. The "long" in any given composition was either 2 or 3 times longer than the "short," but the "short" occurred 2 to 3 times, respectively, more often than the "long." In this context it is worth noting that Morse code, the only temporal alphabet ever developed, has only two units, "long" and "short," with "long" being twice as long as "short."

***Time Division for a Concert Pianist.***   Just because musically untrained listeners/performers keep track of only three or four relative time values does not mean that rhythmic organization in Western music can't be complex. We

contrast Povel's (1981) results with those of Clarke (1985), who has reported
the timing data for 3 performances of Erik Satie's "Gnossienne No. 5" by the
concert pianist, John McCabe. Satie's notation for the right hand contains
representations for 16 different durations, 10 of which are divisions of the beat.
Some representative beat divisions are shown in Fig. 6.1. From Satie's score,
it is clear that a concert pianist must know how to divide the beat (an eighth-
note in this example, played at the tempo of 48 beats/min or 1.25 sec/beat)
into *equal temporal intervals* as halves, thirds, quarters, and so on. In one case,
the eighth-note beat is divided equally into sevenths (see Fig. 6.1, Item 9). The
ability to divide the beat into *equal* portions accounts for the production of 6
different temporal intervals that are equal to ⅛th, ⅐th, ⅙th, ¼th, ⅓rd or ½

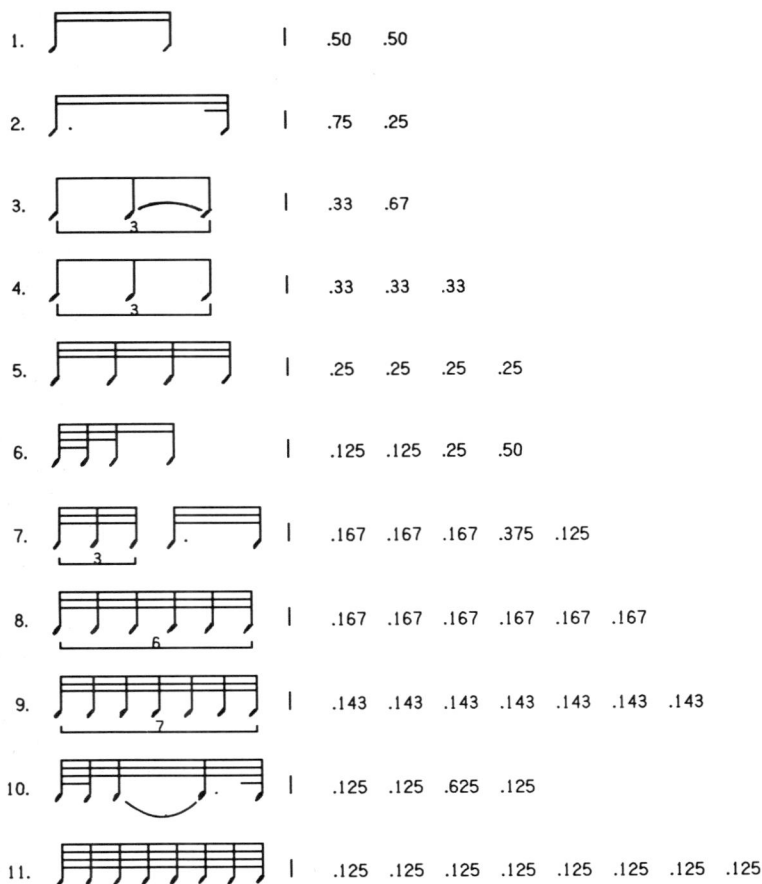

FIG. 6.1.   Some divisions of the eighth-note beat in Erik Satie's *Gnossienne No.
5*. Proportions of the beat that are formed in the given examples are: 1/8, 1/7,
1/6, 1/4, 1/3, 3/8, 1/2, 5/8, 2/3, and 3/4.

the length of an eighth-note (1.25 sec), corresponding to approximate periods of 156, 179, 208, 313, 417, and 625 ms, respectively. The ability to divide the beat or half-beat accurately into unequal proportions of 2:1 or 3:1 accounts for the production of three additional different intervals that are equal to 3⁄8ths, 2⁄3rds, or 3⁄4ths of the length of an eighth-note, that is, approximate periods of 469, 833, and 938 ms, respectively. Altogether, these abilities account for 9 of the 10 different intervals that are subdivisions of the eighth-note beat in Satie's score.

Clarke measured the note durations of McCabe's performances as inter-onset intervals (IOIs) from one note to the next and, in particular, the accuracy of the different eighth-note beat subdivisions. Most of the performed durations followed the notated durations very accurately, with standard deviations of 1% of the beat value or less. In fact, the difference between the total length of the slowest performance of the whole piece and the fastest was less than 2%!

On the basis of his analysis, Clarke concluded that *usually only the beat interval is directly timed*. His argument is based on the fact that the lengths of timed units should covary positively or have zero covariance if they are not subject to a higher order timing constraint. Clarke found that in two cases durations were not timed independently of the beat duration. First, *the lengths of uneven beat divisions covary negatively* (when one gets longer, the other gets shorter) and therefore are constrained by the timing of the beat; second, when there are a large number (five to eight) of even divisions of the beat, the pianist plays them as evenly as possible while confining them within the beat length.

On the other hand, when the beat is divided into a small number of equal intervals (two to four), *the covariance among the lengths of these even divisions is positive*, and, as a consequence, the size of the beat may "drift," getting slightly smaller or larger in the interest of maintaining evenness at the level of the sub-division. We suggest that this is a small bit of evidence for the psychological reality of a second metrical level above the rhythmic surface: The concert pianist may have two nested interval "clocks": a beat clock (eighth-note level) and a clock moving twice as fast for evenly dividing the beat (sixteenth-note level).

Clarke suggested that performers fit uneven time divisions within the beat as "short-long" or "long-short" contours without actively timing them. Further evidence of the difference in performance between uneven and even beat division was that *the variance of ratios from notated temporal values was an order of magnitude higher for uneven beat division than for even beat division* (see Clarke, 1985). Clarke (1987, Experiment 1) showed that listeners also make a very sharp categorical distinction between the even and uneven division of beats if they are heard in metrical contexts.

Because evidence indicated that usually only the beat interval is timed, Clarke (1985) questioned the emphasis of Povel's (1981) rhythmic model on the accurate production of temporal ratios, especially across beat boundaries. Clarke further pointed out that Povel's model was unable to handle Satie's temporal

notation that indicates the presence (presumably Clarke means the psychological presence or psychological reality) of (a) binary and ternary metrics, as well
as (b) equal and unequal divisions of the beat at (c) each of two or three hierarchical levels (e.g., eighth-, sixteenth-, and perhaps the thirty-second note levels).

Povel and Essens (1985) corroborated the importance of the first two of these
components in rhythm perception and production: (a) an internal clock or beat;
and (b) the nature of time division within clock units (even or no division vs.
uneven division of beats) for both musically naive and trained listeners. In their
second experiment, on each trial these researchers played a "double sequence"
comprising a repeating high-pitched monotonic rhythmic pattern together with
a low-pitched isochronic sequence (see Examples 6.4a & 6.4b, slashes indicate
note onsets). The low-pitched sequence was meant to induce a clock or metric
every three or four grain-intervals. The subjects' task was to reproduce the
high-pitched pattern by tapping.

Results indicated, first, that the presence (vs. the absence) of the low-pitched
clock sequence increased the accuracy and reduced the latency of reproduction
of the high-pitched sequence. Second, 90% of listeners who heard the same

```
a.      Sequence X  3     1 1 1 2   1 3        High-pitched

                    / . . / / / / . / / . . |

        Sequence Y  4 . . . 4 . . . 4 . . . | Low-pitched (4-clock)

                    / . . . / . . . / . . . |

                    31        112     13       Beat subdivision code

b.      Sequence X  3     1 1 1 2   1 3        High-pitched

                    / . . / / / / . / / . . |

        Sequence Z  3 . . 3 . . 3 . . 3 . . | Low-pitched (3-clock)

                    / . . / . . / . . / . . |

                    Empty Even  21   Empty    Beat subdivision code

c.      Sequence X  3     1 1 1 2   1 3

                    / . . / / / / . / / . . |

                    >     >     >     >        Natural temporal accent
```

Example 6.4.   Sequence X in "double sequence" A is almost never recognized
as identical to Sequence X in double sequence B (Povel & Essens, 1985). B is
judged simpler than A because its 3-clock (Sequence Z) both provides for a simpler beat subdivision code and coincides with positions of natural temporal accenting as shown in C.

high-pitched sequence (Sequence X in Examples 6.4a & 6.4b, as shown) with different low-pitched clocks, did not realize that it was the same sequence! *This suggests that meters of different length promote different subdivisions and coding of the same temporal sequence.* Third, listeners heard pairs of double sequences and rated them for simplicity. The double sequence of Example 6.4b with triple meter was judged simpler than 6.4a, presumably because beats that are empty or divided evenly are easier to code than those that have two or more uneven elements. A second, related reason that the 3-clock may sound simpler is that its "ticks" correspond to positions of *natural temporal accent* (see Example 6.4c and the previous section on accent and timing). Povel and Essens (1985) have argued that isolated tones in temporal patterns sound accented; the most accented are those beginning long intervals (usually empty beats) and then those that follow long intervals and begin strings of three or more intervals (usually evenly divided beats).

## Musical Time is Multidimensional

Based on the foregoing observations and following Clarke's (1985) comments about Satie's notation, we suggest that the multidimensional scheme in Fig. 6.2 might roughly represent a "temporal psychological space" for a concert pianist. There are three dimensions or bases for measurement or categorization: (a) the

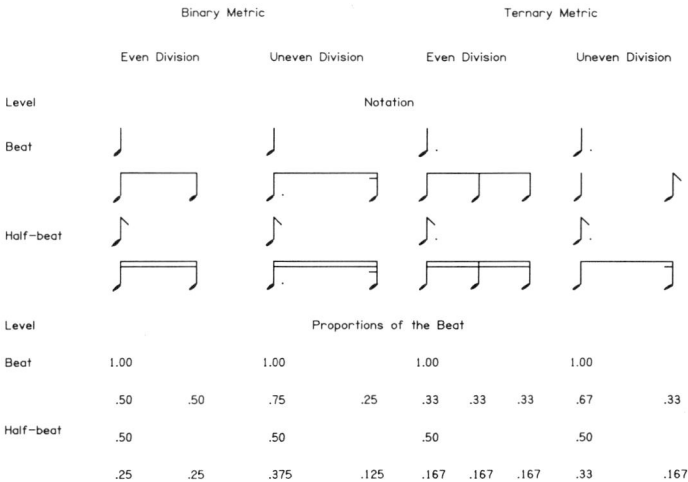

FIG. 6.2.   Representation of a concert pianist's temporal schema. There are two meters, duple and triple. There are two kinds of time division in each meter, even and uneven. In duple meter, time division is in the ratio of 3:1; in triple meter, it is in the ratio of 2:1. There are two levels of hierarchy above the rhythmic surface, thus not only may the beat be divided but also the half-beat.

metrical prime or base; (b) shape or form of time (beat) division; and (c) hierarchical level or depth of time division within the metric. We are claiming here
that the rhythmician must keep track of several time values just as the melodist
must keep track of many pitches. This is more easily done within a redundant
multidimensional temporal scheme.

*The Metrical Base.* Categorization into binary and ternary metrics is
reasonable given that most Western music is written in duple or triple meter
(Fraisse, 1982). Scholes (1964) and Monahan (1984) suggested that Western
musicians primarily employ two different temporal alphabets or scales: binary
and ternary. Listeners perceive different beat subdivisions for the same temporal sequence depending on which meter is evoked (Povel & Essens, 1985).
Evidence for the psychological importance of metrical categorization also comes
from multidimensional scaling studies showing that meter (duple vs. triple) is
a highly salient perceptual dimension for listeners (Gabrielsson, 1973; Monahan & Carterette, 1985). Yeston (1976) has suggested the possibility of other
metrical bases, notably 5 and 7, but also 11, 13, 17, and 19. However, Monahan (1984) noted that because of short-term memory limitations, coherence of
temporal patterns is likely to decrease as the length of the metrical base increases.

From the standpoint of performance, categorization into different metrical
bases also seems imperative. Even virtuosos may have some difficulty in making successive bipartite and tripartite beat divisions (Clarke, 1985), and relatively untrained performers make such divisions with little accuracy. Povel (1981)
reported that his subjects found that reproducing a repeating pattern of 33222
nearly impossible. This pattern is shown in Example 6.5 and may be thought
of as having two (dotted quarter-note) bars or beats with the first divided in
half (as two dotted eighth-notes) and the second divided in thirds (as three eighth-
notes). Clarke (1985) would attribute the difficulty of this figure to the fact that
there are two different metrical divisions required at the dotted-quarter beat
level.

In addition, the pattern in Example 6.5 sounds *syncopated* to most listeners;
that is, there is a clash, between two different metrical strata—evidence that
both strata are psychologically "real." In a recycling pattern, motion at the rate
of the dotted eighth-note starts out and then is denied because no note onset
occurs at point x where it is anticipated. The same is true of the eighth-note
rate of motion, which is denied because there is no onset at point y where it
is expected. Gabrielsson (1973 Experiments 9 and 10) has shown that listeners
classify rhythmic patterns as similar depending on whether they sound syncopated.

Yeston (1976) has called metrical structures that contain two or more differently rated strata *rhythmically dissonant.* When one stratum is strongly superimposed on the other, as just noted, the result is syncopation. The listener does

| Beat rate | 6 . . . . . 6 . . . . . etc. |
|---|---|
| Notation | ♪. ♪. ♩♩♩ |
| Relative intervals | 3   3   2  2  2 |
| Surface onsets | / . . / . . / . / . / . |

Example 6.5.   A rhythmic pattern where the beat is successively divided by two differently-rated subdivisions. The pattern sounds syncopated, that is, the clash between the two metrics is perceived.

not know how to interpret the surface metrically because two competing beat frameworks are equally salient. The metrical patterning is ambiguous. As discussed in the following Western music generally avoids rhythmically dissonant structures.

*The Shape of Beat Division.*   Categorization of rhythms into those having equal or unequal beat subdivisions seems necessary as there are both perceptual and performance differences for these categories. Uneven beat division is usually judged "more complex" (Povel & Essens, 1985) and leads to more variable production (Clarke, 1985). Clarke (1987) has argued that the two types, 1:2 and 1:3 (Fig. 6.2), are not categorically distinct from one another when they occur within the same meter; rather, they are seen on a continuum of "unevenness." On the other hand, when 1:2 and 1:3 occur in triple and duple meter, respectively, performance becomes quite stable.

Other possibilities within the beat have not been exhausted. Accent pattern within beats is highly salient in multidimensional scaling studies (Gabrielsson, 1973; Monahan & Carterette, 1985). Musician subjects in the latter study grouped "accent-first" patterns (long-short and long-short-short) together and opposed them to groupings of "accent-last" patterns (short-long and short-short-long). Povel and Essens (1985) have remarked that the beat framework or clock is more easily set up if longer subdivisions begin a beat (i.e., if the subdivision is 31, 21, or 211, rather than 13, 12, 112, or 121). They also note that untrained listeners are especially likely to assume that a naturally accented tone that begins a long interval marks a beat boundary—which may or may not be the case. This suggests that it is not just equal or unequal time division, but also the contour of the time division that sets up local temporal accenting that is important (Clarke, 1985; Gabrielsson, 1973; Hutchinson & Knopoff, 1987; Monahan, 1984; Monahan & Carterette, 1985; Monahan et al., 1987).

*Hierarchical Level.* As was noted, Povel and Essens (1985) consider only two levels of coding in rhythm perception: (a) the induced internal clock or beat, and (b) its subdivisions. Example 6.6 shows seven common divisions of the beat (arbitrarily a quarter-note) in duple meter. In Povel's and Essens' model, only Examples 6.6a and 6.6b constitute even beat division, the rest are uneven. Clarke's (1985) model agrees with Povel and Essens' model in considering 13, 31, and 121 as irregular or uneven beat division and 22 or 1111 as even division. However, he still does not consider the 112 and 211 divisions to be uneven or irregular. These divisions have regular onsets at the half-beat (every eighth-note) and thus are said to preserve the eighth-note rate or level of motion. Clarke showed that note durations in patterns like these are independently timed and are not constrained by the duration of the beat. Thus, apparently, one internal clock may control divisions at the beat level and the other at the half-beat level.

Further evidence of the psychological reality of hierarchical level comes from an observation by Clarke (1985), who has suggested that the difficulty of playing a rhythmic figure is predicted by the number of metrical levels that are skipped between one beat divisor and another. He argued that Pattern A in Example 6.7, which moves from the quarter-note to the 32nd note level without any intervening steps, is far more difficult to play accurately than Pattern B, which contains the intervening 8th- and 16th-note metrical levels.

In conclusion, the evidence for the psychological reality of nested levels of motion above the beat level is slight in terms of temporal perception or performance. Below the beat level, concert performers apparently may readily access at least one other clock at the half-beat level for the active timing of events. Perception research has been concentrated on the processing of monotonic rhythmic stimuli from a single source, thus there is little evidence from that quarter for the psychological reality of hierarchically nested clocks or rates of motion that do not conflict with one another.

## HOW DO PITCH AND TIME GO TOGETHER?

We turn now to the situation where there is more than one source of salience and grouping. As noted by Monahan and Carterette (1985) and Monahan et al.

Example 6.6.   Common divisions of the quarter-note beat.

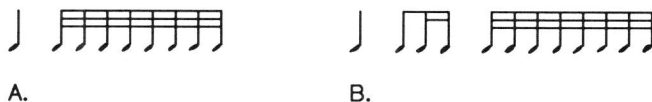

Example 6.7.   A. Transition from quarter-note to thirty-second note in one step and B. with intervening eighth- and sixteenth-note steps. According to Clarke (1985), B. is more accurately performed than A.

(1987), there may be accenting from pitch-level, tonal, timbral, manner (legato-staccato), loudness, and temporal differences. These may come from the same line of music or from multiple lines with more than one voice. Here we are most concerned with the mutual relationships of pitch and temporal sources of accenting.

## The Difference Between Pitch and Time Relationships

Temporal features must of necessity occur in a particular order that makes them very different from pitch features. Subgroups (rhythms) in time are literally nested within larger groupings, unlike the tones of the diatonic scale, which are a subgroup of the larger pitch set only in an abstract sense. As we have already seen with the 33222 pattern (Povel, 1981), we cannot easily change the periodicity of subgroupings because that conflicts with the periodicity of previous subgroupings. Neither can we change meter easily because that will obscure the original meter and change the composition of subgroups.

Western music generally avoids patterns that have more than one metrical interpretation. In order for pitch relations to be clearly perceived among tones or chords, they must come at a predictable rate (Monahan & Carterette, 1985; Monahan et al., 1987). With Balzano (1987), we might suppose that cultures that do not have the weight of a tonal tradition would have a more rhythmically rich tradition to add to the interest of their music.

## Three Metrical Structures

Yeston (1976) has classified metrical structures into three categories: rhythmic consonance, out-of-phase consonance, and rhythmic dissonance. These structures idealize the combined effects of several rates of motion. We use these structures to look at accent patterning that emanates from more than one source.

*Rhythmic Consonance.*   Most of Western music is classified as rhythmically consonant. In consonant structures (see Fig. 6.3A) all rates of motion are nested so that the accented onsets marking slower rates necessarily coincide with those at faster rates. If the composer defines the rate of motion at Level B (the quarter-note rate) as the meter, then no conflict with this meter is offered

**A.**

**B.**

**C.**

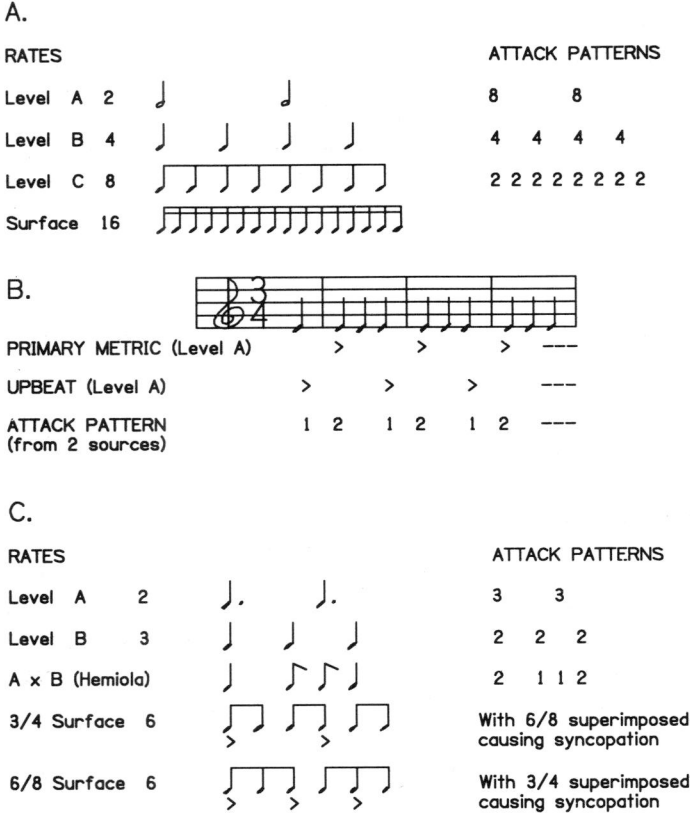

FIG. 6.3.   Three metrical structures: A. Three consonant hierarchical levels of motion above the rhythmic surface; B. Out-of-phase consonance where the dynamic accenting of the upbeat regularly precedes the notated downbeat causing syncopation; C. Hemiola a case of rhythmic dissonance. If a passage is to receive a single metric interpretation, one level of motion is marked as primary by the time signature (3/4 marks Level B as primary and 6/8 marks Level A as primary). The alternate level of motion is strongly superimposed on the primary level, which is the meaning of syncopation.

by accented onsets on Levels C (the eighth-note rate) or A (the half-note rate). Similar arguments may be made for levels A and C if they are taken as defining the meter.

***Out-of-Phase Consonance.***   Yeston has described a metrical structure that is the result of consonant hierarchies that are superimposed so that their accent structures are out of phase with each other as shown in Fig. 6.3B. Here, upbeats may be thought of as the basis of displaced motion occurring at the same metrical level or rate as downbeats; if the chain of upbeats is dynamically stressed, then syncopation is created through displaced or *out-of-phase consonance*. Such patterns are common in Chopin's mazurkas; there is no resting place or point at which out-of-phase metrics agree and listeners can be confused as to whether the notated upbeat or downbeat is "really the downbeat." Such patterns are like auditory reversible figures and are relatively rare in Western music.

### Rhythmic Dissonance

**Polyrhythms.** Rhythmic dissonance is the division of time by two or more differently rated strata. One form is called *polyrhythm*, in which two or more prime metrics divide the same time period (Handel & Oshinsky, 1981). The simplest polyrhythm (2 × 3, called *hemiola*) divides the same time period equally by three and by two simultaneously. Western music, in avoiding more than one metrical interpretation, marks patterns "in 6" either as 3/4 (3 groups of 2) or 6/8 (2 groups of 3; cf. Example 6.3). When hemiola occurs, the composer has marked one of the two groupings as primary in the time signature. The composer usually indicates the other level of motion to be superimposed on it by dynamic or phrase markings (see Fig. 6.3C). The marker for the possibility of metrical ambiguity is what is called a *temporal retrograde* in the attack point pattern: hemiola generates 2112. Example 6.8 shows that a 3 × 7 polyrhythm generates 331232133 at the rhythmic surface.

This pattern is the same read backwards or forwards. As we have seen, by itself the attack point pattern does not define the groupings in the pattern because these are psychological phenomena. However, a temporal retrograde is a sign that there *can* be metrical ambiguity.

Handel and his colleagues (Handel & Lawson, 1983; Handel & Oshinsky, 1981; Oshinsky & Handel, 1978) investigated different polyrhythms whose different levels might have different pitches. They asked listeners to "tap to the beat." They found that tapping depended on the rate of presentation of the whole structure. At the very fastest tempos, listeners tapped to the rate of the whole polyrhythm (termed a *unit response*). At fast tempos, listeners tapped at the rate of the slowest level (e.g., Level A, in Example 6.8); at moderate tempos they tapped at the rate of the faster level (Level B, in Example 6.8). Only at the slowest tempos did they tap to the cross-rhythms formed by the two levels.

```
Level A     7       7       7       etc.
Level B     3 3 3 3 3 3 3   etc.
Attack Pattern   3..3..12.3..2.13..3..etc.
```

Example 6.8.   Representation of a 3 × 7 polyrhythm which results in a 331232133 attack pattern (temporal retrograde) at the rhythmic surface.

*Modal Time Organization.* Pressing (1983) has reported about several modal organizations of time that he termed *perceptually multistable*. One of these patterns is shown in Fig. 6.4. The structure is organized around the attack pattern of the bell: 2212221. Note that this is the very same organization for temporal intervals as the major diatonic scale is for pitch intervals. (Perhaps Aristoxenes was right!) Any time organization that has a total of 12 units in the attack pattern can be evenly divided by 2, 3, 4, and 6. Amongst the Ewe tribe of West Africa, the lead musician plays the bell pattern and different groups of people clap every 2, 3, 4, or 6 units. None of these metrics is very stable because each of the clap patterns coincides with silence in the bell pattern at least once per cycle (see Fig. 6.4). So, again we have the case of a rhythmic surface that has several metrical (and rhythmic) interpretations: an auditory reversible figure. As with polyrhythmic structures (see the previous section), the only point at which modal patterns are completely temporally stable is when the whole unit (or "isorhythm" of the bell) is repeated; almost all the clap patterns coincide with the bell pattern at the beginning of the unit.

A second characteristic of modal patterns is that they are played very quickly, often at the limits of human performance. Pressing (1983) gave a range of shortest-interval rates from 225/min to 600+/min. Presumably, this serves to focus attention on the pattern as a whole and permits the recycling of a very long temporal unit within the range of temporal short-term memory. Recall that Handel and Oshinsky (1981) reported that the unit response, that is, tapping to the repetition of a whole polyrhythmic cycle, emerged only at faster tempos.

Complex modal organizations of time assist in the formation of sensorimotor schemata. West African and Balkan children who listen to and ultimately perform such patterns learn them just as Western children learn the diatonic pitch scales of their culture. Just as pitch scales serve as the basis for categorical perception and the production of interval relations, so temporal schemata serve

| Rhythmic levels of motion | Attack point patterns | | | | | | | | | | | |
|---|---|---|---|---|---|---|---|---|---|---|---|---|
| 2-claps/cycle | 6 | . | . | . | . | . | 6 | . | . | . | . | . | \| |
| 3-claps/cycle | 4 | . | . | . | 4 | . | . | . | 4 | . | . | . | \| |
| 4-claps/cycle | 3 | . | . | 3 | . | . | 3 | . | . | 3 | . | . | \| |
| 6-claps/cycle (a) | 2 | . | 2 | . | 2 | . | 2 | . | 2 | . | 2 | . | \| |
| 6-claps/cycle (b) | . | 2 | . | 2 | . | 2 | . | 2 | . | 2 | . | 2 | \| |
| 7-stroke modal bell pattern | 2 | . | 2 | . | 1 | 2 | . | 2 | . | 2 | . | 1 | \| |
| 12 equal intervals per/cycle | . | . | . | . | . | . | . | . | . | . | . | . | \| |

FIG. 6.4. Example of "multistability": metrical clap cycles superimposed on a modal time pattern. None of the metrical clap cycles is stable because at least once per cycle of the 7-stroke bell pattern, each clap cycle coincides with silence or no onset in the modal bell pattern. Numbers indicate point of note attacks and the number of intervals until the next attack in each clap or bell cycle. Dots mark off equal intervals and show points where there is no note onset.

to organize musical time. People used to listening to modally organized time patterns should be adept at reproducing metrically ambiguous patterns. Povel (1987, personal communication) has reported testing a nonmusician Thai subject who was able to reproduce all the metrically ambiguous patterns in his experiment equally quickly and correctly. It is perhaps no coincidence that a large body of Thai songs are in 7/4 meter (Pressing, 1983).

The conclusion to be drawn is that when we measure Western listeners' response to metrically ambiguous patterns we are measuring their familiarity with nested metrical time patterns and their lack of experience with polyrhythmic or modal time organization. The need for cross-cultural studies of temporal pattern perception and temporal pattern learning experiments is obvious.

## Examples of Rhythmic Consonance and Dissonance in Western Music

Consonant patterning has a great deal in common with Martin's (1972) hierarchical scheme and Lerdahl's and Jackendoff's (1983) tree-structure grammar for equally distributed accents. The hierarchical view of speech or music is generally opposed to a "concatenative" point of view, which suggests that physical correlates of accent are to be located "on" syllables or notes themselves. We have previously pointed out the major correlates of accent in most languages and music. However, there is no simple correspondence between any one or a combination of these acoustic characteristics of a syllable or note and the perception of relative accent (Cooper & Meyer, 1960; Fry, 1968; Ladefoged, 1967; Lehiste, 1970).

On the other hand, a large body of evidence has grown up supporting the notion of a hierarchy of equally distributed accents in music and speech. For examples, see Martin (1970), Huggins (1972a, 1972b), Shields, McHugh, and Martin (1974), Deutsch (1980), Jones, Boltz, and Kidd (1982), Handel, Weaver, and Lawson (1983), Boltz and Jones (1986), Monahan et al. (1987), Fourakis and Monahan (1988), and Drake, Dowling, and Palmer (1991). One striking result in favor of the equally distributed accent hypothesis was reported by Sturges and Martin (1974). They showed that listeners' memory for binary high-buzz and low-buzz sequences was better for eight-element than for seven-element patterns. Thus, an eight-element pattern like 10101000 (where 1 is the high buzz and 0 is the low buzz) was better recognized than a seven-element pattern like 1010100. This is a nonintuitive result from the concatenative point of view. However, it fits well with the notion of equally distributed accent because primary accents can be equidistant from one another in eight-element patterns but not in seven-element patterns. One must be cautious about the generality of such results because again, we may be measuring Western listeners' lack of familiarity with more complex time structures such as 7/4 meter.

*"Three Blind Mice."*   The example we have chosen here is perhaps over-worked but is still a paragon of rhythmic consonance in Western music. Figure 6.5 shows the pattern of "Three Blind Mice." The pitch pattern is shown in semitones where the tonic (G) or key was assigned the value of zero; it is also shown in diatonic scale steps. The pitch contour that indicates the direction of pitch change from note to note as well as pitch-level accenting is shown. Tonal motion of pitch is shown: the pattern moves from pitches of the tonic to dominant chords (chords based on the first or fifth step of the diatonic scale, T or D, respectively). Organization of the time pattern is shown as the attack point pattern and as the number of beats from one note to the next. The temporal contour and positions of natural temporal accenting are also shown.

All these variables are lined up neatly in a nested hierarchy. Two periodicities are especially worthy of note. First, the tonic always lines up with natural temporal accenting (each occurring and coinciding every two beats). Second, a lengthening ( + ) in the temporal contour always precedes the largest (upward or + ) skips—as well as inflections ( + − ) in the pitch pattern. Thus pitch-level and natural temporal accenting are also metrically related in a consonant man-

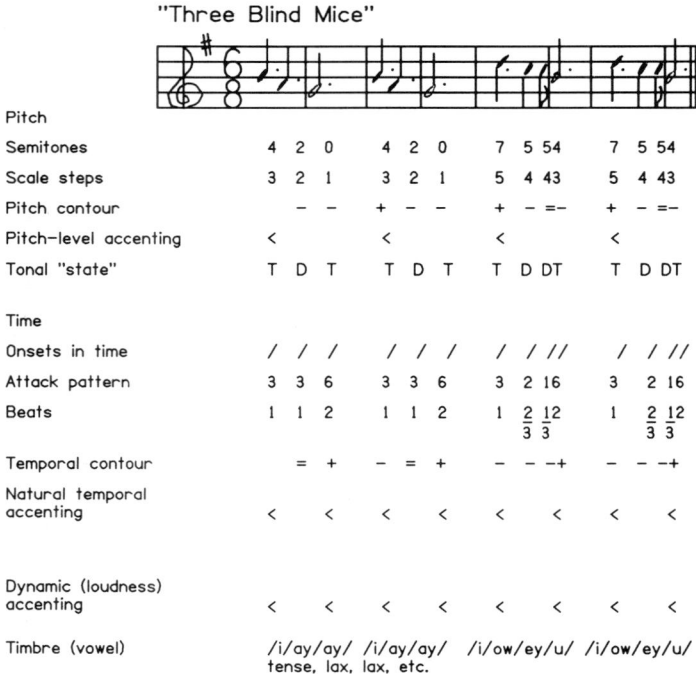

"Three Blind Mice"

| Pitch | | | | | | | | | | | | |
|---|---|---|---|---|---|---|---|---|---|---|---|---|
| Semitones | | 4 | 2 | 0 | 4 | 2 | 0 | 7 | 5 54 | 7 | 5 54 |
| Scale steps | | 3 | 2 | 1 | 3 | 2 | 1 | 5 | 4 43 | 5 | 4 43 |
| Pitch contour | | | − | − | + | − | − | + | − =− | + | − =− |
| Pitch-level accenting | < | | | < | | | < | | | < | |
| Tonal "state" | T | D | T | T | D | T | T | D DT | T | D DT |

| Time | | | | | | | | | | | | |
|---|---|---|---|---|---|---|---|---|---|---|---|---|
| Onsets in time | | / | / | / | / | / | / | / | / // | / | / // |
| Attack pattern | | 3 | 3 | 6 | 3 | 3 | 6 | 3 | 2 16 | 3 | 2 16 |
| Beats | | 1 | 1 | 2 | 1 | 1 | 2 | 1 | 2 12<br>3 3 | 1 | 2 12<br>3 3 |
| Temporal contour | | = | + | − | = | + | − | − | −+ | − | − −+ |
| Natural temporal accenting | < | < | < | < | < | < | < | < |

| Dynamic (loudness) accenting | < | < | < | < | < | < | < | < |
|---|---|---|---|---|---|---|---|---|
| Timbre (vowel) | /i/ay/ay/  /i/ay/ay/  /i/ow/ey/u/  /i/ow/ey/u/<br>tense, lax, lax, etc. | | | | | | | |

FIG. 6.5.   "Three Blind Mice" showing the patterning of pitch-level, tonal, timbral, temporal and dynamic accenting, as well as pitch and temporal contours and intervals. This is an example of rhythmic consonance.

ner, with the former occurring every four beats and the latter every two beats. We have included at the bottom of the figure the likely dynamic accenting. Also included are the vowels of the words to ''Three Blind Mice'': the tense vowel /i/ begins every phrase. This kind of patterning for timbre has been noted by Kendall and Carterette (1991) who have conceived a model for timbre as a time-ordered sequence of state changes that are in or out-of-phase with the consonant pitch and time organization. They suggest singing ''Three Blind Mice'' with the vowels alternating between /i/ and /a/. This would constitute a case of rhythmic dissonance.

Perhaps some would say that strictly consonant structure is ''boring'' because it is so predictable. However, Boltz and Jones (1986) have shown that musical dictation with this kind of consonant structure is more accurate. Also, Monahan et al. (1987) showed that pitch difference detection for notes in rhythmically consonant patterns is more accurate than in out-of-phase consonant or dissonant patterns. Recently, Drake, Dowling, and Palmer (1991) showed that children and adult pianists reproduced simple novel tunes more accurately when there was consonant nested structure between pitch-level and temporal accenting. Dynamic accenting had no effect on reproduction accuracy. Neither dynamic nor pitch-level accenting had an effect on the reproductions of rhythm. This result confirms Monahan's and Carterette's (1985) finding in a multidimensional scaling study that similarity among simple melodies is primarily determined by temporal structure rather than by pitch structure.

*The "America" Tango.*    Consider Fig. 6.6, which shows ''America'' as it was originally written with the time pattern of a stately galliard in simple triple meter. With the exception of dynamic and timbral patterning, the same variables are shown in this figure as were considered previously in our discussion of ''Three Blind Mice.'' The main characteristic to note about this pattern is that pitch-level accenting and temporal accenting combine to mark a clear downbeat every three beats. *Usually, the combination of pitch-level and natural temporal accenting will clarify the position of the bar or measure.*

Consider now the pattern in Fig. 6.7, which is called ''America Tango'' because the present author took its pitch pattern from the song called ''America'' (or ''God Save the Queen'') and its time pattern from the tango, a simple duple meter with a characteristic dotted rhythm (3122). *In several hundred presentations of "America Tango" to musically trained and untrained listeners, about 30% of musicians but only about 10% of nonmusicians could immediately identify the melody as "America."* Apparently, ''America Tango'' is not a ''permissible'' transformation or variation of ''America.''

There is no consonance of accenting in the first six notes of this pattern. Pitch-level accenting divides the six notes into two groups of three, whereas natural temporal accenting divides them into three groups of 2. Thus we have rhythmic dissonance (hemiola) between the pitch-level accenting and the tem-

"America" as a Galliard

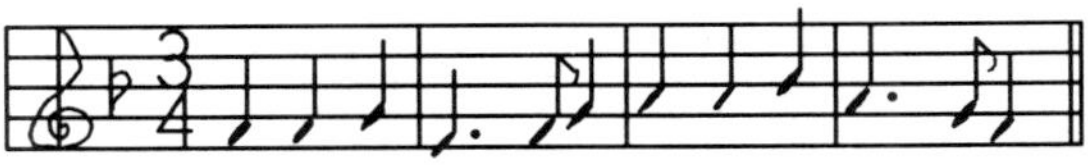

[musical notation]

| Pitch | | |
|---|---|---|
| Semitones | 0 . 0 . 1 .−1 . . 0 2 . 4 . 4 . 5 . 1 . . 0 2 . | |
| Scale steps | 1 . 1 . 2 . 7̄ . . 1 2 . 3 . 3 . 4 . 3 . . 2 1 . | |
| Pitch contour | = + − + + + = + − − − | |
| Pitch−level accenting | <   < <   <   < | |
| Tonal "state" | T . T . D . D . . T D . T . T . D . T . . D T . | |

| Time | | |
|---|---|---|
| Onsets on equal-interval time−line | / . / . / . / . . / / . / . / . / . / . . / / . | |
| Attack pattern | 2 . 2 . 2 . 3 . . 1 2 . 2 . 2 . 2 . 3 . . 1 2 . | |
| Beats | 1 . 1 . 1 . $\frac{3}{2}$ . . $\frac{1}{1}$ 1 . 1 . 1 . 1 . $\frac{3}{2}$ . . $\frac{1}{1}$ 1 . | |
| Temporal contour | = = + − + = = = + − + | |
| Natural temporal accenting | <   <   <   <   < | |
| Combined pitch−level and natural temporal accenting | < . < < . < < . < < . < | |
| Attack point pattern of combined accenting | 2 . 1 2 . 1 2 . 1 2 . 1 | |
| Downbeats | <   <   <   < | |

FIG. 6.6. "America" as a galliard showing the patterning of pitch-level, tonal, and temporal accenting as well as pitch and temporal contours and intervals. This is an example of rhythmic consonance.

poral accenting. Note that the attack pattern for the combination of pitch-level and temporal accents contains the signature of a temporal retrograde, 2112.

## Two Conclusions

**_The Effects of Good and Poor Gestalts._** "America Tango" is a poor gestalt. It is confusing because the listener cannot group the pitch patterning every three notes while the time pattern groups them every two notes. The listener will almost certainly group the pattern by temporal accenting because that is far more salient than pitch-level accenting (Monahan & Carterette, 1985). One could learn to play the "America Tango" but it would almost certainly take longer than learning the original as a galliard. Drake, Dowling, and Palmer (1991) have suggested that the reason for this is that consonant accenting draws attention to the same points in time and then segmentation of the sequence into smaller units is efficient and reproductions are good. However, when attention

"America" as a Tango

| Pitch | | |
|---|---|---|
| Semitones | | 0 . . 0 2 .-1 . 0 . . 2 4 . 4 . 5 . . 4 2 . 0 . | |
| Scale steps | | 1 . . 1 2 .⌐. 1 . . 2 3 . 3 . 4 . . 3 2 . 1 . | |
| Pitch contour | | = +   -   +   + +   =   +   - -   -   | |
| Pitch-level accenting | <     <   <       <     <     | |
| Tonal "state" | T . . T D . D . T . . D T . T . D . . T D . T . | |

| Time | | |
|---|---|---|
| Onsets on equal-interval time-line | / . . / / . / . / . . / / . / . / . . / / . / . | |
| Attack pattern | 3 . . 1 2 . 2 . 3 . . 1 2 . 2 . 3 . . 1 2 . 2 . | |
| Beats | $\frac{3}{4}$ . . $\frac{1}{4}\frac{1}{2}$ . $\frac{1}{2}$ . $\frac{3}{4}$ . . $\frac{1}{4}\frac{1}{2}$ . $\frac{1}{2}$ . $\frac{3}{4}$ . . $\frac{1}{4}\frac{1}{2}$ . $\frac{1}{2}$ . | |
| Temporal contour |   - +   =   +   - +   =   +   - +   =   | |
| Natural temporal accenting | <     <   <     <     <     <   | |
| Combined pitch-level and natural temporal accenting | < .   < <   < .   < .   < .   < . | |
| Attack point pattern of combined accenting | 2 .   1 1   2 .   2 .   2 .   2 . | |

FIG. 6.7. "America" as a tango showing the patterning of pitch-level, tonal, and temporal accenting as well as pitch and temporal contours and intervals. This is an example of rhythmic dissonance.

is drawn to too many points in time, segmentation is less efficient and reproductions are poorer.

Highly consonant structures are excellent schema for training children to have expectancies in time and in pitch space. According to Jones (1981), initially, expectancies are "ideal or simplified . . . continuous, rhythmically generated paths . . . that allow us to guide our attention to approximately correct neighborhoods" (p. 571). Our conclusion is that if music is to be memorable and relatively "performer-" and "performance-proof" it must have natural temporal accenting and pitch-level accenting that occur in a manner that generates a regular metric in their combined attack pattern.

***The Identity of Musical Entities and the Salience of Grouping by Time.*** The reason that listeners cannot identify the tune of "America" with a tango rhythm is that the tango rhythm does not preserve the relative temporal information of the original (temporal contour and relative interval sizes). Pitches that were salient in the original are now less salient, and vice versa, because they coincide with different durations. This transformation, unlike changing the tempo, destroys the very identity of a known musical entity. As a child, I recall reading the description of a new recording of Schubert's *Eighth (Unfinished) Symphony*. The writer pointed out that the pitch pattern of the four-tone opening motif was the same as the theme that preceded the popular television series, "Dragnet." I was surprised that I hadn't recognized that the two melodies were identical. But I have since found that, as with "America Tango," two different temporal contours combined with the same melody are two different entities.

Example 6.9 shows the two themes along with their attack patterns, pitch, and temporal contours, as well as pitch-level, temporal, and combined patterns of accenting. The attack point pattern for combined accenting shows clearly that the Schubert motif is in triple meter and the "Dragnet" theme is in "four" or duple meter. Most observers report that the Schubert motif has "more tension" than "Dragnet"; the reason seems to be that pitch-level and temporal accenting are out-of-phase at the third tone; this is not the case in the "Dragnet" motif. The point is that one would never consider either of these well-known patterns as an acceptable variation of the other—they're simply too different. Similarly, in the realm of speech, the same pair of syllables with different accent patterns attached are *not* the same word: for example, *ob'ject* has a different identity (and meaning) than *ob ject'*. While using the word *ob'ject*, one usually does not think of *ob ject'* or its meaning, or vice versa. It seems probable from these observations that melodies, like words, are stored together with their relative accent patterns as entities in long-term memory.

Everyone agrees that adding a new pitch pattern to the same temporal pattern creates a new entity. There are thousands of waltzes, tangos, rhumbas, and so on, comprising different melodies attached to distinctive classes of rhythms. Isn't it odd that thousands of melodies should be classified by their rhythm patterns? Yet we can hear a temporal pattern's regularity when it's combined with almost any pitch pattern that stays in the range of one octave. This also fits with the earlier observations that we don't immediately recognize the very same pitch pattern attached to different-contour rhythms. Both point to the fact that grouping by temporal accenting is enormously more salient than grouping by pitch-level or tonal accenting (see Monahan & Carterette, 1985).

## SUMMARY

### Parallels Between Pitch and Time

1. The primary physical scales underlying both domains may be represented *either* as frequencies or periods (durations).

2. There are critical ranges of frequency (or period) for perception and production of music in both domains. For instance, melodies typically occur with-

| Theme | Schubert's "Eighth" | "Dragnet" |
|---|---|---|

| | Schubert's "Eighth" | "Dragnet" |
|---|---|---|
| Attack pattern | 3 . . 2 . 1 3 . . | | 3 . . 1 2 . 2 . | |
| Pitch contour | + + − | | + + − | |
| Temporal contour | − − + | | − + = | |
| Pitch–level accent | < < | | < < | |
| Temporal accent | < < < | | < < | |
| Combined accent | < < << | | < < | |
| Attack pattern of combined accents | 3 2 1 3 | | 4 4 | |
| Downbeats | < < < | | < < | |

Example 6.9. The first four notes of Schubert's *Eighth Symphony* and of the "Dragnet" theme have the same relative pitches but different relative timing; hence, they are different musical entities.

in the range of one octave, active timekeeping or "keeping the beat" occurs in the range of 4 to .67 events/sec. Relatively isolated tones in either domain sound accented and generate pattern grouping. The most common interval sizes in musical pitch and time provide comparable amounts of redundancy relative to measures of discriminability.

3. The basic psychological scales underlying pitch and time perception are different: The perceptual scale for pitch is logarithmic because octaves are perceived as equivalent; the perceptual scale for time is linear.

4. Humans are usually perceivers of relative rather than absolute values in both domains. Even though the basic perceptual scales are different, there are parallel transformation rules that preserve relative (but not absolute) pitch and time information in patterns: these are *transposition* and *tempo change rules* respectively. Thus "Yankee Doodle" played fast or slow, high and low, is still "Yankee Doodle." Transposition is experienced as addition or subtraction of a constant value; tempo change is experienced as the speeding (multiplication) or slowing (division) of the beat rate.

5. Western music divides the octave into both chromatic and diatonic scales. A third scale, "key distance," is represented by the Circle of Fifths.

Pitch is multidimensional because the effects of pitch height, pitch chroma of the diatonic scale (tonality), and key distance (nonlinear relationships among tone chroma represented by the Circle of Fifths) have all been shown to "have psychological reality" in that they affect perception and memory for melodies.

6. Western music divides time into a beat or metrical framework. The ability to set up a beat framework is a matter of musical experience and the location of natural temporal accent. Metrical frameworks have different lengths or prime bases. Divisions of time within frameworks differ depending on whether they are even or uneven. There is evidence that highly trained musicians may be able to construct two hierarchical levels of timekeeping above the rhythmic surface.

7. Psychologically speaking, time, like pitch, is multidimensional. For time, the major dimensions are beat frameworks of different length and their rhythmic subdivisions. A third variable for performers may be the hierarchical level of the subdivision. Composers, performers, and listeners make use of these scales and categories so that each has "psychological reality."

## How Pitch and Time Go Together

1. Relationships in time are literally nested in a hierarchical manner. Pitch relationships are only abstractly arranged as subgroups. That is, diatonic scale chroma comprise only an abstract subgroup of the chromatic scale; on the other hand, two eighth-notes are literally nested within a quarter-note. This means that setting up new beat frameworks with different lengths of subdivision will necessarily conflict with and destroy the old framework. On the other hand, occurrence of nondiatonic pitches temporarily disturb, but do not easily upset, the sense of tonal center in most pieces.

2. Different sources of salience may have different rates of motion. These regularly accent and group the tones of a piece of music. We considered three arrangements (suggested by Yeston, 1976) among different regular levels of motion: rhythmic consonance, out-of-phase consonance, and rhythmic dissonance. Most pieces of Western music are consonant, which means rates of motion are neatly nested and in phase with one another so that they do not conflict. Particularly important is the nested metrical relationship of pitch-level accenting with natural temporal accenting. We suggested that the reason Western music is so biased toward consonant structures is because of its rich tonal tradition. Tonal patterns that are regularly grouped in time are easily chunked and remembered: Consonant structures accomplish regular segmentation.

Other cultures without a rich tonal tradition often have a complex rhythmic tradition to add interest to their music: this aesthetic is different from that of the West. We considered polyrhythms and modal time patterns as cases of rhythmic dissonance. These structures support two or more metrical (and rhythmic) interpretations and are often perceived as syncopated, which means two or more metrics are in conflict.

3. We considered examples of rhythmic consonance ("Three Blind Mice") and rhythmic dissonance ("America Tango"). We suggested that because of its extreme regularity, rhythmic consonance presents children with an excellent schema for directing attention and thus learning expectations about the locations of "when" (time) and "where" (pitch) in music.

4. We concluded that rhythmic dissonance was a poor gestalt because it allowed two or more conflicting interpretations of the same piece of music. This conclusion assumes the general Western aesthetic that one and only one interpretation of the rhythmic surface should be salient.

A second conclusion was derived from our experiment with "America Tango" and other examples. Musical entities are created not only by attaching the same rhythm pattern to different pitches (e.g., How many waltzes are there?) but also by attaching the same pitch pattern to different-contour temporal patterns (the theme from "Dragnet" and the opening motif of Schubert's *Eighth Symphony* are different entities despite the fact that they have the same pitch pattern). It is the unique combination of pitch and time contours and relative intervals that creates a musical entity. Last, given that we hear the time pattern of a waltz despite the thousands of melodies that might be attached to it and given that we do not hear the same pitch pattern when it is combined with a different-contour rhythmic pattern, demonstrates the salience of temporal accenting and grouping over pitch-level or tonal grouping.

## ACKNOWLEDGMENTS

This work was supported by OCAST Grant HSO-005, by a grant from the Presbyterian Health Foundation to the Department of Communication Disorders at the University of Oklahoma, and by Air Force Grant AFOSR-87-0382 to the Central Institute for the Deaf at Washington University Medical Center, St. Louis, MO, where the author was a post-doctoral research scientist. Thanks are extended to Edward C. Carterette, W. Jay Dowling, Blas Espinoza-Varas, and Ira J. Hirsh for their comments on earlier versions of this manuscript.

## REFERENCES

Balzano, G. J. (1987). Measuring music. In A. Gabrielsson (Ed.), *Action and perception in rhythm and music* (pp. 177–199). Stockholm: Royal Swedish Academy of Music.

Bharucha, J. J., & Pryor, J. H. (1986). Disrupting the isochrony of underlying rhythm: An asymmetry in discrimination. *Perception & Psychophysics, 40,* 137–141.

Boltz, M., & Jones, M. R. (1986). Does rule recursion make melodies easier to reproduce? If not, what does? *Cognitive Psychology, 18,* 389–431.

Bregman, A. S., & Campbell, J. (1971). Primary auditory stream segregation and perception of order in rapid sequences of tones. *Journal of Experimental Psychology, 89*, 244–249.

Clarke, E. F. (1985). Some aspects of rhythm and expression in performances of Erik Satie's "Gnossienne No. 5." *Music Perception, 2*, 299–328.

Clarke, E. F. (1987). Categorical rhythm perception: An ecological perspective. In A. Gabrielsson, (Ed.) *Action and perception in rhythm and music* (pp. 19–33). Stockholm: Royal Swedish Academy of Music.

Cooper, G. W., & Meyer, L. B. (1960). *The rhythmic structure of music*. Chicago, IL: University of Chicago Press.

Deutsch, D. (1980). The processing of structured and unstructured tonal sequences. *Perception & Psychophysics, 28*, 381–389.

Dowling, W. J. (1968). *Rhythmic fission and perceptual organization of tone sequences*. Unpublished doctoral dissertation, Harvard University, Cambridge, MA.

Dowling, W. J. (1973). The perception of interleaved melodies. *Cognitive Psychology, 5*, 322–337.

Dowling, W. J., & Harwood, D. L. (1986). *Music cognition*. Orlando, FL: Academic Press.

Drake, C., Dowling, W. J., & Palmer, C. (1991). Accent structures in the reproduction of simple tunes by children and adult pianists. *Music Perception, 8*, 315–334.

Fourakis, M., & Monahan, C. B. (1988). Effects of metrical foot structure on syllable timing. *Language and Speech, 31*, 283–306.

Fraisse, P. (1982). Rhythm and tempo. In D. Deutsch (Ed.), *The psychology of music* (pp. 149–180). New York: Academic Press.

Fry, D. (1968). Prosodic phenomena. In B. Malmberg (Ed.), *Manual of phonetics* (pp. 365–410). Amsterdam: North Holland.

Gabrielsson, A. (1973). Similarity ratings and dimension analyses of auditory rhythm patterns. I. *Scandinavian Journal of Psychology, 14*, 138–160.

Garner, W. R. (1974). *The processing of information and structure*. Potomac, MD: Lawrence Erlbaum Associates.

Grant, K. W. (1987). Identification of intonation contours by normally hearing and profoundly hearing-impaired listeners. *Journal of the Acoustical Society of America, 82*, 1172–1178.

Handel, S., & Lawson, G. R. (1983). The contextual nature of rhythmic interpretation. *Perception & Psychophysics, 34*, 103–210.

Handel, S., & Oshinsky, J. S. (1981). The meter of syncopated auditory polyrhythms. *Perception & Psychophysics, 30*, 1–9.

Handel, S., Weaver, M. D., & Lawson, G. R. (1983). Effect of rhythmic grouping on stream segregation. *Journal of Experimental Psychology: Human Perception & Performance, 9*, 637–651.

Heise, G. A., & Miller, G. A. (1951). An experimental study of auditory patterns. *American Journal of Psychology, 64*, 68–77.

Hirsh, I. J. (1959). Auditory perception of temporal order. *Journal of the Acoustical Society of America, 31*, 759–767.

Hirsh, I. J., Monahan, C. B., Grant, K. W., & Singh, P. G. (1990). Studies in auditory timing. 1: Simple patterns. *Perception & Psychophysics, 47*, 215–226.

Huggins, A. W. F. (1972a). Just noticeable differences for segment duration in natural speech. *Journal of the Acoustical Society of America, 51*, 1270–1278.

Huggins, A. W. F. (1972b). On the perception of temporal phenomena in speech. *Journal of the Acoustical Society of America, 51*, 1279–1290.

Hutchinson, W., & Knopoff, L. (1987). The clustering of temporal elements in melody. *Music Perception, 4*, 281–303.

Jones, M. R. (1981). Only time can tell: On the topology of mental space and time. *Critical Inquiry, 7*, 557–576.

Jones, M. R., Boltz, M., & Kidd, G. R. (1982). Controlled attending as a function of melodic and temporal context. *Perception & Psychophysics, 32*, 211–218.

Julesz, B., & Hirsh, I. J. (1972). Visual and auditory perception—An essay of comparison. In E. E. David & P. B. Denes (Eds.), *Human communication: A unified view* (pp. 283–340). New York: McGraw-Hill.

Kendall, R. A., & Carterette, E. C. (1991). Perceptual scaling of simultaneous wind timbres. *Music Perception, 8,* 369–404.

Krumhansl, C. L. (1990). *Cognitive foundations of musical pitch.* New York: Oxford University Press.

Kubovy, M. (1981). Concurrent pitch segregation and the theory of indispensable attributes. In M. Kubovy & J. R. Pomerantz (Eds.), *Perceptual organization* (pp. 55–98). Hillsdale, NJ: Lawrence Erlbaum Associates.

Ladefoged, P. (1967). *Three areas of experimental phonetics.* London: Oxford University Press.

Laloy, L. (1904). *Aristoxène de Tarente et la musique de l'antiquité* [Aristoxenes of Tarente and The Music of Antiquity]. Paris: Société Française d'Imprimerie et de Librairie.

Lehiste, I. (1970). *Suprasegmentals.* Cambridge, MA: MIT Press.

Lerdahl, F., & Jackendoff, R. (1983). *A generative theory of tonal music.* Cambridge, MA: MIT Press.

Lindsay, P. H., & Norman, D. A. (1977). *Human information processing.* New York: Academic Press.

Longuet-Higgins, H. C., & Lee, C. S. (1982). The perception of musical rhythms. *Perception, 11,* 115–128.

Martin, J. G. (1970). Rhythm-induced judgments of word stress in sentences. *Journal of Verbal Learning and Verbal Behavior, 9,* 627–633.

Martin, J. G. (1972). Rhythmic (hierarchical) versus serial structure in speech and other behaviors. *Psychological Review, 79,* 487–509.

Miller, G. A., & Heise, G. A. (1950). The trill threshold. *Journal of the Acoustical Society of America, 22,* 167–173.

Monahan, C. B. (1984). *Parallels between pitch and time: The determinants of musical space.* Unpublished doctoral dissertation, University of California, Los Angeles.

Monahan, C. B., & Carterette, E. C. (1985). Pitch and duration as determinants of musical space. *Music Perception, 3,* 1–32.

Monahan, C. B., & Carterette, E. C. (1987). The influence of temporal contour and interval information on the discrimination of rhythmic patterns. *Journal of the Acoustical Society of America, 81* (Suppl. 1), S91.

Monahan, C. B., & Hirsh, I. J. (1989). Studies in auditory timing. 2: Temporal interval patterns. *Perception & Psychophysics, 47,* 227–242.

Monahan, C. B., Kendall, R. A., & Carterette, E. C. (1987). The effect of melodic and temporal contour on recognition memory for pitch change. *Perception & Psychophysics, 41,* 576–600.

Oshinsky, J. S., & Handel, S. (1978). Syncopated auditory polyrhythms: Discontinuous reversals in meter interpretation. *Journal of the Acoustical Society of America, 63,* 936–939.

Povel, D. J. (1981). Interval representation of simple temporal patterns. *Journal of Experimental Psychology: Human Perception and Performance, 7,* 3–18.

Povel, D. J. (1984). A theoretical framework for rhythm perception. *Psychological Research, 45,* 315–337.

Povel, D. J., & Essens, P. (1985). Perception of temporal patterns. *Music Perception, 2,* 411–440.

Povel, D. J., & Okkerman, H. (1981). Accents in equitone sequences. *Perception & Psychophysics, 30,* 565–572.

Pressing, J. (1983). Cognitive isomorphisms in pitch and rhythm in world musics: West Africa, the Balkans, Thailand, and Western tonality. *Studies in Music, 17,* 38–61.

Scharf, B. (1970). Critical bands. In J. V. Tobias (Ed.), *Foundations of modern auditory theory (Vol. I,* pp. 157–202). New York: Academic Press.

Scholes, P. A. (1964). *The concise Oxford dictionary of music.* London: Oxford University Press.

Shepard, R. N. (1982a). Geometrical approximations to the structure of musical pitch. *Psychological Review, 89,* 305–333.

Shepard, R. N. (1982b). Structural representations of musical pitch. In D. Deutsch (Ed.), *The psychology of music* (pp. 343–390). New York: Academic Press.

Shields, J. L., McHugh, R., & Martin, J. G. (1974). Reaction time to phoneme targets as a function of rhythmic cues in continuous speech. *Journal of Experimental Psychology, 102,* 250–255.

Steedman, M. J. (1977). The perception of musical rhythm and metre. *Perception, 6,* 555–570.

Sturges, P. T., & Martin, J. G. (1974). Rhythmic structure in auditory temporal pattern perception and immediate memory. *Journal of Experimental Psychology, 102,* 377–383.

Thomassen, J. M. (1982). Melodic accent: Experiments and a tentative model. *Journal of the Acoustical Society of America, 71,* 1596–1605.

van Noorden, L. P. A. S. (1975). *Temporal coherence in the perception of tone sequences.* Eindhoven, The Netherlands: Institute for Perception Research.

Vos, P. G. (1977). Temporal duration factors in the perception of auditory rhythmic patterns. *Scientific Aesthetics, 1,* 183–199.

Warren, R. M. (1982). *Auditory perception.* New York: Pergamon Press.

Yeston, M. (1976). *The stratification of musical rhythm.* New Haven, CT: Yale University Press.

Zwislocki, J. (1965). Analysis of some auditory characteristics. In R. D. Luce, R. R. Bush, & E. Galanter (Eds.), *Handbook of mathematical psychology.* (Vol. III, pp. 1–97). New York: Wiley.

# III

# DEVELOPMENT OF MUSIC PERCEPTION

Thomas J. Tighe
*University of Connecticut*

The question of the origins of musical abilities and of musical tastes has long intrigued and baffled. The abilities to produce, perform, and appreciate music differ widely among individuals, as does musical taste. Do these differences arise primarily from the biological structure of the species and the individual or from environmental experience? We know that many of the world's most distinguished composers and performers of music were prodigies, exhibiting superior musical abilities at early ages. But we know too that many prodigies had still earlier and intensive exposure to musical experience and training. Until quite recently, such speculative balancing of opposing "evidence," often derived from anecdotal or retrospective biographical reports, has characterized efforts to account for the origins of musical skills and tastes. However, the last two decades have seen a dramatic increase in objective studies, indeed in quantitative and experimentally derived measures, of early musical abilities. The three chapters in this section, by Trehub, Zenatti, and Pick and Palmer, provide excellent examples of this new, scientific literature. The work of these leading investigators has moved the analysis of the original question to new and fascinating levels of inquiry. Collectively, their work indicates significant roles for both innate and environmental determinants of music cognition, but in ways that are both more surprising and challenging than could have been expected from earlier analyses.

The reader might well expect that a new methodology, perhaps complex and technical, underlies the new approach and findings on early musical abilities. A new method, yes, but hardly complex or dependent on technology. The methodology, similar to that employed in earlier but still essentially contemporary studies of infant visual perception, merits commentary here, both as an interesting example of the development of science and for what it tells us about the significance of musical stimulation to the infant and young child.

Throughout the first half of this century, infancy and early childhood received scant attention from researchers. Under the prevailing behaviorist doctrine, which held that knowledge and skills develop through interaction with the environment, the infant was viewed as essentially a helpless, incompetent organism of limited perceptual, and few, if any, cognitive skills. Little perceptual or cognitive development was thought to take place in infancy, for how could environmental shaping take place in the absence of the interactions with the world that only locomotion and language make possible? But in the 1960s, and following the creative lead of Robert Fantz (1962; 1963), investigators of infant visual perception began simply to look at what the infant looks at. The method is as uncomplicated as it sounds—a visual stimulus, which might be a natural or artificial pattern, is presented and the frequency and duration of the infant's visual fixation is noted. Alternatively, two patterns might be presented and the infant's visual preference, again measured by actual looking time, is measured. The findings, especially remarkable in the bleak expectations of the prevailing view of infant competencies, were that infants tend to persistently fixate virtually any novel stimulus, visually attend in systematic ways, and exhibit clear visual preferences. Extensive follow-up studies of infants' looking made clear that they are capable of organized visual percepts, can tell the differences among a wide variety of visual patterns, and are sensitive to a great deal of the information in visual stimulation. Further, experimenters found that infants will predictably lose interest in a repeatedly presented novel stimulus but will reliably renew looking if that stimulus is changed in some way or a new stimulus is presented in place of the initial one. This pattern of initial attention, attention loss, and attention recovery upon change (termed the *habituation paradigm*), is of fundamental importance because it indicates that infants spontaneously construct representations (or memories) of the stimuli that capture their attention, and that those representations in turn serve as comparators in the detection and direction of attention to altered or novel input. That is, only if a persisting internal representation of a given stimulus has been formed could the infant possibly tell if a new or altered stimulus has been presented in its place, as evidenced by the renewal of attention. In essence, by "looking at what the infant looks at" investigators had found a simple yet highly effective means of asking the infant what it is able to perceive and learn about its visual world. And the picture that emerged from these studies is that of an organism capable of meaningful discrimination of its visual world and intrinsically motivated to seek and store information about that world through directed visual attention.

Experimenters were quick to extend the same method and questions to other forms of stimulation, and of interest here of course is auditory stimulation. Will an infant attend to a sequence of tones and form a representation of that sequence? After repeated exposure to the sequence, will the infant renew attention to some alteration of the pattern, such as a change in pitch, loudness, or rhythm? What properties of auditory stimulation are infants capable of discriminating, as inferred from the habituation-recovery pattern? This general approach, adapted for particular stimuli and age levels, has been used to excellent advantage in the work of Trehub, and of Pick and Palmer, as will be described in the present chapters, and is the basis for a number of their conclusions about the musical capacities of infants and young children. Although Zenatti, working with somewhat older children, utilizes a stimulus preference procedure, this technique nevertheless shares with the attentional paradigm a reliance on the subject's selective response to stimuli as the means of defining their musical abilities and tastes, for example, a preference for consonant versus dissonant chord structures. In the new methodology, then, the infant and young child, although lacking in verbal skills, nevertheless "tell" the experimenter about their abilities and tastes by the way they freely orient to or prefer diagnostic samples of stimulation. Perhaps the most remarkable feature of the methodology is that it testifies to the young child's strong and reliable tendencies to seek, select, and learn about patterned stimulation, because indeed the method is based on these tendencies. In this connection, newborns have been found to prefer musical (tonally organized) auditory input as opposed to random patterns of sound of equivalent intensity and pitch range (Butterfield & Siperstein, 1972). In this light, music, like other forms of meaningful stimulation, appears something the infant and young child are capable of perceiving and are ready to sample, explore, and learn about.

Trehub's contribution to this volume grows out of her long-standing research program on the perception of complex auditory sequences by infants and young children. The data she reports here comprise the most dramatic observations on infants' perception of musical stimuli. She has shown that infants listen to and represent musical sequences in ways surprisingly similar to the manner of adults. Thus, after exposure to a melodic pattern of tones, infants classify as the "same" a pattern that preserves the melodic contour, that is, the relations between the notes, even when the specific notes or specific intervals between the notes themselves change. As Trehub notes, this establishes that infants do not encode the exact notes or pitches of a melody but rather, like adults, represent the melody in terms of the more abstract level of the relations between the pitches. Note that this level is also the more informative level, from the viewpoint of the real-life task of distinguishing among many melodic patterns, which of course often contain notes in common. The sophistication of the infant's listening and representational skills is further attested by Trehub's observation that infants also perceive the common features of a melodic sequence despite changes in its tempo or the duration of its constituent elements.

Such observations surely attest to the hard-wired, that is, biologically determined character of the infant's listening skills and "music appreciation." We should be cautious, however, in such interpretations. Trehub's subjects are about 6 months of age. Although experience with musical sequences per se is generally quite limited at this age, it is nevertheless likely to exist to some appreciable degree, and quasimelodic patterns of auditory stimuli may be quite pervasive in infant experience. Trehub speculates in her chapter that adult–infant speech interactions, which characteristically contain distinctive and salient patterns of intonation and rhythm, may contribute to the infant's perception of melodic patterns. We know, too, that within hours of birth, infants are capable of discriminating speech in their native language, that is, the language of the parents, from speech in another language (Mehler et al., 1988) suggesting that prenatal auditory experience contributes to learning the intonations and rhythms of the complex auditory patterns comprising language.

That learning may play a key role in the development of music perception is further attested by a number of Pick and Palmer's observations reported herein. For example, using the habituation paradigm, they found that 3-month-old infants treated a simple transposition of a melody (which preserves its contour) as a new or different melody, but *did* transpose the melody when the habituation training involved repeated exposure to the melody in varying keys. In contrast, 5-year-olds transposed immediately across both near and distant key scales. Finally, although 5-year-olds could recognize a melody across transformations in its original key and rhythm, they treated a transformation involving pitch interval changes as a different song, even when those changes preserved the melodic contour. However, Pick and Palmer also report measures indicating that the 5-year-olds were capable of perceiving some degree of contour similarity in the latter condition.

The picture that emerges from consideration of the Trehub and Pick and Palmer data is that of very early appearance of adult-like listening strategies coupled with progressive elaboration and refinement of listening skills as the child gains increasing exposure to the melodies within the culture.

This theme is extended in the work of Zenatti, who finds that between the ages of 5 to 10 children show a sharp increase in their preference for culturally favored musical patterns. Specifically, children's preference for consonant chords, tonal structures, and metrically organized rhythms (as opposed to the opposite structures) rose from about 60% at age 5 to roughly 95% at age 10. Similarly, adding an atonal context to the task of discriminating a tonal scale sequence did not affect the performance of 6- to 7-year-old girls, but did retard the discrimination by 8- to 9-year-olds, indicating that the latter subjects were beginning to acquire the dominant musical framework of their culture. These and other observations by Zenatti suggest that children become progressively attuned to the musical structures defined as "good" by the prevailing culture. Although the collective data of these several chapters make such a trend incontrovertible, the story cannot be so simple, because Zenatti also presents provocative evidence that the ditonic scale, which is present in the primitive music of many civilizations, may have a primary, that is, biologically determined, character.

Pick and Palmer also provide a theoretical framework that appears capable of encompassing a broad array of findings on the development of music perception. Drawing upon the ecological theory of perception and perceptual development as formulated by Eleanor and James Gibson (1969; 1979), they note that music affords excellent opportunities for the kind of perceptual learning emphasized by the Gibsons. A basic assumption is that ecological (naturally occurring) stimuli, including the auditory sequences that comprise music, typically contain more information than is likely to be detected on initial or limited exposure. That information is assumed to be specific to structural aspects of the stimulus, and as a consequence of experience with the stimulus, the subject becomes increasingly sensitive to those features. This process of coming to perceive more of what is present in stimulation is termed *differentiation*. Differentiation of stimulus input is intrinsically driven and its self-reinforcing consequences are that the organism becomes more sensitive to properties of the stimulus and perceives with greater specificity, precision, and economy. From this theoretical perspective, differentiation of stimulus input is a major pathway to both perceptual and cognitive development.

As applied to the development of music perception and cognition, an assumption of Pick and Palmer's analysis is that music, including even relatively simple melodic structures, affords opportunities for perception at multiple levels. Pick and Palmer nicely show how music provides such opportunities for differentiation in terms of its structural aspects and in relation to differing levels of development. Certainly the differentiation concept appears to fit the increasing music discrimination skills of the developing child as well as the observed trend toward attunement of the developing child to the predominant musical framework encountered. But the theory also rationalizes a number of other observations from Pick and Palmer's own studies and from other laboratories. For example, Zenatti reports an intriguing discrepancy among her findings that might well fit Pick and Palmer's analysis. In one of her tests, children were asked to choose between excerpts from works by contemporary composers that were atonal in character as opposed to tonal transformations of these excerpts. Not surprisingly in light of Zenatti's overall observations, beginning around the age of 6, children rejected the composers' excerpts in favor of the tonal transformations. However, the trend toward increasing preference of the tonal transformations began to level off at age 7 to 8 and a reversal of this preference was observed among 9- to 10-year-olds, a small number of whom repeatedly chose the original, less tonal excerpts. Zenatti hypothesized that the latter children had reached a stage of development wherein they have become receptive to aesthetic aspects of atonal melodies. From the Pick and Palmer viewpoint, it is tempting to speculate that the 9- to 10-year-olds had progressed from detection of the relatively obvious regularities of the tonally organized stimuli to the less detectable but no less real structural subtleties and corresponding attunements within the original excerpts. After all, tonality and atonality are, like dissonance and consonance, parts of a continuum.

As embodied in the work of Trehub, Zenatti, and Pick and Palmer, the scientific study of music perception and its development has progressed a long way in a short time. Their data establish that the infant and young child are far more perceptive and skilled appreciators of music than would have been credited just a decade ago. Their work also outlines important developmental changes in the child's perception and knowledge of music. The development of music perception remains overall a relatively uncharted domain, yet the experimental and theoretical analyses in this section represent an exciting and promising beginning.

## REFERENCES

Butterfield, E. C., & Siperstein, G. M. (1972). Influence of contingent auditory stimulation upon nonnutritional suckle. In J. Bosma (Ed.), *Oral sensation and perception: The mouth of the infant* (pp. 313–334). Springfield, IL: Charles C. Thomas.

Fantz, R. L. (1963). Pattern vision in newborn infants. *Science, 140,* 296–297.

Fantz, R. L., Ordy, J. M., & Udlef, M. S. (1962). Maturation of pattern vision in infants during the first six months. *Journal of Comparative and Physiological Psychology, 55,* 907–917.

Gibson, E. J. (1969). *Principles of perceptual learning and development.* New York: Appleton-Century-Crofts.

Gibson, J. J. (1979). *The ecological approach to visual perception.* Boston, MA: Houghton-Mifflin.

Mehler, J., Jusczyk, P., Lambertz, G., Halsted, N., Bertoncini, J., & Amiel-Tison, C. (1988). A precursor of language acquisition in young infants. *Cognition, 29,* 143–178.

# The Music Listening Skills of Infants and Young Children

Sandra E. Trehub
*University of Toronto, Mississauga*

In recent years there has been increasing interest in music education for preschool children (see Hargreaves, 1986; Peery, Peery, & Draper, 1987), with the focus on instrument training, ear training, or some combination of the two. It is reasonable to assume, in the case of instrument training, that novice students will be unskilled with respect to the instrument in question. It is obviously unreasonable to presume, however, that preschoolers will be entirely without music listening skills or with skills poorly suited to the task. Rather, this is an issue to be settled by research on the music listening skills of youngsters who have not received systematic instruction or exposure.

From anecdotal and published reports we know that many musical prodigies have had intensive exposure to music very early in life, often by musically talented parents. In such cases, it is difficult, if not impossible, to disentangle the contribution of an enriched musical environment from that of inherited predispositions. Perhaps we will never succeed in separating the influence of genetic and experiential factors on musical achievement, but it should still be possible to determine whether musical proficiency or enjoyment can be enhanced by early formal or informal exposure. Clearly, this is a worthwhile direction for future research. For the present, however, there is reason to believe that infants as young as 6 months of age may be rather capable listeners and that preschoolers possess additional skills that are required for the understanding of emotional and notational conventions in the music of our culture.

## A PROCEDURE FOR STUDYING LISTENING SKILLS
## IN INFANCY

Over the past several years, my colleagues and I at the University of Toronto
have been attempting to uncover some of the abilities that infants and young
children bring to the task of listening to complex auditory sequences such as
melodies (see Trehub, 1990; Trehub & Trainor, 1990, in press). What we do,
in a nutshell, is to train infants (6 months or older) to turn toward a loudspeaker
(the sound source) whenever they hear a change in a sound pattern. In a sound-
attenuating booth or very quiet room, we present a repeating melody over a
loudspeaker located to one side of the infant (see Fig. 7.1). Initially, the infant
keeps turning toward the loudspeaker during sound presentation but ultimately, he or she loses interest in this regularly repeating melody (the background
melody) and attends more closely to the tester, who manipulates various puppets directly in front of the infant. From time to time, when the infant is watching the puppets (i.e., looking directly ahead), we substitute a new melody or
make some change, substantial or subtle, to the original melody. Infants tend
to turn toward the source of this novel auditory event if and when they detect
the change. We reward such turns to the sound change by presenting one of
several animated toys near the loudspeaker (see Fig. 7.1). Most infants are
delighted with the toys, and quickly learn that they can control their presentation by simply responding to changes in the sound patterns emanating from the
loudspeaker.

Following a training period during which infants are required to respond
correctly to sound changes (i.e., turn toward the loudspeaker) four times in
succession, we present approximately 30 test trials, half of which involve a
change in sound, the other half being control trials with no change. The control trials allow us to determine the extent to which infants turn for reasons
other than the presence of a sound change (e.g., restlessness, to see their
mother). If infants turn more frequently on trials with a change than on those
without a change, this implies that they can detect the change in question.
To preclude the possibility that a well-intentioned tester or parent (on whose
lap the infant sits) inadvertently provides cues for the infant, we require both
to wear headphones that deliver competing sounds. Thus, the individual who
plays with puppets in front of the infant and who records the occurrence of
head turns toward the loudspeaker (by pressing a button linked to a computer) is unaware of the nature and occurrence of sound changes. The attending computer keeps track of sound changes and infant head turns and, when
appropriate (i.e., for turns immediately following a sound change), delivers
reinforcement in the form of illumination and activation of one of several animated toys. (For further methodological details, see Trehub, Thorpe, & Morrongiello, 1987).

FIG. 7.1.   Upper panel: Infant watches the tester and puppet directly ahead while the familiar sound pattern is presented repeatedly. Lower panel: Infant turns to the loudspeaker when the pattern changes, receiving visual reinforcement for a correct response.

## Detecting Melody Changes: Contour

It is well-known that we recognize familiar melodies not because of any specific notes or pitches but rather because of the relations between notes in each melody, specifically, the pattern of *intervals* (see Dowling & Harwood, 1986). Intervals refer to the pitch distance or number of semitones that separates adjacent notes of a melody. When a melody has the same intervals as another melody but different component notes, it is considered to be a *transposition* of that melody. Moreover, a familiar melody is generally recognizable when played or sung in any key, regardless of the key (or set of notes) in which we habitually hear it. For example, regular listeners of the NBC network were able to recognize its three-note signal (the NBC chimes) but could not identify which transpositions embodied the exact pitches of the original (Attneave & Olson, 1971). This suggests that our mental representation or image of a familiar melody is abstract yet precise, involving specific information about the relations between adjacent notes (i.e., intervals) but little information about the notes themselves. With unfamiliar melodies, our mental representation seems to involve less precise information about the relations between notes. Soon after hearing a novel melody, we no longer have access to the exact pitches or intervals, but only to the pattern of ups and downs or what is termed the *melodic contour* (Dowling, 1978). For example, on hearing the opening phrase of ''Frère Jacques'' for the very first time, we would likely confuse it with other four-note patterns that have ascending pitch except for the final descending note.

In a series of studies, my colleagues and I attempted to determine whether infants use listening strategies that are similar to or different from those of mature listeners. Would infants adopt a different strategy, remembering some or all of the exact pitches of a brief melody? Alternatively, would they use a global or adult-like strategy of retaining the melodic configuration or contour? Using the procedure outlined earlier, we familiarized infants with a specific repeating melody and tested for their detection of various changes to that melody (Trehub, Bull, & Thorpe, 1984), including contour changes (i.e., the same notes reordered), same-contour melodies (i.e., different notes and intervals but the same pattern of ups and downs), and transpositions (i.e., different notes but the same intervals). What we found seemed to indicate that infants paid careful attention to the contour but not to the exact pitches. In other words, they reliably detected changes in contour whether these changes involved reordering the same notes, substituting all new notes (Trehub et al., 1984), or even a single new note in one position of a six-note melody (Trehub, Thorpe, & Morrongiello, 1985). On the other hand, infants tended to ignore transpositions as well as same-contour melodies, treating these as if they were familiar. We demonstrated that their failure to respond to transpositions and to same-contour melodies was not based on an inability to *discriminate* the relevant differences but rather on their failure to *remember* details about the exact pitches or intervals. Our findings indicate that infants perceived these pitches and intervals initially but did not incorporate them into their mental representation of the melody. As a result, when the original and comparison melody were separated by 2 or more seconds, infants no longer noticed the pitch or interval changes that they readily detected in melodies separated by less than a second (Trehub et al., 1984).

In further research, we were able to establish that infants perceived the *similarity* across discriminable transpositions of a melody (Trehub et al., 1987). To do so, we used the procedure described earlier, except that the repeating background melody was transposed for each presentation (i.e., different pitches from the immediately preceding sequence), in contrast to the fixed repeating background (i.e., identical pitches) of the previous study. As before, we required infants to respond to melodies with a contour change but we also required them to ignore (i.e., not respond to) the pitch and interval changes of each successive presentation. The contour changes were also presented in a different key from the immediately preceding comparison melody. This meant that infants could not use absolute pitch cues to guide their behavior. Instead, they had to extract and retain either the contour or the pattern of intervals from the original sequences so that they could respond to the sequences with contrasting contour. That they did so with ease confirms their global or configurational bias when listening to melodies. In short, when infants listened to test melodies that embodied pitch or interval changes but no change in contour, they behaved as if they were thinking as follows: "I hear new pitches but it's the same old song." With contour changes, their thoughts might have been as follows: "There's a new one, at last."

We have also been able to determine that infants can discriminate two-note patterns with rising pitch (i.e., ascending) from those with falling pitch (i.e., descending), even when the two notes are separated by as little as one semitone and the patterns are transposed on each repetition (Thorpe, 1986). This task is difficult for some adults, who can detect the change but cannot discern the direction of change when the pitch differences are small. Nevertheless, these findings underline infants' relational orientation to listening. What is puzzling, when considering infants' success in this endeavor, is the repeated failure of other investigators to demonstrate pitch direction discrimination (i.e., ascending vs. descending sequences) with preschool and young school-aged children (e.g., Hair, 1977). It is unlikely that this ability deteriorates between infancy and later childhood. What is more likely is that young children *can* discriminate rising from falling pitch but that the tasks used to date have been either too complex or insufficiently interesting for the participants.

## Detecting Temporal or Rhythm Changes

When we listen to melodies or other sequential auditory patterns, we group elements within the overall melody or pattern. Such groupings are influenced by the duration of individual elements and also by the pattern of pitches and accents. Even when the elements are uniform with respect to duration, pitch, and stress, we still tend to group them. Such grouping processes seem to enhance our memory for auditory patterns and our perception of speech. If infants imposed such groupings on auditory sequences, this might also have favorable consequences for their perception and retention of complex patterns.

In one series of experiments (Thorpe & Trehub, 1989; Thorpe, Trehub, Morrongiello, & Bull, 1988), we generated a simple tone sequence with three tones of one kind followed by three others that differed from the first three in pitch, timbre (sound quality), or loudness (e.g., XXXOOO). Despite the fact that all of the notes were equally spaced, adult listeners seemed to hear two groups of tones separated by a pause. One consequence of this mental organization of the pattern was that adults had greater difficulty detecting a pause inserted *between* tone groups (i.e., XXX OOO) compared to one inserted *within* a group (i.e., XXXO OO). Much to our surprise and delight, infants behaved in a similar manner, exhibiting difficulty detecting brief pauses *between* groups of tones contrasting in pitch or timbre but no such difficulty detecting comparable pauses *within* a tone group. What this suggests is that infants group or chunk auditory sequences into smaller units and, in so doing, create rhythmic patterns or figures. The resulting percept highlights the structure of the sequence and likely contributes to its memorability.

In a further study (Trehub & Thorpe, 1989), we sought to determine whether infants' mental representation of the temporal structure of a melody is global, as is their representation of its melodic structure. Just as adults recognize a melody independent of specific notes or pitches, they also recognize it in the context of changes in tempo or rate of presentation (i.e., faster or slower). Having established that infants recognize melodies in the context of changes in their component pitches, we set out to ascertain whether they could perceive the invariance of melodies across changes in tempo. We used the same procedure as for our melody discrimination tasks, with the exception that infants were required to respond (i.e., turn) to changes in rhythm: either a 2, 1 pattern (XX X) contrasted with a 1, 2 pattern (X XX), or a 2, 2 pattern (XX XX) contrasted with a 3, 1 pattern (XXX X). As in our more complex melody discrimination tasks, we used a variable as opposed to fixed background. That is, the original and contrasting patterns were presented at five different tempos or rates and at five different pitch levels. Thus, each repetition of the original pattern (or instance of the contrasting pattern) embodied a different tempo and pitch from the immediately preceding pattern, requiring infants to focus on the rhythmic changes (which could bring visual rewards) and to ignore the tempo and pitch changes (which brought no reward). Infants' behavior indicated that they could recognize and respond to the overall temporal structure of a pattern independent of the specific durations and pitches of individual elements.

## Detecting Interval Changes in *Good* Melodies

For the most part, infants extract the contour and the rhythmic pattern of a melody. But this is not the entire story. Rather, there are indications that infants, like adults, remember more details of *good* as opposed to *bad* melodies.

In this case, the designation *good* applies to melodies that conform to Western musical conventions (i.e., typical melodies) and the designation *bad* to those that deviate from such conventions to a greater or lesser degree (i.e., atypical melodies). Most scholars have assumed, quite reasonably, that adults' superior memory for *good* melodies stems from familiarity with the relevant musical idiom, gained from formal or informal exposure to the music of their culture. Is it possible, however, that some patterns are inherently *good* or congenial to our auditory system, even without listening experience?

To clarify the issue, some background information on Western tonal music might be helpful. Each octave is divided into 12 equal intervals or steps that form the *chromatic* scale. It is notable, however, that Western tonal music is not based on this chromatic scale but rather on the *diatonic* scale, an unequal-interval scale of seven notes drawn from the chromatic scale. Various notes and subsets of notes from the diatonic scale are considered to have special significance. One of these subsets is the *major triad* (the first, fifth, and seventh position of the chromatic scale or the first, third, and fifth position of the diatonic scale), which occupies a central role in Western music theory, occurs frequently in Western compositions for adults and children, and is considered to be the prototype of Western tonal structure.

In a few studies (Cohen, Thorpe, & Trehub, 1987; Trehub, Thorpe, & Trainor, 1990), my colleagues and I evaluated infants' ability to detect subtle same-contour changes (i.e., a one-semitone change in one position of a five-note melody) in *good* and *bad* melodies. The *good* melodies in all cases were based on the major triad, for example, C E G E C and its transpositions, or $B_3$ $D_4$ $G_4$ $E_4$ $C_4$ (the subscripts designating specific octaves) and its transpositions. The *bad* melodies had the same simple contour (rising–falling) and overall pitch range as the *good* melodies, but had one or more notes outside the appropriate diatonic scale; for example, C E G♯ E C (G♯ being a wrong note in this case) or C F♯ B F C♯ (two highly dissonant intervals, C to F♯ and B to F). Surprisingly, infants succeeded in detecting the semitone change in the context of the *good* melodies but not the *bad* ones. This implies that there is something about these melodies, perhaps diatonic structure in general or the major triad in particular, that is inherently *good*, in the sense of being a reasonable match to our auditory pattern-processing predispositions. This is not to suggest that Western music is more appropriate or better than non-Western music in any way. On the contrary, it is likely that Western as well as foreign musical systems have capitalized on *good*, although different, melodic and rhythmic structures to generate appealing musical patterns that are readily learned. It is also likely, however, that some aspects of Western as well as foreign musical structure are not inherently *good*, but rather require exposure before they are perceived as *good* or typical. Research with infant and child listeners can help us distinguish those features of Western music that are naturally *good* from those that become *good* after some period of familiarization.

# FURTHER PERSPECTIVES ON MUSIC LISTENING
# IN INFANCY

It is clear, then, that infants are hardly incompetent or naïve with respect to some of the skills that are critical for music listening. Can we conclude that they are born with such skills or that these skills emerge without specific training or experience? That may well be the case, but recent research has revealed some aspects of early parent–infant interaction that may be relevant to the development of such perceptual skills or at least to their use in early life.

When parents speak to their young infants, they do so with higher pitch, slower tempo, more regular timing, smoother and more highly modulated intonation contours, and greater repetitiveness than when they speak to adults (Fernald, 1984; Fernald, Taeschner, Dunn, Papoušek, de Boysson-Bardies, & Fukui, 1989). The intonation patterns of parental speech to young infants are often characterized as melodies (Fernald, 1989; Papoušek & Papoušek, 1981), with melodic contours being the most salient aspects of such speech. In fact, some researchers have identified similar melodic contours in the speech of American, British, French, Italian, German, Japanese, and Chinese caregivers (Fernald et al., 1989; Grieser & Kuhl, 1988), with specific contours used for eliciting or maintaining infant attention and others used for soothing distressed infants (Fernald, 1989; Papoušek & Papoušek, 1981; Stern, Spieker, & MacKain, 1982). The existence of common speech adjustments across gender and culture, coupled with the match between parental adjustments and infant perceptual skills, has led researchers to posit the existence of biologically preadapted parenting skills that foster social, emotional, and communicative development (e.g., Papoušek & Papoušek, 1987). One implication of this view is that the route to the child's native language may be musical.

Indeed, there is considerable evidence to suggest that infants, in the early months of life, attend more to the intonation patterns of speech than to the consonant and vowel sounds (Fernald, 1992; Lewis, 1951). Infants can recognize their mother's voice (DeCasper & Fifer, 1980; Mehler, Bertoncini, Barrière, & Jassik-Gerschenfeld, 1978), although the basis for such recognition is unclear. Perhaps they identify its distinctive timbre or the specific contours that carry social and emotional messages. Another possibility, as yet unevaluated, is that infants apply an interval-processing strategy to maternal melodies, just as they do with *good* melodies and as adults do with *familiar* melodies. Such a strategy could provide infants with access to unique aspects of their mother's vocal signature, notably its interval patterning.

Recently, we have been delving into other potential parallels between speech and music by focusing on the *lullaby*, a musical form that shares some interactional functions with infant-directed speech (Trehub, Unyk, & Trainor, in press; Unyk, Trehub, Trainor, & Schellenberg, 1992). Like infant-directed speech, the lullaby is an intimate, vocal communication between caregiver and infant, one presumably replete with emotional qualities. Although lullabies have been found in all countries and in all periods of recorded history, there has been no psychological research on their form or function. Nevertheless, we have recently established that adults have some intuitive knowledge of lullabies in the sense that they can distinguish lullabies from adult songs even when the musical culture is entirely unfamiliar. In one study, we presented adults with 30 pairs of musical excerpts, one of these being a lullaby from a foreign culture, the other being a non-lullaby with equivalent tempo from the same culture. Adults were successful, although considerably less than perfect, in identifying the lullabies, and there were indications that simplicity and pattern *goodness* played a role in their judgments. We are currently working on detailed musicological descriptions of the lullabies, with the goal of uncovering the specific musical features that signal lullabies as opposed to adult-directed songs. We are also attempting to determine whether lullabies and non-lullabies have differential effects (e.g., motoric, emotional) on infant listeners. Although ethnomusicologists have largely abandoned their relatively unsuccessful search for universal features of music, we are hopeful that our efforts will uncover some universal features of lullabies.

## DETECTING MELODY CHANGES
## IN THE PRESCHOOL PERIOD

We have also examined the listening skills characteristic of the preschool period. Not only is the preschooler more intellectually sophisticated and motorically capable than the infant, but he or she has also experienced a good deal of informal exposure to the music of our culture. In assessing the discrimination skills of children 4 to 6 years of age, we typically ask them to respond nonverbally by clapping, raising a hand, pressing a button, or pointing to pictures. Usually, we present a series of four or five repetitions of an unfamiliar melody and ask children to respond if, and only if, the final melody differs from the preceding repetitions. Otherwise, they must withhold their response. Like infants, children readily detect melodic changes that alter the contour of a melody but they also detect some changes that alter the interval size (Morrongiello, Trehub, Thorpe, & Capodilupo, 1985). If we increase the difficulty of the task (e.g., substantially reducing the tempo), we find greater disruption in the discrimination of interval changes compared to contour changes (Morrongiello et al., 1985). This underlines the priority of contour in preschoolers' mental representation of unfamiliar melodies. When preschoolers are presented with familiar melodies such as "Happy Birthday" or "Twinkle, Twinkle, Little Star" and various changes to such melodies, they unequivocally accept transpositions as the original melody, reject changes that alter contour, and are uncertain about changes that preserve contour but alter interval size (Trehub, Morrongiello, & Thorpe, 1985). We have also found that the optimal tempo for melody presentation to preschoolers is considerably faster than our customary tempo for infants (2.5 tones per second) (Morrongiello et al., 1985).

In other work (Trehub, Cohen, Thorpe, & Morrongiello, 1986), we tested children 4 to 6 years of age for their detection of a semitone change in a five-note *good* melody (C E G E C) based on the major triad and a *bad* melody (C E G♯ E C) with one nondiatonic note, both melodies having been used previously with infants. The children listened to the repeating diatonic or nondiatonic pattern and judged (by responding or not responding) whether the final pattern of the series was different from those preceding it. We reasoned that children would remember more details of the *good* melody, thereby facilitating the detection of the subtle semitone change. Indeed, preschoolers detected the change more readily when listening to the *good* melody, either because of its inherent *goodness* or memorability (as suggested for infants) or because of their implicit knowledge of Western scale structure gained by informal musical exposure. Recent research indicates that preschool and school-age children who have received formal music instruction are more proficient at detecting subtle melodic changes than are children without such training (Lynch & Eilers, 1991; Morrongiello & Roes, 1990; Morrongiello, Roes, & Donnelly, 1989). It is difficult to conclude that musical training, in itself, is responsible for such enhanced performance. Children with *natural* musical talent (if it exists) or interest are more likely to receive training, as are the offspring of parents who are very interested in music. Moreover, such training may facilitate performance on music perception tasks by enhancing children's attention to musical materials or by altering their perceptual organization of musical input. As usual, there are no simple answers to such complex questions.

## UNDERSTANDING THE EMOTIONAL MEANING OF MUSIC

Claims that music is the language of the emotions have been based on the consensus of musically trained and untrained adults on the emotional meanings expressed by various kinds of music. In our research, we have attempted to determine whether preschoolers and young school-aged children have some understanding of these conventional emotional meanings. We played very simple melodic sequences to children 4 to 8 years of age as well as to adults, and asked them to rotate a pointer to a sad face, happy face, or neutral face (see Fig. 7.2) (Trehub, Cohen, & Guerriero, 1987). In one experiment, we presented a repeating alternation of two notes that varied in pitch range (two notes from a high or

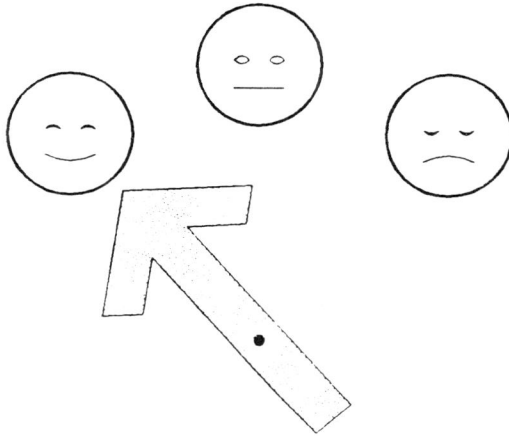

FIG. 7.2.   Schematic faces, providing three choices of emotional expression (happy, neutral, sad) for preschool listeners.

low pitch range) and rate (fast or slow). For all ages, the typical response to high-fast sequences (high pitch, fast rate) was *happy* and to low-slow sequences, *sad*. In a further experiment, we used nine-note sequences that were ascending or descending, with notes from the major or minor scale. Ascending sequences led to *happy* judgments and descending sequences to *sad* judgments. Responses to major and minor sequences were inconsistent, except for musically trained adults, who provided the conventional association of major with *happy* and minor with *sad*.

It is clear that children in the preschool and early school years have access to at least some of the conventional emotional meanings expressed through music, even though these aspects are unlikely to have been the target of adult instruction. What remains unclear is whether the melodic sequences that led to children's ratings of *happy* and *sad* actually made them feel somewhat happy or sad or whether the children understood, in adult-like fashion, that such patterns simply conveyed emotional meaning. What is also unclear is whether these associations between musical parameters and emotional meaning are culture-bound, derived from exposure to specific songs and their meanings, or whether they represent primitive universal responses to music. One way of addressing this issue in the future is to videotape very young infants as they listen to patterns that vary in pitch and tempo. If differences in motoric and facial responses are systematically related to the pitch or tempo of the sound patterns, this would provide support for a universal, biological basis for some emotional meanings in music.

## PREREQUISITES FOR THE ACQUISITION
## OF MUSICAL VOCABULARY

Those who study music acquire a specialized vocabulary or jargon for use in the precise description of various aspects of music. Even in everyday life it is common to use some descriptions derived from conventions of written music; for example, *high* or *low* as applied to pitch, and *ascending* or *descending* as applied to the direction of pitch movement. Despite the use of identical terminology to describe the relative pitch of sounds and the relative height of visual elements, there is little correspondence between the auditory and visual sensations or between the concepts of relative pitch and height. Rather, the application of the spatial terms *high* and *low* to the domain of pitch can be considered abstract or metaphorical for those unfamiliar with the convention. In fact, young school children experience considerable difficulty understanding and using conventional verbal labels for pitch (high, low) and pitch direction (up, down). Reasoning that the verbal labels as opposed to the underlying concepts might present problems, we had 4-, 5- and 6-year-olds listen to a melody played at one of two different pitch levels (high or low) and to indicate which of two brightly colored drawings "goes with" the "song" (Trehub & Trainor, 1989). The object of greatest interest was positioned high in one drawing and low in the other (see Fig. 7.3). All age groups succeeded on the task although the 6-year-olds performed best.

In a further study (Trainor & Trehub, 1992), we used this nonverbal approach to explore rather different aspects of musical meaning. We selected four 15-second excerpts from Prokofiev's *Peter and the Wolf*, corresponding to the composer's musical depictions of the wolf, bird, cat, and duck in the story. Children 3, 4, and 6 years of age who were unfamiliar with the music or story (by parental report) were tested on their ability to match the musical excerpts to drawings of the animals. On each trial, 4- and 6-year-olds heard one musical excerpt and had to choose one of four animal pictures. The task was simplified for 3-year-olds, who were required to choose a picture from two alternatives. All age groups were successful on the task although the 6-year-olds performed best. Moreover, children performed better on the *wolf* and *bird* excerpts than on the *cat* and *duck* excerpts. To clarify whether this reflected children's limited understanding or the composer's expressive limitations, we tested adults unfamiliar with the music and story on the four-choice task. Although adults' performance was more accurate than that of the oldest children, they showed similar patterns of confusion for the *cat* and *duck* excerpts. It is clear, then, that children can relate nonmusical meanings to music, but the musical features relevant to this process remain unclear. Perhaps the low pitch, high intensity, and full chords of the *wolf* music and the rapid tempo, distinctive instrumentation, and large pitch range of the *bird* music help confer such extramusical meanings.

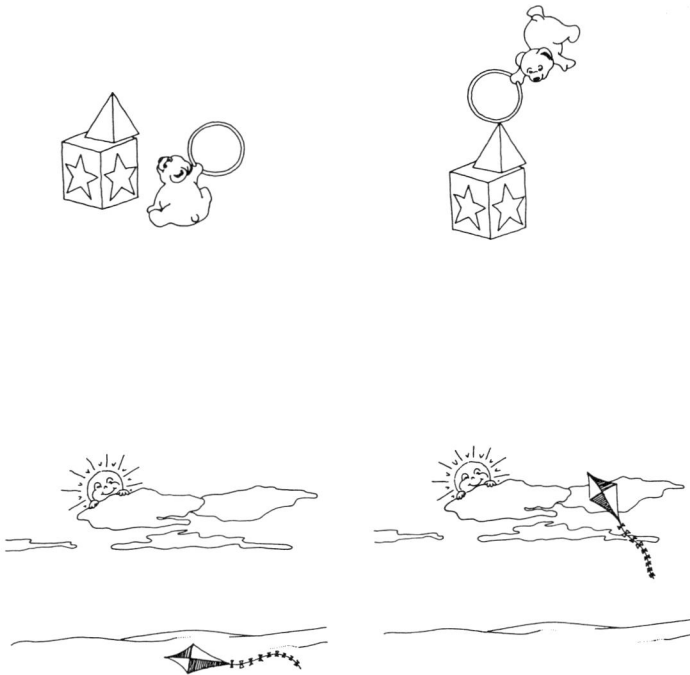

FIG. 7.3.   Upper and lower pairs are examples of pictures that accompanied musical excerpts played at high and low pitch levels.

Children's comments on their picture choices were instructive, revealing a liberal use of analogy. For example, many children said that the *wolf* music was "scary," leading them to choose the most feared animal in the set, namely the wolf. By contrast, their comments about the bird excerpt revealed a more transparent analogy: "sounds like a bird."

What is the role of experience in these developing associations between musical forms and extramusical concepts? By 3 years of age, children have had ample opportunity for linking musical and nonmusical events so that it is difficult, if not impossible, to separate the effects of nature from nurture. In principle, however, one could distinguish between analogies that arise universally from music (e.g., primitive emotional associations) and those that are by-products of acculturation. As we have seen, relations between meaning and form in maternal utterances to preverbal infants are not arbitrary and there are suggestions that the meaning of such speech is to be found in its melody (Fernald, 1989). In this sense, opportunities for exploring relations between musical and extramusical experiences are available from the earliest days of life.

## CODA

The foregoing research would seem to indicate that infants and young children are relatively astute listeners, even in the absence of systematic exposure or training. Can these findings provide guidance for parents and educators who are interested in maximizing musical opportunities for their young charges? Unfortunately, the answer is negative. All one can say, with assurance, is that infants and young children use listening strategies that are remarkably similar to those of adults. Perhaps listening *preferences* as opposed to listening *skills* can be influenced by exposure to music in general and to certain types of music, as is the case for older children and adults. For example, it is no accident that most of us derive pleasure from the music of our culture (whether popular, folk, or art music) but have difficulty appreciating some of the very discrepant musical forms from other cultures (and even our own).

If acceleration is the goal, as is often the case for North American parents, then there is some evidence that this may be attainable with an enriched musical environment. Kelly and Sutton-Smith (1987) observed three infants over their first 2 years of life, documenting musical events initiated by the parents and musical behaviors exhibited by the infants. In two of the three homes, singing was a central aspect of caretaking and social activities, but in the third, music played a subsidiary role, being initiated primarily in response to the child's interest. The two children from musically oriented homes were more attentive to music and exhibited earlier vocal and gross motor responses to music. On the expressive side, these children produced glissandos and discrete pitches substantially earlier than the child from the nonmusical home. In the acquisition of songs, the two children from musically oriented homes proceeded from melodic contour to rhythm to words, in contrast to the other child, who proceeded from words to rhythm and then to melody. As was characteristic of their caretakers, the two "musically reared" tots tended to sing as they played, whereas the third sang as a distinct activity.

Although these effects of very early exposure to musical activities must be regarded as tentative, being derived from a study of very limited scope, they are provocative in suggesting that musical development can be influenced by environmental factors, even in infancy. What remains unclear is whether this initial acceleration in musical development has long-term consequences for the ultimate level of musical achievement and for the motivation to engage in musical activities. It is also unclear whether the observed effects were attributable to the positive emotional tone that accompanied musical activities in the two musical households (i.e., pleasant associations) or to the accumulated musical experience. It is therefore presumptuous to regard these findings as a mandate for *musical parenting* or for alternative musical curricula for infants and toddlers. A wiser and more moderate course would be for parents and caregivers to share pleasurable pursuits, musical and nonmusical, with infants, toddlers, and children.

## ACKNOWLEDGMENTS

The preparation of this manuscript was assisted by grants from the Natural Sciences and Engineering Research Council and the Social Sciences and Humanities Research Council of Canada.

## REFERENCES

Attneave, F., & Olson, R. K. (1971). Pitch as a medium: A new approach to psychophysical scaling. *American Journal of Psychology, 84,* 147–166.

Cohen, A. J., Thorpe, L. A., & Trehub, S. E. (1987). Infants' perception of musical relations in short transposed tone sequences. *Canadian Journal of Psychology, 41,* 33–47.

DeCasper, A. J., & Fifer, W. P. (1980). Of human bonding: Newborns prefer their mothers' voices. *Science, 208,* 1174–1176.

Dowling, W. J. (1978). Scale and contour: Two components of a theory of memory for melodies. *Psychological Review, 85,* 341–354.

Dowling, W. J., & Harwood, D. L. (1986). *Music cognition.* Orlando, FL: Academic Press.

Fernald, A. (1984). The perceptual and affective salience of mothers' speech to infants. In L. Feagans, C. Garvey, & R. Golinkoff (Eds.), *The origins and growth of communication* (pp. 5–29). Norwood, NJ: Ablex.

Fernald, A. (1989). Intonation and communicative intent in mothers' speech to infants: Is the melody the message? *Child Development, 60,* 1497–1510.

Fernald, A. (1992). Meaningful melodies in mothers' speech to infants. In H. Papoušek, V. Jurgens, & M. Papoušek (Eds.), *Nonverbal vocal communication: comparative and developmental approaches* (pp. 262–282). New York: Cambridge University Press.

Fernald, A., Taeschner, T., Dunn, J., Papoušek, M., de Boysson-Bardies, B., & Fukui, I. (1989). A cross-language study of prosodic modifications in mothers' and fathers' speech to preverbal infants. *Journal of Child Language, 16,* 477–501.

Grieser, D. L., & Kuhl, P. K. (1988). Maternal speech to infants in a tonal language: Support for universal prosodic features in motherese. *Developmental Psychology, 24,* 14–20.

Hair, H. I. (1977). Discrimination of tonal direction on verbal and nonverbal tasks by first grade children. *Journal of Research in Music Education, 25,* 197–210.

Hargreaves, D. J. (1986). *The developmental psychology of music.* Cambridge: Cambridge University Press.

Kelley, L., & Sutton-Smith, B. (1987). A study of infant musical productivity. In J. C. Peery, I. Weiss Peery, & T. W. Draper (Eds.), *Music and child development* (pp. 35–53). New York: Springer-Verlag.

Lewis, M. M. (1951). *Infant speech.* London: Routledge & Kegan Paul.

Lynch, M. P., & Eilers, R. E. (1991). Children's perception of native and nonnative musical scales. *Music Perception, 9,* 121–131.

Mehler, J., Bertoncini, J., Barrière, M., & Jassik-Gerschenfeld, D. (1978). Infant recognition of mother's voice. *Perception, 7,* 491–497.

Morrongiello, B. A., & Roes, C. (1990). Developmental changes in children's perception of musical sequences: Effects of musical training. *Developmental Psychology, 26,* 814–820.

Morrongiello, B. A., Roes, C., & Donnelly, F. (1989). Children's perception of musical patterns: Effects of music instruction. *Music Perception, 6,* 447–462.

Morrongiello, B. A., Trehub, S. E., Thorpe, L. A., & Capodilupo, S. (1985). Children's perception of melodies: The role of contour, frequency, and rate of presentation. *Journal of Experimental Child Psychology, 40,* 279–292.

Papoušek, H., & Papoušek, M. (1987). Intuitive parenting: A dialectic counterpart to the infants' integrative competence. In J. Osofsky (Ed.), *Handbook of infant development* (2nd ed., pp. 669–720). New York: Wiley Interscience.

Papoušek, M., & Papoušek, H. (1981). Musical elements in the infant's vocalization: Their significance for communication, cognition, and creativity. In L. P. Lipsitt (Ed.), *Advances in infancy research* (Vol. 1, pp. 163–224). Norwood, NJ: Ablex.

Peery, J. C., Peery, I. W., & Draper, T. W. (Eds.). (1987). *Music and child development.* New York: Springer-Verlag.

Stern, D. N., Spieker, S., & MacKain, K. (1982). Intonation contours as signals in maternal speech to prelinguistic infants. *Developmental Psychology, 18,* 727–735.

Thorpe, L. A. (1986, April). *Infants categorize rising and falling pitch.* Paper presented at the International Conference on Infant Studies, Los Angeles.

Thorpe, L. A., & Trehub, S. E. (1989). Duration illusion and auditory grouping in infancy. *Developmental Psychology, 25,* 122–127.

Thorpe, L. A., Trehub, S. E., Morrongiello, B. A., & Bull, D. (1988). Perceptual grouping by infants and preschool children. *Developmental Psychology, 24,* 484–491.

Trainor, L. J., & Trehub, S. E. (1992). The development of referential meaning in music. *Music Perception, 9,* 455–470.

Trehub, S. E. (1990). The perception of musical patterns by human infants: The provision of similar patterns by their parents. In M. A. Berkley & W. C. Stebbins (Eds.), *Comparative perception: Vol. 1. Basic mechanisms* (pp. 429–459). New York: Wiley.

Trehub, S. E., Bull, D., & Thorpe, L. A. (1984). Infants' perception of melodies: The role of melodic contour. *Child Development, 55,* 821–830.

Trehub, S. E., Cohen, A. J., & Guerriero, L. (1987, April). *Children's understanding of the emotional meaning of music.* Paper presented at the meeting of the Society for Research in Child Development, Baltimore.

Trehub, S. E., Cohen, A. J., Thorpe, L. A., & Morrongiello, B. A. (1986). Development of the perception of musical relations: Semitone and diatonic structure. *Journal of Experimental Psychology: Human Perception and Performance, 12,* 295–301.

Trehub, S. E., Morrongiello, B. A., & Thorpe, L. A. (1985). Children's perception of familiar melodies: The role of intervals, contour, and key. *Psychomusicology, 5,* 39–48.

Trehub, S. E., Thorpe, L. A., & Morrongiello, B. A. (1985). Infants' perception of melodies: Changes in a single tone. *Infant Behavior and Development, 8,* 213–223.

Trehub, S. E., Thorpe, L. A., & Morrongiello, B. A. (1987). Organizational processes in infants' perception of auditory patterns. *Child Development, 58,* 741–749.

Trehub, S. E., Thorpe, L. A., & Trainor, L. J. (1990). Infants' perception of *good* and *bad* melodies. *Psychomusicology, 9,* 5–15.

Trehub, S. E., & Thorpe, L. A. (1989). Infants' perception of rhythm. Categorization of auditory sequences by temporal structure. *Canadian Journal of Psychology, 43,* 217–229.

Trehub, S. E., & Trainor, L. J. (1989, April). *Preschoolers' understanding of the attributes of musical sound.* Paper presented at the Society for Research in Child Development, Kansas City, MO.

Trehub, S. E., & Trainor, L. J. (1990). Rules for listening in infancy. In J. Enns (Ed.), *The development of attention: Research and theory* (pp. 87–119). Amsterdam: Elsevier.

Trehub, S. E., & Trainor, L. J. (in press). Listening strategies in infancy: The roots of language and musical development. In S. McAdams & E. Bigand (Eds.), *Cognitive aspects of human audition.* London: Oxford University Press.

Trehub, S. E., Unyk, A. M., & Trainor, L. J. (in press). Adults identify infant-directed music across cultures. *Infant Behavior and Development.*

Unyk, A. M., Trehub, S. E., Trainor, L. J., & Schellenberg, E. G. (1992). Lullabies and simplicity: A cross-cultural perspective. *Psychology of Music, 20,* 15–28.

# Children's Musical Cognition and Taste

Arlette Zenatti
*Centre National de la Recherche Scientifique, Paris*

To suggest a cognitive factor in connection with musical taste might at first seem paradoxical. Emotional responses to music are primordial—you either like or dislike a particular piece or a particular composer. Even if a professional musician and a musically untrained listener have different perceptions of a work because of their different backgrounds—even if their cognitive processing of musical information differs, as well as the network of memory associations that information evokes—in what way could those cognitive mechanisms influence their emotional reactions?

In fact, a variety of factors enter into the formation and development of musical taste, which is itself a complex phenomenon. Studying the development of music preference in children, LeBlanc (1980, 1987) exposed an interactive theory, in which he proposed a hierarchical model with eight levels starting with the input of musical information and progressing all the way to the acceptance or rejection of that information. Among the variables that LeBlanc considered were those pertaining to the stimuli, media, family and cultural milieu, physiological enabling conditions, basic attention, current affective state, individual differences of personality, musical training, maturation, information processing by the brain, and whether the person is eager to arrive at a judgment or wants to explore the stimulus further. Numerous studies of musical taste and musical preferences have focused on one or another of these aspects and their interactions; for example, studies by Wapnick (1976), Radocy and Boyle (1979), Abeles (1980), Haack (1980), and Hargreaves (1986). Farnsworth (1958) emphasized the influence of cultural milieu, and Konecni (1982) that of social factors.

The formation and evolution of taste can be approached from the point of view of information theory. The message transmitted—that is, the piece of music—is not decoded in the same way by everyone. That decoding process depends essentially on the degree of maturation of the nervous system, which in turn depends on the age of the child, a variety of biological factors, the musical experience acquired in a given milieu, and on the musical education received. For information theory, the information received is considered in terms of its banality or originality: whether it is predictable and thus tells the listener nothing new, or whether it is novel and unpredictable. The notion of originality and banality are important in the artistic domain, and are fundamental to a distinction between *interest* and *aesthetic pleasure*. With visual stimuli Berlyne (1971) showed that interest grew to the extent that the message became less banal, whereas aesthetic pleasure grew to a certain degree of originality and then declined when originality became too pronounced. These tendencies have also been observed in the musical domain (Crozier, 1974; McMullen, 1974; Vitz, 1966, 1974).

Information theory permits us to sketch a simple scheme for the reception of a message by an individual. However, that approach fails to capture all of the complexity of the psychological processes brought into play. From a cognitive perspective, the processing of information takes a new dimension as the information is organized in structures characteristic of a musical idiom.

The cultural factor is very important in music because sounds are organized differently in different civilizations and periods. Musical information from the environment thus needs to be defined with respect to a specific cultural milieu. At present a number of quite different musical traditions coexist in Western civilization, and their transmission in the environment differs as well. Diverse studies show that when they listen to musical broadcasts, many people in Western culture choose program material based on the tonal system. That system served as a framework for most works written between 1650 and 1900. Lully, Bach, Mozart, Beethoven, Schumann, and Ravel are representative names among a large number of composers who wrote within the tonal framework, and most contemporary popular music uses that system as well. As parents, these listeners place their children in a well-defined musical environment, out of which their musical acculturation develops. The psychological term *acculturation* "designates the process of learning through which the child receives the culture of the society or milieu to which he or she belongs" (Bastide, 1968, pp. 102–103). Francès (1958/1988) was one of the first to have used the term in connection with experimental research in the psychology of music.

The idea that the environment exerts a selective influence is generally accepted. "The environment confirms or discourages, selecting behavioral possibilities . . . We now know that at least certain domains such as vision and primary language acquisition develop by means of such procedures" (de Schöonen & Bresson, 1983, p. 17). Musical development clearly follows the

same laws. To speak of acculturation thus does not imply the denia,
psychological capacities. To speak of the *interaction* among the influe,
the environment and those depending on human nature implies, besides, tha,
the individual chooses selectively from the information present in the environment on the basis of its physical characteristics and the formal organization of
musical structure. This choice devolves from a tendency inherent in the human
mind. "There is an overwhelming amount of evidence throughout all areas of
psychology that human ability to structure the environment is genetically highly
determined. We see no reason why musical capacity should be any exception"
(Lerdahl & Jackendoff, 1983, p. 301).

In their *Generative Theory of Tonal Music*, Lerdahl and Jackendoff (1983)
hypothesized that once a listener "becomes familiar with the idiom, the kind
of organization that he attributes to a given piece will not be arbitrary, but will
be highly constrained in specific ways" (p. 3). According to their point of view,
"a theory of a musical idiom should characterize such organization in terms of
an explicit formal musical grammar" (p. 3). Without going into the details, it
is important to emphasize certain aspects of their theory:

- It takes as its reference an acculturated listener.
- It raises a problem concerning "the source of the experienced listener's
knowledge. To what extent is it learned, and to what extent is it due to an innate musical capacity or general cognitive capacity?" (Lerdahl & Jackendoff,
1983, p. 4). These innate propensities are connected with "universal" principles that are "subject to verification or falsification by historical and ethnomusicological research" (p. 282).
- It is centered on musical structures involving "such factors as rhythmic
and pitch organization, dynamic and timbral differentiation, and motivic-thematic
processes" (p. 6).
- Although it takes the listener's capacities for perceptual organization into
consideration, it nevertheless emphasizes the importance of studying the affective aspects of music that are not dealt with in the theory. "By treating music
theory as primarily a psychological rather than a purely analytical enterprise,
we at least place it in a territory where questions of affect may meaningfully
be posed" (p. 8).

My study of children's musical taste was carried out between 1967 and 1980,
before the publication of this theory (Zenatti, 1969, 1974, 1976a, 1976b, 1976c,
1980, 1981). It was therefore not designed to address specific points of the theory. Nevertheless, it provides empirical confirmation of it in broad outline with
regard to the melodic, harmonic, and rhythmic structures commonly encountered in the tonal system, as well as addressing the question of preferences
for "universal" structures. In all, 3,376 experimental trials have been recorded.

The development of children's taste is especially interesting to study because it allows us to examine two particular aspects of cognitive functioning. The first of these aspects concerns the way in which children deal with music, depending on how familiar it is as a result of their gradual acculturation in the midst of their environment. The second aspect concerns psychoacoustic and psychophysiological factors involving relationships between the physical properties of the sounds and their effects on human audition, and between rhythmic organization and motor responses. I do not intend to draw a simplistic contrast between these two aspects; they both contribute in complementary ways to musical development. The problem is to show how structures that differ in their musical or rhythmic composition are appreciated by children, and to what degree that appreciation can be explained by a combination of environmental and psychophysiological influences. The problem is to understand the ways in which the environment and the individual interact in connection with musical taste.

## TASTE CONCERNING MUSICAL STRUCTURES INVOLVING CONSONANCE, TONALITY, AND METER

### Evaluation of Taste

In evaluating taste it is important to devise tests that are accessible to young children, especially in the sorts of response required. Failure to obtain statistically significant results should be interpreted with caution, as it often happens that too difficult a test obscures the phenomena being studied. In that case it is necessary to test a larger number of children in attempting to produce evidence of such phenomena; and then it is the pattern of results that is important and not the exact age at which they first appear, as that will be determined simply by the most precocious children. Among the usual types of response, specifying preference on a scale from "most-liked" to "least-liked" is particularly difficult for young children. A quite different technique, accessible to young subjects, consists of leaving the children free to choose the piece they want to hear by pressing buttons, and by measuring the listening times (Geringer, 1982).

The procedure adopted here for assessing taste involved having children compare items in pairs. Each pair consisted of two items that differed in some structural characteristic, but remained identical in other respects. The contrast of the two items was as clear as possible in musical terms in order to facilitate their comparison. I tape recorded the items using a piano, and played the tape for each child. The child indicated which of the two items he or she preferred or found "prettier." Using concrete materials allowed me to avoid relying on verbal responses that are often difficult to obtain with young children.

## Construction of the Tests

Seven tests, each consisting of eight pairs of items, focused on particular harmonic, melodic, and rhythmic features essential to the historical placement of a piece: the consonance of chords, the presence of tonal organization in melody and harmony, and the presence of metrical organization of the rhythms. Sample trials from these tests are shown in Fig. 8.1. The first three tests were constructed with the aim of avoiding interference with other variables. In *Consonance Test 1* (C1), very consonant chords (major triads) were contrasted with very dissonant chords of equal duration. In *Tonality Test 1* (T1), scale and arpeggio fragments based on intervals in the tonal system were contrasted with alterations of those patterns that had an unusual character with respect to the tonal system. In *Rhythmic Test 1* (R1), rhythmical structures containing a metrically organized periodic pulsation were contrasted with nonmetrical structures, both with tonal melodies.

The next four tests drew on works from the musical repertoire, thus testing musical taste as it might be found in real life. In these tests there was an interaction of harmony, melodic chroma, and rhythmic structure. Three of these tests were based on contemporary works by such composers as Milhaud, Jolivet, and Schönberg, contrasting excerpts that were dissonant, atonal, or nonmetrical with items that were consonant, tonal, and metrical transformations of those excerpts. *Consonance Test 2* (C2) contrasted consonant and dissonant chords, using metrical rhythms. *Tonality Test 2* (T2) contrasted tonal and atonal melodic structures, using rhythmic patterns that occasionally had an underlying meter. *Rhythmic Test 2* (R2) contrasted metrical and nonmetrical structures, both with atonal melodies.

FIG. 8.1.   Musical examples from tests of consonance (C1), tonality (T1), rhythm (R1), and tonal structure (T3). The examples contrast consonant (1) versus dissonant (2) in test C1; tonal (3) versus atonal (4) in test T1; metrical (5) versus nonmetrical (6) rhythm in test R1; and a tonally organized excerpt from Clementi's Sonata, Op. 36 (7) versus a disorganized version of the same structure (8) in which the modulations have been altered.

The seventh test, *Tonality Test 3* (T3), varied the organization of musical discourse in terms of coherence of tonal organization versus its alteration. Items exhibiting tonal organization were drawn from the works of classical composers such as Clementi, Diabelli, and Haydn, and began by establishing a principle tonality and included passing modulations to closely related keys. Contrasting items were altered so as to include modulations to distant keys that destroyed the coherence of tonal organization.

## Development of Taste with Age

Because the effects of gender were not statistically significant, the results for boys and girls were grouped together for analysis.

The first three tests (C1, T1, R1) showed that from about 5 years on, consonant chords, tonal structures, and metrically organized rhythms were distinctly preferred in comparison with dissonant chords, atonal structures, and nonmetrical rhythms. These preferences increased with age, reaching (respectively) 95%, 90%, and 90% of judgments on the three tests by the age of 10 (see Fig. 8.2). These trends in taste appeared, though less markedly, in Tests C2 and T2, indicating a distinct rejection of the contemporary composers sampled beginning around the age of 6. That is, the children preferred the more consonant and tonal transformations to the original excerpts. That preference was not statistically significant for 5-year-olds, which may have been due both to the relatively small number of subjects at that age, and to the structural, especially rhythmic, complexity of these stimuli compared with those of Tests C1, T1, and R1. Between 6 and 8 years of age, the results of Tests T1 and T2 were identical.

The development of preferences shown by Tests R1 and R2 were, however, clearly different, probably because of the influence of melodic structure. In most pieces metrical structure is usually associated with tonal or modal melodies, and rarely with atonal melodies. The unusual context in test R2, in which metrical and nonmetrical patterns were contrasted using atonal melodies, may have had an influence on preferences. Disruption on a perceptual level may also have occurred, because other studies have shown that for ages 8 to 10, discrimination of rhythmic alterations is not as good in an atonal melodic context as in a tonal one (Zenatti, 1976c, 1981).

According to the results of the seventh test, T3, beginning at the age of 6 children preferred the excerpts from classical composers that preserved the organization of the tonal system. This result converges with those of Davidson, McKernon, and Gardner (1981) and Bartlett and Dowling (1980), showing that the stability of a tonality—a musical "key"—is acquired around the age of 5 or 6. According to Davidson et al. children of 5 are able to maintain a single tonality in singing a song. That is, they use notes from the same tonal scale and the song sounds more or less "in tune" to adults. Bartlett and Dowling

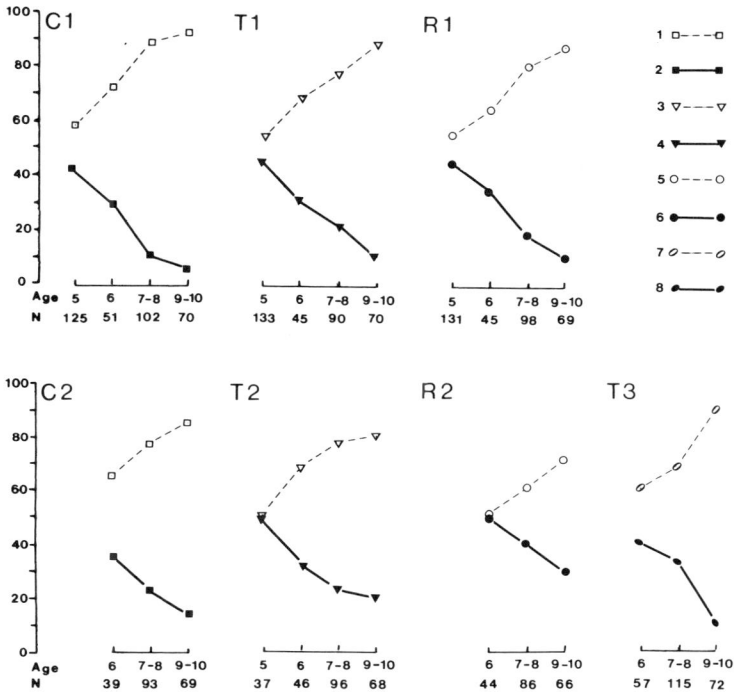

FIG. 8.2. Evolution of judgments of taste with age, as indicated by tests of consonance (C1, C2), tonality (T1, T2, T3), and rhythm (R1, R2). C1, C2: Percent choices of the consonant (dashed line) vs. the dissonant (solid line) item. T1, T2: Percent choices of the tonal (dashed line) vs. atonal (solid line) item. R1, R2: Percent choices of the metrical (dashed line) vs. nonmetrical (solid line) item. T3: Percent choices of the structurally organized (dashed line) versus disorganized (solid line) item.

showed that 5-year-olds could distinguish between near and far key relationships. Two presentations of a familiar melody such as "Twinkle, Twinkle, Little Star," the first in one key and the second in another closely related key, appeared identical to the children even when there were slight alterations of melodic intervals. However, when the second version was in a distant key (in which there were several changes in the pitches of the notes of the tonal scale), it appeared different to the children, even when the melodic intervals were transposed exactly in the comparison melody. In Test T3 the children likewise differentiated between the preferred modulations to near keys and the less preferred modulations to distant keys. This is especially important since Test T3 consisted not of familiar melodies but of unfamiliar materials. This confirms the children's grasp of invariants of organization of the tonal system of their culture.

## Stability of Preferences

No review of the development of taste with age can succeed in doing justice to the complexity of the observed facts. Whereas it is true that a general tendency in taste appears clearly in the data, there are interesting aspects to be found in individual patterns as well. For example, though most of the children preferred the more traditional patterns, there were some children who preferred the excerpts from contemporary composers. However, we can start by evaluating the overall consistency of the children's responses.

The consistency of the children's responses, and the degree to which they depart from what we would expect on the basis of chance, can be seen in Fig. 8.3. The top line (marked BD) in Fig. 8.3 shows how likely various outcomes from eight test items would be if responses were determined randomly—say by flipping a coin. In that case, outcomes such as four heads and four tails, three heads and five tails, or five heads and three tails would be quite likely, and in fact occur about 71% of the time in the long run. The middle 71% of line BD in Fig. 8.3 is indicated with a dashed and dotted line, representing the 71% of

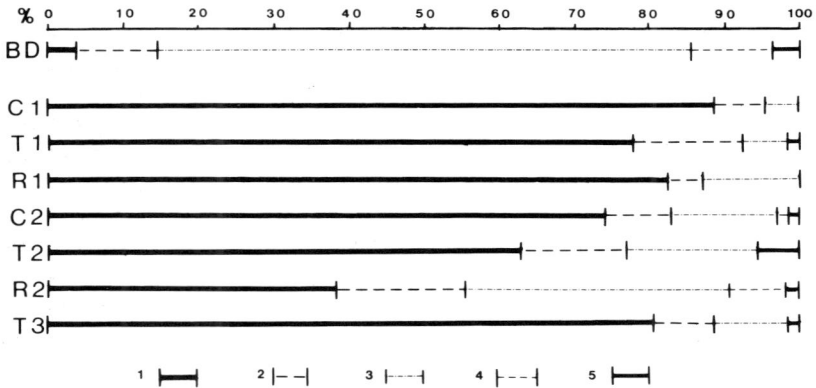

FIG. 8.3. Distribution of judgments of taste for groups of age 9 and 10 yr. Line BD: Binomial distribution. Lines C1, T1, R1, C2, T2, R2, T3: The results of the seven tests. The heavy solid line (1) indicates percent of outcomes in which the consonant, tonal, or metrical item was chosen 8/8 or 7/8 of the time (an outcome that has a chance probability of 3.51 percent indicated in line BD); the heavy dashed line (2) indicates the percent of outcomes in which the consonant, tonal or metrical item was chosen 6/8 of the time (chance probability = 10.94%); the solid and dashed line (3) indicates the percent of outcomes in which the consonant, tonal or metrical item was chosen 5/8, 4/8, or 3/8 of the time (chance probability = 71.10%); the light dashed line (4) indicates the percent of outcomes in which the consonant, etc., item was chosen 2/8 of the time (chance probability = 10.94%); and the light solid line (5) indicates the percent of outcomes in which the consonant, etc., item was chosen 1/8 or 0/8 of the time (chance probability = 3.51%).

cases with outcomes four-four, three-five, and five-three. Splits of six-two or two-six each occur about 11% of the time by chance, and those are indicated by dashed lines to the right and left of the middle area, respectively. Splits of eight-zero and seven-one are rare, occurring altogether only about 3.5% of the time. The same is true of zero-eight and one-seven splits. Those outcomes are represented by the solid bars at the right and left ends of line BD. The shortness of the bars indicates the rarity of their occurrence by chance.

Each of the remaining lines in Fig. 8.3 shows the outcome of one of the seven tests of the 9- and 10-year-olds. In the line for Test C1, for example, the solid bar starting from the left end indicates that 89% of the children chose the more consonant alternative either seven or eight times out of their eight choices—considerably more than the 3.5% to be expected on the basis of chance. In fact, for all the tests except R2 a large majority of the children chose the more consonant, tonally structured, or metrical alternative over the more dissonant, less structured, or nonmetrical alternative at least seven out of eight times. And on Test R2 almost 40% chose the metrical alternative—still considerably greater than chance. (The difficulty of Test R2 can be seen in the 35% of subjects who did not clearly choose either alternative, indicated by the dashed and dotted line.) This shows the stability of the children's choices. It is highly unlikely that such a preponderance of choices could have arisen from random responding. The results provide clear evidence of stability of the children's aesthetic judgments.

A small number of 9- and 10-year-olds preferred the contemporary excerpts, especially in Test T2 where 6% of the subjects chose the original, less tonal, version on at least seven trials. Those children have reached a stage of cognitive development in which they are receptive to atonal melodies.

The study of the evolution of musical taste included a control group of adults without musical education who belonged to diverse social and occupational categories (Zenatti, 1981). Their judgments in melodic Test T1 were less stable than those of the 9- and 10-year-olds. According to the explanations given by these adults, in certain instances the tonal and atonal melodies were at times not well differentiated, and in other cases there was a conflict between the two cultural influences, tonal and atonal, so that neither appeared to predominate. The results of harmonic Test C1 and rhythmic Test R1 failed to disclose differences in preference between the adults and the 9- and 10-year-olds. In the absence of musical education, patterns of taste remain stable throughout the course of one's life.

These various results obtained in France may be compared with those of a study by Sloboda (1985) carried out in England (Zenatti, 1991a). This involves a post-hoc comparison as the studies had already been separately published. In both cases the studies were based on aesthetic judgments of children in the same age groups, as well as of adults. The experimental methods were the same, and the musical structures used were more or less comparable. There was a difference in the nature of the judgments made, however. In Sloboda's experiments, subjects were asked to indicate which structures they judged "correct," which involved an assessment of conformity to rules. In my experiments, on the other hand, subjects judged which were "pretty," which involved an expression of taste. Comparative analysis reveals that judgments expressed by children in both countries tend to be similar, supporting the hypothesis that the formation of musical taste rests at least in part on cognitive mechanisms. With some adults, the appreciation of the aesthetic aspect of melodic structures remained distinct from judgments of "correctness"—in Sloboda's test the number of structures chosen as "correct" approached the upper limit possible—revealing the specificity and evolution of taste.

## Instability of Preferences in Pathological Cases

Seeking to clarify the nature of the cognitive mechanisms involved in the formation and evolution of preferences for structures C1, T1, and R1, I became interested in two types of disorders: cases of dyslexic children (Zenatti, 1980, 1981, 1991b) and of adults with cerebral lesions (Zenatti, 1980, 1991b). The results showed that the preferences of a group of 18 dyslexic children for tonal melodic structures were very significantly less stable than those of a control group of normal children, whereas preferences for consonant and metrically regular structures were comparable in the two groups. Thus a cognitive deficit outside of the verbal domain might be associated with dyslexia in the child, only appearing when a culturally determined melodic organization of tones comes into play.

An experiment with 78 adults with cerebral lesions, compared with the results of a control group without lesions, demonstrated significant deficits in the capacity to express stable preferences associated with lesions of the right cerebral hemisphere, and of the left hemisphere with involvement of a conduction aphasia and a transcortical aphasia. In these latter cases the following dissociations appeared in the data: (a) among the results of the three tests of aesthetic judgments, disclosing an influence of the organization of the tones, and providing a control with regard to the subjects' comprehension of the tasks; and (b) between capacities of aesthetic judgment and those of perceptual discrimination, which were the focus of three tests. This last is extremely interesting, as it discloses the existence of two levels of processing of musical information. On the one hand, the two aphasic subjects were found to be unable to give stable preferences when harmonic and melodic structures were involved, but to perform without difficulty the rhythmic test. On the other hand, their discrimination and short-term memory were not impaired. In the case of cerebral lesions, instability of taste could be interpreted as a form of amusia in which the organization of certain musical structures, which were familiar in childhood, is no longer recognized.

Extensive investigations may possibly provide a specification of the modalities of cerebral functions in the case of musical taste. As Marin (1982) said, "One cannot study the neuropsychology of complex behavior without a prior understanding of the cognitive structures of the system involved" (p. 454). The research on the cognition and musical taste of normal children facilitates the observation of pathological deficits, and perhaps opens a new route to the understanding of brain function.

## THE PREDOMINANCE OF CULTURAL INFLUENCE ON TASTE

To draw conclusions concerning the influence of acculturation from experimental research, we need to satisfy the following conditions. First, we need to find statistically significant differences between responses to two types of structures: one type common in the environment and the other unusual. (This we found in the preceding section.) Second, these differences should not appear with younger children in the same environment, specifically, in a task in which those children are capable of better-than-chance responding. Though the results shown in Fig. 8.2 show a definite increase in culturally favored responses with age, we still need to show that this is not simply due to the younger children's general inability to perform better than chance on such tests. For that we need other experimental procedures and different rhythmic and musical structures.

### Acculturation of Tonality

The development of tonal acculturation was demonstrated successfully in two types of tests. This acculturation appeared at a particular age, and it did not appear with younger children who nevertheless performed at better-than-chance levels. These results were produced by subjects selected for their ability to perform the required task.

The first task involved the discriminative learning of two melodic structures. In one case, the discriminative learning bore on pentatonic structures (essentially similar to standard tonal structures), and in another case on atonal structures. The two types of structures were taught to two different groups of boys, which were matched on the basis of a pretest used to select subjects who could perform the task. The boys' performances on the two types of structures were comparable at the age of 4 or 5 years, and different at 6 or 7 years, where the atonal structures were harder to learn (Zenatti, 1973, 1981). The second task required the discrimination of melodic changes. This was significantly easier when the organization of sounds composing melodic pattern of three notes corresponds to the one that is most often used in the tonal system, and was more difficult when the melodic structure formed at the time of the presentation and the repetition of the pattern is not frequent. The results, selected from the performance of the best subjects, failed to show a significant effect of tonal scale-step chroma for 6- and 7-year-old girls, and the discrimination of melodic changes was not as good for 8- and 9-year-olds in a less frequent context. For 6-year-old boys, tonal acculturation observed in tasks of discriminative learning was found again in the case of discrimination of melodic changes. It is interesting that statistically significant results were obtained with short sequences (Zenatti, 1969, 1970, 1985).

In conclusion, when taste and perception are involved, the influence of tonal acculturation appeared at different ages, between 5 and 8 years, depending on the constitution of melodic structures and the nature of psychological processes: aesthetic judgments, discriminative learning, discrimination of modifications.

## Acculturation of Rhythm

Can the preferences we observed in 5-year-olds for metrical structures be explained by the beginnings of musical acculturation laid down in the practice of songs and dances involving strong rhythmic organization? I tested this via judgments of taste that contrasted two types of patterns composed of tones on the same pitch: a rhythmical pattern versus one in which the notes occurred at equal time intervals (see Fig. 8.4). I used the same method as before, and repeated each item eight times in the course of the test. As shown in Fig. 8.4, around the age of 4 years the children expressed a preference for the completely regular pattern, yet this tendency reversed itself for children 4½ years and older. The early preference for the regular patterns can probably be explained by the simplicity of their structure, which facilitates their perception. The reversal in taste indicated by preference for the rhythmically grouped patterns can be attributed to the influence of acculturation.

These results should be placed in the context of other behavior patterns of children at this age. According to Moorhead and Pond, as cited in Shuter-Dyson and Gabriel (1981), the first musical attempts of a child are characterized by a "regular, unaccented beating" (p. 113), probably physical in origin. This was observed with a child of 3 years, 8 months. Davidson and McKernon (cited in Sloboda, 1985, p. 206) found a significant difference between the ages of 4 and 5 in children's learning of a new folk song. Five-year-olds were able to organize their reproductions in terms of an underlying pulse or beat, which was not the case at the age of 4. It does not contradict these observations to note that a regular temporal beat appears earlier in the case of *spontaneous* singing. As Dowling and Harwood (1986) noted, "during the second year of life, children impose the regular beat on longer and longer time spans, a trend that continues throughout childhood" (p. 194). Regularity of rhythmic structure appears earlier in spontaneous behavior than with novel materials and in tests, but the overall trend is one of increasing control over rhythmic organization. The present results suggest that between the ages of 4 and 5 children gain sufficient organizational

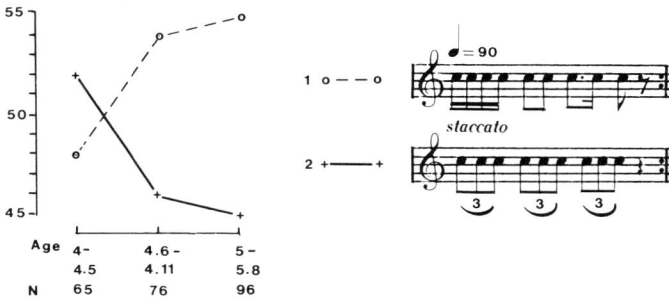

FIG. 8.4.    Judgments of rhythmic taste at the ages of 4 and 5 yrs., showing choices of rhythmically grouped item (dashed line) versus completely regular item (solid line).

capacity to impose a regular structure on the rhythmically grouped patterns. At both ages children select a pattern that sound *regular* to them, but the more complex patterns that sound regular to 5-year-olds strike the 4-year-olds as disorganized.

An important problem concerns the connections between psychomotricity and rhythmic structure. Music with strong metrical accents provokes involuntary muscle contractions that are clearly visible on electromyographic tracings. The physiological basis of this motoric induction is not well understood, and its influence on taste has not been rigorously examined. Nevertheless a reasonable hypothesis is that this influence overlaps with that of acculturation in the case of a taste for highly rhythmic music. As far as the evolution of taste with age is concerned, the preference for rock music, for example, starts to develop at the second grade level (7 years), and increases markedly between the third and fourth grades (Greer, Dorow, & Randall, 1974).

## THE PROBLEM OF STRUCTURAL INFLUENCE ON TASTE

Are there musical structures that are fundamental by virtue of the relationships among the tones that make them up? A standard example is that of the similarity perceived more or less strongly between tones an octave apart. The relations that exist among tones raise in a general way the problem of the importance of psychoacoustic and psychophysiological factors associated with physical properties of the sounds. There is a wide divergence of views of the importance of such factors. Representing the cognitive–structural approach, Shepard (1982), referring to Chomsky's theories of language, proposed that "our musical competence may presuppose an implicit knowledge of underlying structures (e.g., diatonic scales, hierarchies of tonal functions)" (p. 350). Such an approach places tonal relationships in a musical context and considers certain intervals such as the octave and perfect fifth to be especially significant. It has at times been hypothesized that certain simple structures have a privileged status at the time of musical composition and that those same structures will have particular importance in the cognitive processing of information gathered from the environment. An ethnomusicological approach is indispensable in testing this hypothesis, in which we would examine the main streams of musical expression from the historical origins of diverse civilizations in an attempt to find certain structures that they have in common—for example, certain melodic patterns. And then experimental research would be required to evaluate the importance of those structures for human cognition.

## Ditonic Scale Structure and Dissonant Melodic Structures

The ditonic scale, composed of the intervals of the octave, fifth, and fourth, and arising from the cycle of fifths, is present in the primitive music of numerous civilizations (Chailley, 1951; Marcel-Dubois, 1963; Wiora, 1963). In that sense it can be considered a fundamental structure. Is this primacy found in patterns of taste of children of 4 to 6? An experiment was designed to explore that possibility. Tests like T1 and T2 had required the comparison of melodies having the same melodic contour, which was a difficult task for the young children. Therefore, to facilitate their performance I used melodies that differed distinctly in their overall shapes. Melodic contour undoubtedly exerts an influence on preference, thus I controlled for it in the design by using three melodic structures in the experiment (see Fig. 8.5). This allowed us to examine the influence of the pitch chromas in the melodies (differences in pitch relationships such as those between Melodies 1 and 2 in Fig. 8.5) while preserving the possibility of opposition between melodies differing in contour (as between Melodies 1 and 3). The three structural patterns underlying the melodies (as illustrated in Fig. 8.5) were: (1) the ditonic scale; (2) a structure with the same contour as the first, but with chromatic alterations in the scale; and (3) a tonal structure differing in contour from the first two. The structure of Melody 2 was intended to find out if including intervals that would be dissonant in simultaneous presentation would lead to rejection in the preference test when presented in melodic succession.

The children judged the melodies in pairs, and each pair was presented eight times in the course of the test. Two groups of subjects participated in four phases of the experiment during a 2-week period. Group A first compared Structures 1 versus 3, then participated in a period of discrimination learning with those structures, and were given a retest on 1 versus 3. Finally, Group A was given a test comparing Structures 2 and 3. Group B followed the same general pattern, concentrating on Structures 2 and 3 during the first three phases of the

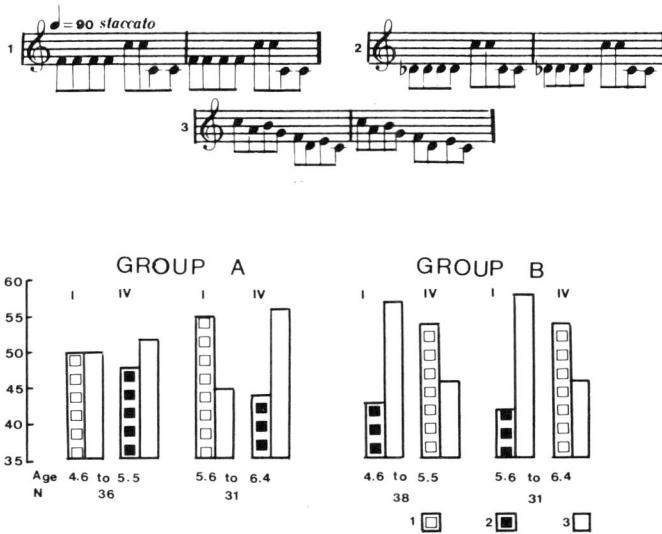

FIG. 8.5. Judgments of three melodic structures by children in two age ranges centered on 5 and 6 yrs.: (1) ditonic melody; (2) dissonant chromatic melody; (3) diatonic tonal melody. Groups A and B performed the tests in different orders, making choices between patterns (1) and (3) (bars with open squares versus open bars) or between patterns (2) and (3) (bars with filled squares versus open bars).

experiment, and judging Structures 1 and 3 in the fourth phase. The results of the tests given in the first and fourth phases for two age ranges centered on 5-year-olds and on 6-year-olds are shown in Fig. 8.5. The ditonic (1) and dissonant, chromatic (2) structures were appreciated quite differently by these subjects, in spite of their similar melodic contours. No group preferred the chromatic Structure 2 to the diatonic tonal Structure 3. However, all but the younger children in Group A preferred the ditonic Structure 1 to Structure 3.

These results clearly indicate the rejection of Structure 2, which can be attributed to its dissonant character, in spite of the successive presentation of the pitches. Though this result is difficult to explain, it has been observed before, as Moore (1982) and Burns and Ward (1982) have noted. Along the same lines, the preferences for the ditonic structure (1) compared with the diatonic tonal structure (3) could be attributed to consonance of the intervals of the octave and fifth, even when presented via successive tones. An equally possible explanation is that the simplicity of Structure 1 facilitated perception—the same explanation proposed previously in connection with regular rhythmic structures. These results are important from a cognitive perspective in that the preferences confirm the fundamental psychological importance of the ditonic scale, recognized as a universal structure from the ethnological point of view.

## Age of Emergence of Preference
## for Musical Consonance

Preference for consonance poses problems that have not yet been fully clarified. Nevertheless, we can succeed in focusing on certain aspects. This is truly one of those essential problems whose investigation will sooner or later lead us to a better understanding of the kinds of interaction that occur between the individual and the environment.

A distinction has been established between *tonal* (Plomp & Levelt, 1965) or *sensory* (Terhardt, 1976) *consonance*, and *musical consonance*. This distinction was already made by Helmholtz (1863), who also observed that the limit separating consonance and dissonance had varied considerably with national and individual taste. From a cognitive perspective musical consonance, which is defined psychologically by its pleasant qualities, is a genuinely meaningful concept. No sharp dichotomy is established between consonance and dissonance, and chords are more or less consonant, or more or less dissonant, the pleasurableness of such and such a type of chord varying according to the individual. It is useful to note that this concept of the relativity of consonance, which can be developed in different ways according to different conceptualizations, "has been set forth by Schönberg and Koechlin in their treatises on harmony" (Chailley, 1951, p. 11).

Concerning tonal or sensory consonance, to call attention to relationships between factors that depend on the constitution of human beings and physical factors connected with the pattern of sounds, would seem to imply that those relationships exist from birth. Experimental results show, however, that children display preferences only later for intervals and chords classified as very consonant. We can explain this by supposing that it is only then that they become aware of their preferences. This serves to define the notion of taste that is acquired at that time.

Experimental studies with children show an evolution of preference between 1910 and 1985, indicated by a lowering of the age at which a preference for consonance appears. This is likely to be due to the effects of the mass media. Valentine (1913) found that in judgments of taste children began to differentiate between intervals presented to them around the age of 9 years in the case of elementary school children, and around the age of 6 or 7 years for children in a preparatory school where they had more intensive musical education. According to Imberty's (1968) results, a preference for consonant chords (open fifths and major triads) was present to some extent at 7 years, stronger at 8 years, and had become quite significant by the age of 10. According to the very similar results of Sloboda (1985) and Zenatti (1974) reviewed earlier, a preference for consonance appeared to a significant extent starting at age 5. We can ask whether these effects observed at the age of 5 might be observed at even younger ages with more sensitive experimental methods.

## CONCLUSIONS

Musical taste rests in part on a cognitive base. Observations of the evolution of taste confirm this. We know that musical taste has evolved over the centuries, and personal experience tells us that our own taste changes throughout our lives. Concurrent with the development of capacities for processing richer and more complex varieties of information, musical taste develops and, especially under the effects of education, "serious" contemporary music can come to be preferred to classical or popular music. The distinction made by Abeles (1980) between *preference* and *taste* is important: Preferences are transitory, whereas taste remains relatively stable throughout the life of the individual. This distinction is important in that it poses the problem of the age (probably variable) at which taste ceases to evolve. It may be that the stability of taste can explain the often observed divergences in taste between persons of different generations.

A crucial question arises with regard to contemporary music: Is it possible to like any kind of music? A necessary condition appears to be that the listener should be able to grasp some organization in the music that he or she hears. For Lerdahl and Jackendoff (1983),

> Nonhierarchical aspects of musical perception (such as timbre and dynamics) tend to play a greater, compensatory role in musical organization. But that is not compensation in kind; the relative absence of hierarchical dimensions tends to result in a kind of music perceived very locally, often as a sequence of gestures and associations. (p. 298)

Nevertheless, regarding the formation and evolution of children's taste, the mechanisms underlying the internalization of the tonal language provide an "explanation for the psychological assimilation of other musical languages, taking account of the structures belonging to those languages, supposing that those structures consist of elements sufficiently salient to be picked up by the child" (Zenatti, 1981, p. 254).

The relationships between musical cognition and taste in children have mainly been studied from the perspective of the child's receptivity to music. Instrumental and vocal sound production is another source of pleasure for children, and comes equally into play in the formation of musical taste. There exists an entire scale of behaviors that permits us to follow the stages of that development, from sensorimotor play (shaking a rattle, e.g.) to the time at which some children have the opportunity to explore the world of sound that an instrument provides (as in the case of the family piano). The relationships that exist on a perceptual level among cognitive development, interest, and taste, reappear at the level of musical production. Musical training is dependent on the interest that motivates that training. A variety of pedagogical methods can play an essential role in the musical awakening of young children and the broadening of taste during childhood and adolescence; for example, by means of singing (Kodaly), playing the violin (Suzuki), or collections of simple instruments (Orff), or instruments especially constructed for their diversity of timbre (Baschet), or the use of computers that facilitate initiation to electro–acoustic music (Xenakis). Just as on the verbal level we couldn't imagine the child being content to listen without speaking, so in music we stimulate the child's capacity for expression through vocal and instrumental improvisations that provide for the spontaneous organization of sounds and develop creativity. Through learning to sing and to play instruments such as the piano, violin, and so on, children learn to love the music they work on. These interpreters recreate works that go beyond the symbols inscribed in the score, expressing more or less well their understanding of them. Whether the faltering performance of a beginner or the easy interpretation of a great artist, giving life to a work is an oft-experienced source of joy for the interpreter, of whatever age.

## ACKNOWLEDGMENT

I wish to express my thanks to W. Jay Dowling for translating this chapter from French with all of his competence as a psychologist of music.

## REFERENCES

Abeles, H. F. (1980). Responses to music. In D. A Hodges (Ed.), *Handbook of music psychology* (pp. 105–140). Lawrence, KS: National Association for Music Therapy.

Bartlett, J. C., & Dowling, W. J. (1980). The recognition of transposed melodies: A key-distance effect in developmental perspective. *Journal of Experimental Psychology: Human Perception & Performance, 6*, 501–515.

Bastide, R. (1968). Acculturation [Acculturation]. *Encyclopedia Universalis, 1*, 102–107.

Berlyne, D. (1971). *Aesthetics and psychobiology.* New York: Appleton-Century-Crofts.

Burns, E. M., & Ward, W. D. (1982). Intervals, scales, and tuning. In D. Deutsch (Ed.) *The psychology of music* (pp. 241–270). New York: Academic Press.

Chailley, J. (1951). *Traité historique d'analyse musicale* [Historical treatise of musical analysis]. Paris: Leduc.

Crozier, J. B. (1974). Melodic perception. *Sciences de l'Art/Scientific Aesthetics, 9*, 63–71.

Davidson, L., McKernon, P., & Gardner, H. (1981). The acquisition of song: A developmental approach. In *Documentary report of the Ann Arbor Symposium* (pp. 301–315). Reston, VA: Music Educator National Conference.

Dowling, W. J., & Harwood, D. L. (1986). *Music cognition.* New York: Academic Press.

Farnsworth, P. R. (1958). *The social psychology of music.* New York: Holt, Rinehart & Winston.

Francès, R. (1988). *The perception of music* (W. J. Dowling, Trans.). Hillsdale, NJ: Lawrence Erlbaum Associates. (Original work published in French, 1958).

Geringer, J. M. (1982). Verbal and operant music listening preference in relationship to age and musical training. *Psychology of Music, 10*, 47–50.

Greer, R. D., Dorow, L. G., & Randall, A. (1974). Music listening preferences of elementary school children. *Journal of Research in Music Education, 22*, 284-291.
Haack, P. A. (1980). The behavior of music listeners. In D. A. Hodges (Ed.) *Handbook of music psychology* (pp. 141-182). Lawrence, KS: National Association for Music Therapy.
Hargreaves, D. J. (1986). *The developmental psychology of music*. Cambridge, England: Cambridge University Press.
Helmholtz, H. (1863). *Die Lehre von den Tonempfindungen als physiologische Grundlage für die Theorie der Musik* [On the sensations of tone as a physiological basis for the theory of music]. Braunschweig: Fr. Viewig u. Sohn.
Imberty, M. (1968). Recherche sur la genèse du sentiment de consonance [Research on the origins of the feeling for consonance]. *Sciences de l'Art/Scientific Aesthetics, 5*, 29-44.
Konecni, V. J. (1982). Social interaction and musical preference. In D. Deutsch (Ed.) *The psychology of music* (pp. 497-516). New York: Academic Press.
LeBlanc, A. (1980). Outline of a proposed model of sources of variation in musical taste. *Bulletin of the Council for Research in Music Education, 61*, 29-34.
LeBlanc, A. (1987). The development of music preference in children. In C. Peery, I. W. Peery, & T. W. Draper (Eds.), *Music and child development* (pp. 137-157). New York, Berlin: Springer-Verlag.
Lerdahl, F., & Jackendoff, R. (1983). *A generative theory of tonal music*. Cambridge: The MIT Press.
Marcel-Dubois, C. (1963). Présence ou absence de la constante de quarte, de quinte et d'octave: Son rôle structurel dans l'ethnologie européenne [Presence or absence of the constant of fourth, fifth, and octave: Its structural role in European ethnomusicology]. In E. Weber (Ed.), *La résonance dans les échelles musicales [Resonance in musical scales]* (pp. 143-148). Paris: Centre National de la Recherche Scientifique.
Marin, O. S. (1982). Neurological aspects of music perception and performance. In D. Deutsch (Ed.) *The psychology of music* (pp. 453-478). New York: Academic Press.
McMullen, P. T. (1974). Influence of number of different pitches and melodic redundancy on preference responses. *Journal of Research in Music Education, 22*, 198-204.
Moore, B. C. J. (1982). *An introduction to the psychology of hearing* (2nd ed.). New York: Academic Press.
Plomp, R., & Levelt, W. J. M. (1965). Tonal consonance and critical bandwidth. *Journal of the Acoustical Society of America, 38*, 548-560.
Radocy, R. E., & Boyle, J. D. (1979). *Psychological foundations of musical behavior*. Springfield, IL: Thomas.
Schönen, S. de, & Bresson, F. (1983). Données et perspectives nouvelles sur les débuts du développement [Data and new perspectives on the beginnings of development]. In S. de Schönen (Ed.), *Le développement dans la première année* [Development in the first year] (pp. 13-23). Paris: P. U. F.
Shepard, R. N. (1982). Structural representations of musical pitch. In D. Deutsch (Ed.) *The psychology of music* (pp. 344-390). New York: Academic Press.
Shuter-Dyson, R., & Gabriel, C. (1981). *The psychology of musical ability* (2nd ed.). London: Methuen.
Sloboda, J. A. (1985). *The musical mind: The cognitive psychology of music*. London: Oxford University Press.
Terhardt, E. (1976). Ein psychoakustisch begründetes Konzept der Musikalischen Konsonanz [A psychoacoustically based concept of musical consonance]. *Acustica, 36*, 121-137.
Valentine, C. W. (1913). The aesthetic appreciation of musical interval among school children and adults. *British Journal of Psychology, 6*, 190-216.
Vitz, P. C. (1966). Affect as a function of stimulus variation. *Journal of Experimental Psychology, 71*, 74-79.
Vitz, P. C. (1974). Experiments on affective reactions to music stimuli. *Sciences de l'Art/Scientific Aesthetics, 9*, 3-14.

Wapnick, J. A. (1976). A review of research on attitude and preference. *Council for Research in Music Education, 48*, 1–20.

Wiora, W. (1963). Présence ou absence de la constante de quarte, de quinte et d'octave: Son rôle structurel dans l'ethnologie européenne [Presence of absence of the constant of fourth, fifth, and octave: Its structural role in European ethnomusicology]. In E. Weber (Ed.), *La résonance dans les échelles musicales [Resonance in musical scales]* (pp. 129–142). Paris: Centre National de la Recherche Scientifique.

Zenatti, A. (1969). *Le développement génétique de la perception musicale [The genetic development of musical perception].* Paris: Centre National de la Recherche Scientifique.

Zenatti, A. (1970). Perception mélodique et acculturation tonale. Etude expérimentale de l'influence du sexe sur les performances d'enfants âgés de 5 à 10 ans [Melodic perception and tonal acculturation. Experimental study on the influence of gender on the performances of children aged 5 to 10 years]. *Sciences de l'Art/Scientific Aesthetics, 7*, 71–76.

Zenatti, A. (1973). Etude de l'acculturation musicale chez l'enfant dans une épreuve d'identification mélodique [Study of children's musical acculturation with a test of melodic identification]. *Journal de Psychologie Normale et Pathologique, 70*, 453–464.

Zenatti, A. (1974). Perception et appréciation de la consonance musicale par l'enfant, entre 4 et 10 ans [Perception and appreciation of musical consonance by children between 4 and 10 years of age]. *Sciences de l'Art/Scientific Aesthetics, 9*, 47–61.

Zenatti, A. (1976a). Influence de quelques variables socio-culturelles sur le développement musical de l'enfant [Influence of some sociocultural variables on the musical development of the child]. *Psychologie Française, 21*, 185–190.

Zenatti, A. (1976b). Jugement esthétique de l'enfant sur la consonance musicale, la tonalité et l'isochronisme de la pulsation rythmique [Aesthetic judgments by children of musical consonance, tonality, and regularity of rhythmic pulse]. *Psychologie Française, 21*, 175–184.

Zenatti, A. (1976c). Jugement esthétique et perception de l'enfant, entre 4 et 10 ans, dans des épreuves rythmiques [Aesthetic judgments and perception of children between 4 and 10 years of age on tests of rhythm]. *L'Année Psychologique, 76*, 93–115.

Zenatti, A. (1980). *Tests musicaux pour jeunes enfants avec applications en psychopathologie de l'enfant et de l'adulte [Musical tests for young children with applications to the psychopathology of children and adults].* Issy-les-Moulineaux, France: Etablissements d'Applications Psychotechniques.

Zenatti, A. (1981). *L'enfant et son environnement musical. Etude expérimentale des mécanismes psychologiques d'assimilation musicale [The child and his musical environment: Experimental study of the psychological mechanisms of musical assimilation].* Issy-les-Moulineaux, France: Etablissements d'Applications Psychotechniques.

Zenatti, A. (1985). The role of perceptual-discrimination ability in tests of memory for melody, harmony, and rhythm. *Music Perception, 2*, 397–404.

Zenatti, A. (1991a). Aesthetics judgments and musical cognition. A comparative study in samples of French and British children and adults, *Psychology of Music, 19*, 65–73.

Zenatti, A. (1991b). Musikalische Akkulturation und ästhetische Urteile. Experimentelle Studien bei normalen und pathologischen Fällen [Musical acculturation and aesthetic judgments: Experimental studies in normal and pathological cases]. *Musikpsychologie, 8*, 91–115.

# 9

## Development of the Perception of Musical Events

Anne D. Pick
*University of Minnesota*

Carolyn F. Palmer
*Vassar College, New York*

Making music is a universal activity and an interesting and important human endeavor. Music is ubiquitous in the environments of even the youngest members of our culture, and it must surely be a rare individual for whom music does not provide some pleasure. Yet pleasure is just the beginning of what music affords us. Even the simplest of melodies is complex, having a unique structure, and requiring repeated listening for complete apprehension.

How does sensitivity to the structure of melodies develop? What do we know about the sources of the melodies we hear—the instruments and voices producing them? To what extent does the development of musical perception depend on learning, and what is the nature of that learning? These are the issues with which the present chapter is concerned. To begin, we consider melodies not as "stimuli" for our receptors, but instead as events that we perceive. We look to contemporary thinking about event perception to help formulate our questions about the development of musical perception.

## MELODY PERCEPTION AS EVENT PERCEPTION

A melody—played or sung—can be thought of as an audible event. Although melodies obviously are heard rather than seen, they share many properties with visible events. The most important of these is a dynamic quality, change over time. The identity of events is only revealed over time. In addition, melodies, like other events, have structure, organization, and unity.

One focus of perceptual development research during the past decade has been on understanding the development of perception of events (Gibson & Spelke, 1983). The theoretical and developmental perspectives of James and Eleanor Gibson have provided the impetus for much of this research. There are at least three reasons why the development of event perception is a central problem of their ecological approach to perception (E. J. Gibson, 1982; J. J. Gibson, 1979). First is the general hypothesis that important properties of objects and surfaces we perceive are revealed in events in which they participate. We learn about objects by seeing and hearing things happen to them, or watching them do things like bounce, or by exploring them, or walking around them and interacting with them. Events, in short, are important sources of information about the world.

A second aspect of events that makes understanding their perception particularly interesting is their embedded or nested quality. Events are embedded in larger events and perceiving them entails perceiving nested structure. A rendition of a melody, for example, is a complexly structured event, with the possibility of perceiving its structure at several levels—discerning the superordinate structure and how the units embedded in it relate to it.

A third significant characteristic of many perceived events is that they are multi-modally specified; their properties are detected by looking and listening as, for example, when we perceive musical instruments being played. An important developmental question about event perception is how we perceive the unity of events that are multi-modally specified. When a baby sees and hears her father singing a lullaby, how does she know that the face she sees is the source of the sound she hears? How do we know that the drum and violin we see are the sources of the percussive and string sounds we hear respectively, and not the other way around?

Events, then, are important units for studying human–environment interaction. Herein we consider how our understanding of the development of event perception is elucidated by what we have been learning about the early development of music perception. In particular, we focus on perception of the *structure* of melodies and the *unity* of musical events.

## Learning to Perceive Melodies

What do babies perceive when they hear music? Can they tell that one melody, "Happy Birthday," is different from another melody, "Mary Had a Little Lamb"? These are the kinds of questions—questions about ordinary perception—we strive to answer.

Think of the structure of a melody as hierarchical or nested. The elements of the structure are the notes of particular pitches and durations, although musical notes themselves have a complex harmonic structure. The next level above the individual notes is the contour, the pattern of rising and falling pitches. Here the relations among the notes are relations of higher and lower. The next level of the hierarchy is the pattern of relative interval sizes among the pitches where there are relations of larger and smaller among the intervals of the contour. Finally, there is the pattern of absolute interval sizes among the pitches of a melody, a pattern defined by the absolute size of relations among intervals.

Our investigation began with questions about the role of notes and scales in children's melody perception (Pick et al., 1988). Notes are elements of the structure of melodies, but are they basic units for listeners' perception of melodies? Even musically untrained adults easily recognize as "the same" melodies played in different scales or keys. However, adults have been hearing and humming songs in different keys for many years. Is it plausible that the course of learning to perceive melodies involves learning to ignore specific pitches, and that young children perceive these properties of melodies even if adults ordinarily do not? Dixon Ward (1970), a scholar of auditory psychophysics, has advanced the hypothesis that we do begin life with perfect pitch that we "unlearn" so to speak, by hearing and singing the same melodies transposed into different scales. Jay Dowling (1978) has argued also that the musical scales of a culture are fundamental properties that one learns about in the course of hearing music during one's early years.

Our first study of the role of musical scales in children's perception of melodies was focused on whether children would recognize the same melody across a change of scale. We solicited the participation of 5-year-old children who had had little if any of what we think of as formal music education. The children played a "Special Song Game," which began with their listening to four unfamiliar songs played on a piano. The songs were from 15 to 20 notes in length (averaging about 15 seconds duration). Each song was played in one key, and each rendition of it was played in that same key. One of the four songs was designated the "special" song, and the children's task was to learn to identify that song and to distinguish it from the other three songs. The children didn't have to learn names for the four songs; they only had to learn to recognize the "special" song and distinguish it reliably from the other songs.

After each rendition of a song, the children said whether or not it was the "special" song. The game continued until they reached a designated criterion demonstrating that they recognized that song. Then without any change in the game as far as the children knew, a rendition of the "special" song transposed into a new key was played. Would the children call the new rendition the "special" song, or would they say it was not that song and instead classify it with the "other" songs? The answer was that the vast majority (about 85%) of the children called it the "special" song.

In various conditions of the study, the songs were in minor keys and in major keys, and the transpositions of the target songs were into highly related keys (keys that retained many notes of the original key) or distant keys (keys that retained few notes of the original). Neither of these variables made any difference. Nearly all of the children treated the transformed songs as equivalent to their original version regardless of whether the two renditions were in highly related or distant scales and regardless of whether the scales were major or minor.

Perhaps these young children could not discriminate between two renditions of a song in different keys. If they could not hear a difference between the two renditions, then it is not surprising or even very interesting that the children treated renditions of a melody in different keys as equivalent. In our next study we asked whether children can distinguish between two renditions of a melody played in different keys, and we found that they easily can.

In this second study, 5-year-old children listened to pairs of melodies played on a piano and said whether the two melodies of a pair were the same or different. For this study, the songs were all well-known to the children. They were excerpts (of about a dozen notes each) of "Mary Had a Little Lamb," "London Bridge," and "Jingle Bells."

The children heard some pairs of melodies that were identical; for example, two renditions of "Mary Had a Little Lamb" in the same key. Other pairs of melodies differed only in their key, for example, two renditions of "London Bridge," one in the E flat major scale and the other in the A flat major scale. The children heard six pairs of melodies in all, and they were repeated until the children could judge them all correctly. In fact, after the children were informed that they were to judge two renditions of a song in different keys as "different," most children only required one repetition of the six pairs. They readily distinguished between two renditions of a song in different keys.

For the next phase of the study, the children listened to new pairs of songs, all different from the ones they heard before, but still familiar: "Twinkle, Twinkle, Little Star," "Row, Row, Row Your Boat," and "Old McDonald Had a Farm." The children heard pairs like those in the first phase of the study, and the question was whether they would generalize to the new song pairs the distinction they had learned so easily with the first set of songs. The answer was yes; the children judged nearly all of the song pairs in which the renditions were in different keys to be "different."

From the two studies together, we can say that young children quite easily can distinguish between two renditions of a melody played in different scales, and they also recognize two such renditions as being the same melody. The identity of a melody is specified by properties that remain invariant over a key transposition, and we next began to ask what invariant properties of melodies children perceive.

One property of the structure of a melody that is unchanged over a key transposition is its contour. Does the contour of a melody specify its identity for young listeners? How do young listeners perceive a song whose contour remains unchanged while other properties of its structure, namely the intervals among its notes, are changed? These were the next specific questions we sought to answer. We again asked 5-year-old children to participate in a version of the "Special Song Game." As before, the children listened repeatedly to four songs and learned to distinguish a designated "special" song from the others. This time, each of the songs was played in two keys, sometimes in one and sometimes in the other. In other words, scale variation within each song occurred from the very beginning of the game. Some children listened to four familiar songs: "Frosty the Snowman," "Rudolph the Red-Nosed Reindeer," "Jingle Bells," and "Santa Claus is Coming to Town." Other children listened to four unfamiliar folk songs. We varied familiarity so that we could find out if children's sensitivity to melodic contour might be affected by how well they knew the songs. The songs ranged from 12 to 19 notes in length and, as before, they were played on a piano.

After the children could reliably distinguish the "special" song from the other three songs of a set, they heard, interspersed among other songs, renditions of the target melody that preserved its contour and rhythm but in which the intervals were different. The question was whether the children would judge these transformations to be renditions of the "special" song. For the most part, the answer was no. Most of the children judged these transformations to be instances of "other" songs and not the "special" song. In the earlier phase of the game, when they listened to the target melody and learned to distinguish it from the other melodies, they apparently detected additional properties other than the contour. They learned something about the *intervals* of the melody that enabled them to identify it when they listened to it again. In the new rendition with unchanged contour, the changed intervals specified a different melody.

The children's judgments were similar whether they listened to familiar or to unfamiliar songs. The children who listened to familiar songs provided the most striking results. Nearly 90% of these children said the first transformed melody they heard was not the "special" song. Some children also said that subsequent songs in which the contour of the target song was maintained but its intervals changed were the "special" song. This was true of more children who listened to unfamiliar than to familiar songs. A number of children made comments to the effect that a particular transformation was "sort of" like the target melody, implying sensitivity to the common contour of the target melody and its transformation even when they said the transformation was a different song.

Some musical themes and variations are related by transformations that preserve the rhythm or the rhythm and the contour of the original themes while altering the intervals. These are the kinds of transformations children in this study listened to. Skilled listeners can discern properties of the theme in the variation and with practice one can learn to hear invariant properties of initially seemingly unrelated themes and variations. The children in this study provided evidence that they sometimes discerned invariant properties of the target melodies and transformations even though they mostly judged them to be different songs. Consequently, in our next study we asked directly whether young children detect invariant melodic properties in songs with the same contour and different intervals.

We used familiar melodies in this new study because it was transformations of familiar melodies that the children in the previous study had most frequently said were different melodies. Consequently, we were most interested now to find out if children could detect common properties in familiar melodies and their transformations in addition to being able to distinguish between them.

Again we asked 5-year-old children to participate in the procedure. They listened to a melody they knew very well, the first 14-note segment of "Rudolph the Red-Nosed Reindeer," and they judged a set of other melodies in terms of how similar they were to the familiar "standard" melody. The comparison melodies included transformations that preserved the contour and rhythm of the original melody, transformations that preserved only the rhythm of the original, and excerpts of folk songs that differed in intervals, contour, and rhythm from the "Rudolph" excerpt.

The children made their similarity judgments by dropping a poker chip for each comparison melody into one of three boxes. One box, a white box, was for melodies that were "not at all like Rudolph." A second, pink box, was for melodies that were "a little like Rudolph," and the third, red box, was for melodies that were "a lot like Rudolph." During the procedure the children listened frequently to the Rudolph excerpt in order to make sure they wee judging the similarity of the comparison melodies to that excerpt rather than to each other.

The children's judgments were related systematically to the three types of comparison melodies. The folk song excerpts differing from "Rudolph" in intervals, contour, and rhythm were judged most dissimilar to it. Transformations preserving the rhythm and contour of "Rudolph" were judged more similar to it than were transformations preserving only its rhythm. Thus, the children did perceive the contour of "Rudolph" over interval changes that preserved it. The children could discern similarity between melodies that have the same contour; they perceived that contour across differences in intervals that distinguish different melodies.

From the studies described so far, we have found that young children detect key transposition changes even in familiar melodies and they perceive similarity over key transpositions even in unfamiliar melodies. Children also are sensitive to melodic contour over transformations that preserve it, yet they distinguish spontaneously between melodies with the same contour and different intervals. They perceive the relatedness of different melodies having the same contour.

Does the detection of invariant properties of melodic structure depend on extensive listening experience? Even 5-year-old children who have not had formal music education have heard countless melodies. It is possible, as Ward's (1970) hypothesis noted earlier implies, that the youngest listeners of a culture attend to the notes of melodies, but their experience hearing melodies played in different scales and in different variations eventually leads them to ignore notes and discern a more complex level of melodic structure. This issue motivated our studies of melody perception in infants, which we discuss next (Hennessy et al., 1983).

We used an habituation procedure in which 3-month-old infants looked at a visual display (a slide of a sunny Caribbean sky) while they heard a short melody excerpt (about eight notes long) coming from behind the display. The excerpt was sung repeatedly in a female voice. The babies' looking time to the display was monitored until it decreased to a specified criterion. Then the babies either continued to hear the same melody, or they heard a new melody, or they heard some type of transformation of the original melody. All the melodies were sung by the same person (CP). The babies' looking continued to be monitored to determine what transformations were sufficiently different from the original melody to elicit recovery of their looking at the display.

We investigated infants' sensitivity to transposed melodies in the first study. During the habituation phase, the babies heard a melody excerpt sung repeatedly in the same key. After attaining criterion, different groups of babies (a) continued to hear the same melody in the same key, (b) heard a new melody, and (c) heard the original melody transposed into a new key. The babies in the first group who continued to hear the same melody in the same key remained habituated. The babies in both other groups, those who heard a new melody and those who heard the transposed original melody, renewed looking at the display. Their renewed looking demonstrated that they discerned the changes in what they were listening to, but their behavior didn't indicate whether they detected any invariant property of the original melody over the key transposition.

For our next study we decided to habituate babies to a melody sung in different keys, and then to ask if they detected any invariant property over that transformation. This time, during the habituation phase, the babies heard a melody that was sometimes sung in one key and sometimes in a second key. After their looking times had decreased to a specified criterion of habituation, different groups of babies (a) continued to hear the melody sung in the same two keys, (b) heard the melody sung in two new keys, and (c) heard a new melody sung in two keys. The question of greatest interest was whether the second group of babies would generalize habituation to the "old" melody sung in two new keys. The answer was that they did. Babies in that group showed no more looking at the display than did the babies in the first group who continued to hear the melody sung in its original keys.

The third group of babies who heard a new melody did renew looking at the display, and the magnitude of their looking time overall was comparable to that of the babies in the first study who heard a new melody. However, the variability of looking was considerably greater for this group of babies than for the comparable group in the first study. In fact, the looking time for the third group of babies in the second study made up a bimodal distribution, with some of the babies showing marked significant renewed looking at the display as expected, and the rest showing generalization of habituation to the new melody. It was as though these latter babies had become habituated to any change in the melody rather than specifically to a key transposition change. The results of the two studies together are evidence that 3-month-old babies can discern a key transposition change in a melody and they also can detect an invariant property of a melody over a key transposition.

In a third study we asked whether infants are sensitive to the contour and intervals of a short melody excerpt. The habituation phase of this study was like that of the first study. The babies looked at the visual display while they heard repetitions of a melody excerpt sung repeatedly in one key. When the babies' looking times to the display decreased to the specified criterion, different groups of babies (a) continued to hear the melody sung in the same key, (b) heard a new melody sung in the same key as the original melody, (c) heard a transformation that preserved the contour and rhythm of the original excerpt but changed its intervals, and (d) heard a transformation that preserved the rhythm of the melody excerpt but changed its contour and intervals.

The babies in the first group who continued to hear repetitions of the original melody generalized habituation as expected. The babies in the second group who heard a new melody in the same key as the original renewed looking at the display, although the overall length of time of their renewed looking was less than that for babies who heard new melodies in the previous two studies. Whether the decrease in their post-criterion looking was a consequence of discerning the common property of key (or possibly pitch range) in the habituation and post-criterion melodies is a matter for speculation. This was the first study in which the key of the new melody in the "new song" condition was the same as that for the original melody. The babies in the third group generalized habituation to the transformations preserving the rhythm and contour of the original, suggesting they were not sensitive to the interval changes. Finally, the babies in the fourth group showed some renewed looking upon hearing transformations preserving only the rhythm of the original, but they did not continue looking at the display for very long. Thus, some of them may have detected the contour change, but sensitivity to contour and certainly to the intervals of melodies develops with experience listening to the melodies of one's culture.

The results of our studies of the development of melody perception can be summarized as follows: Young babies have a good start toward detecting invariant properties of melodies across key changes they also can discriminate. Older children can discern similarity between melodies across differences that distinguish them. In particular, 5-year-old children and 3-month-old infants can discern a key transposition change in a melody as well as detecting an invariant property of a melody over a key transposition. Five-year-olds also perceive melodic contour over transformations that preserve it, and they can distinguish between melodies with the same contour and different intervals. Young infants may also detect contour in melodies, but sensitivity to contour and intervals develops with listening to the melodies of one's culture.

What will these babies learn to hear in melodies as they listen to them during the course of their development? What kind of learning is reflected in what a musician can hear in a rendition of a complex piece of music? How does this compare with what a naive listener hears, or what someone hears who listens to a composition for the first time? Underlying these particular questions is a specific assumption about perception that is not shared by all investigators of perceptual development. The assumption is that of *stimulus specificity*: that there is information in the ambient arrays surrounding us that more than adequately specifies its sources in the objects and events of our world.

An alternative assumption, one held by many investigators, is that of *stimulus inadequacy*: that the information available in light and sound is inadequate for unambiguous perception and must be supplemented in some way. The assumption of stimulus inadequacy directs us to study how the perceived world is constructed, what the supplementation processes are, how our perception is mediated. This assumption implies a constructive account of the development of melody perception, one that involves acquiring representations of aspects of melodic structure and using these schemas to help interpret what we hear when we listen to a piece of music (e.g., Krumhansl & Keil, 1982, Shepard & Jordan, 1984).

The assumption of information specificity, and the theory of perception on which it is based—that of James Gibson (1966, 1979)—suggest a very different account of the development of melody perception. Eleanor Gibson (1969; Gibson & Spelke, 1983) has formulated a complementary theory of perceptual development in which differentiation is a key concept. We think the concept of differentiation is important for our eventual understanding of the development of melody perception. Differentiation is a kind of learning; it refers to how perception becomes increasingly precise. When we think of melodies as events, the course of learning to perceive them can be thought of as the differentiation of their embedded structure: the discerning of progressively higher order structure and simultaneously the discovery of their subordinate units and how they fit together.

Eleanor Gibson (1969) documented a developmental trend toward economy in perception, and the development of melody perception is a rich example of this trend. The structure of a melody includes units of many sizes, and skilled listeners can make use of levels of the structure or units of a size that are most relevant for their immediate purpose. For conductors, performers, and novices, these units will be different. Furthermore, skilled listeners can deal at different levels, discerning the superordinate structure and how the units embedded in it relate to it.

## Perceiving the Unity of Musical Events

When we listen to melodies, in addition to perceiving their structure, we also can know something about their sources, that is, the instruments or voices producing them. When a melody is sung, we can perceive properties of the singer as well as what is being sung. We can tell whether the singer is male or female, adult or child; we can identify some musical instruments by listening to melodies being played on them. How is it that we know the source of a sound we are listening to? What properties of instruments and their sounds might be the basis for our perception and what is the course of development of sensitivity to these properties? These are questions about perceiving the unity of musical events, the aspect of the development of music perception we turn to now.

More than a decade ago, researchers discovered that even very young babies perceive the unity of some bimodally specified events. Spelke (1976) showed 4-month-old babies two distinct filmed events side by side, and she played the sound of one of the events from a speaker midway between the two films. She found that the babies spent more time looking at the sound-specified event than at the other event. Furthermore, when the sound was played without the films, the babies looked to the side where the specified event had been seen—as though they were searching for it. Subsequent research focused on what properties of events are the basis for the babies' perception of them. Synchrony of the sight and sound of an event as well as common tempo and rhythm of sights and sounds are properties to which young infants are sensitive (Spelke, 1979; Spelke, Born, & Chu, 1983). These are likely relevant properties for perceiving the unity of musical events as well: When a musical instrument is played, there is synchrony and common rhythm of the player's visible movements and the sounds produced. But researchers also learned that synchrony and tempo are not the only nor even necessary bases for infants' knowledge of sound-specified visible events. Walker-Andrews (1986; Walker, 1982) found that 7-month-old infants recognized the visible affective expression conveyed by an actress even when the sound of the actress' voice was not synchronous with the visible event and even when the rates of speech were common for different expressive events, anger and happiness.

What might be properties of musical events besides synchrony and rhythm that are important for perceiving their unity? Instruments in the same musical family have similar substances and surface layouts, are played in similar ways, and share sound qualities. An idea that has emerged from our research is that musical instrument families may display properties that are relevant for young children's early perception of musical events (Palmer, Jones, Hennessy, Unze, & Pick, 1989). Young children and adults differed predictably in the accuracy with which they could identify by sight a picture of a specific instrument they heard. However, children were highly accurate at knowing what *kind* of instrument they were hearing. They would mistake a violin for a cello, but rarely for a saxophone or a flute. Further, children and adults listening to instruments they probably never had heard before—Chinese instruments—also were very accurate at knowing the kind of instrument they were hearing. They would mistake one they were hearing for others in the same family.

The children who participated in these studies were in the third grade, and we wanted to find out how considerably younger children perceive musical events. We adapted a technique from Spelke (1976) to ask questions about 3- and 4-year old children's perception of musical events (Gross, Miller, Pick, & Palmer, 1987). They watched a video display of two instruments being played in synchrony side by side, and they heard a sound track that was in synchrony with both instruments but specific to one of them. For example, they might watch a trombone and cello being played, and hear the sound of the cello. The children were asked to choose the instrument that was producing the sound they were hearing. They made their choices by pressing a button to make a light come on above the appropriate instrument.

The preschool children in our first study saw 24 musical event displays. Each display showed two musicians playing different musical instruments from the brass, woodwind, and string families. The instruments of each pair were from different families and were selected to have overlapping pitch ranges and sizes. In 12 of the displays the instrument pairs included trumpets, violas, and flutes, four instances of an instrument paired with each of the other two. In the other 12 displays, the instrument pairs included trombones, clarinets, and cellos; again four instances of an instrument paired with each of the other two.

The children were quite accurate at knowing which instruments were producing the sounds they heard. The children's mean number of correct choices was 17 (of 24), and their range was from 12 to 24. The errors were evenly distributed within the 3- and 4-year old age groups and across individual displays except for the trombone, which "captured" the sound when it was seen next to another instrument.

The children correctly identified the instruments of each family—brass, strings, and woodwinds—more often than chance. They were best able to identify brass instruments in general and the trombone in particular. This result reflects, in part, the "capture" of the sound by the trombone whenever it was seen.

Why the trombone compelled the sounds of instruments it was paired with is not altogether obvious. The sweeping arm movements made by a trombone player may contribute to the effect. However, cellists also make sweeping arm movements, and the trombone effect may have had to do with the particular angle and distance of the video camera from the musician.

The children's high level of accuracy overall reflects their ability to use the information available in the displays to perceive the unity of musical events. Pitch range and instrument size as well as synchrony were comparable for the two instruments of a pair. Consequently, other properties, visible and audible, and perhaps specific to instrument families, were the basis for the children's accuracy of instrument identification.

The consistency of the children's performance for instruments within families might reflect the importance for musical event perception of properties common to members of the same instrument family. Instruments from the same musical family share many properties. For example, string instruments are made of wood, are similar in shape, are bowed or plucked, and produce characteristic string sounds when played. Instruments from the brass family are distinguishable from the strings by the substance of which they are made, metal, the manner by which their sounds are produced, blowing, and their characteristic sound quality. Do young children use such information to recognize instruments they see and hear? Are children better able to differentiate members of different families (e.g., a cello and a trumpet) than members of the same family (e.g., a cello and a string bass)? How does this perceptual ability change with development? We asked children of two different age groups, 4 years and 6 years, to participate in our second study, and we varied systematically the properties of family membership and size and pitch range so as to assess directly their relevance for the development of children's perception of musical events.

The task was identical to that of the earlier study. The children watched a video display of two instruments being played side by side in synchrony and they heard a sound track in synchrony with both instruments but specific to only one of them. The children indicated which instrument of a pair was producing the sound.

Four types of instrument pairs were represented with equal frequency in the displays: (a) two instruments from the same family with overlapping pitch ranges and sizes (e.g., violin and viola); (b) two instruments from the same family with different pitch ranges and sizes (e.g., violin and cello); (c) two instruments from different families with overlapping pitch ranges and sizes (e.g., violin and clarinet); and (d) two instruments from different families with different pitch ranges and sizes (e.g., violin and baritone). As in the earlier study, the instruments were from the brass, woodwind, and string families. The specific instruments and the pairs in which they participated are listed in Table 9.1.

The 6-year-olds were more accurate, overall, than were the 4-year-olds. The 6-year-olds' mean number of correct choices was 18 (of 24) and their range was from 13 to 22. The 4-year-olds' mean number of correct choices was 14 (of 24) and their range was from 9 to 21.

With one exception, the children identified the large and small instruments from each family significantly more frequently than chance. The exception was the 4-year-olds' identification of large woodwind instruments. The younger children's difficulty with this group probably was due to the bassoonist's barely discernible finger movements. As in the first study, children in both age groups were best able to identify brass instruments. In addition, the 4-year-olds in this study identified string instruments more accurately than they did woodwind instruments.

TABLE 9.1
Pairs of Instruments Used in Study 2

|  | Family | |
| --- | --- | --- |
|  | Same | Different |
| Overlapping | violin-viola | violin-clarinet |
|  | cello-string bass | cello-trombone |
|  | trumpet-French horn | trumpet-viola |
|  | baritone-trombone | baritone-bassoon |
|  | flute-clarinet | flute-French horn |
|  | saxophone-bassoon | saxophone-string bass |
| Size & Pitch Range |  |  |
| Different | violin-cello | saxophone-trumpet |
|  | viola-string bass | string bass-French horn |
|  | trumpet-baritone | bassoon-viola |
|  | flute-saxophone | flute-cello |
|  | clarinet-bassoon | baritone-violin |
|  | trombone-French horn | trombone-clarinet |

| String Instruments | Brass Instruments | Woodwind Instruments |
| --- | --- | --- |
| violin | trumpet | flute |
| viola | French horn | clarinet |
| cello | baritone | saxophone |
| string bass | trombone | bassoon |

The younger children were more accurate with instrument pairs from different families than with pairs from the same family. In fact, these children's performance with the same-family instrument pairs was not significantly better than chance. Their judgments did not vary systematically with the size and pitch range relation of the instrument pairs.

The family relation of instrument pairs and their size and pitch range interacted in affecting the older children's perception of the musical events. The 6-year-olds were more accurate with instrument pairs differing in family or size than with pairs in which the family and size were the same. For these latter pairs, the older children's performance was not significantly better than chance.

The younger children in this study differentiated among instruments based on audible and visible properties that distinguish among musical instrument families. The older children demonstrated additional sensitivity to the correspondence of physical size and pitch range as a basis for perceiving a unified event.

We also wanted to know about the children's specific knowledge of the instruments they were watching and listening to, so we gave them a multiple-choice posttest after they had watched the displays. For this posttest, an experimenter said the name of an instrument and the children pointed to one of a set of photographs to indicate which instrument they thought was being named.

The children's performance with the musical event displays was not related to their scores on the picture task. Thus, knowing the names of particular instruments and familiarity with them was not necessary for the children to be able to use information available in the dynamic displays to perceive the unity of the events.

When musical instruments are played, multiple sources of information specify the properties of these events. For a perceiver, these events are multimodal experiences. The results of these two studies suggest that children use optical and acoustical information to perceive the unity of musical events. In particular, they use information about properties shared by instruments from the same musical family. Both the 4- and 6-year-old children in the second study were better able to differentiate instruments from different families (e.g., a viola and a flute) than instruments from the same family (e.g., a violin and a viola).

Children's ability to perceive the unity of musical events develops with experience. Overall, of course, the older children in the second study were more accurate than were the younger children. In particular, the 6-year-olds were sensitive to differences in size and pitch range in perceiving these events. When an instrument is played, its physical appearance and the sounds produced (e.g., its size and pitch range; its substance and surface layout and the qualities of sound) are mutually specific, as are the playing of the instrument (e.g., the manner of playing, synchrony of musician's movements) and the sounds produced. Children's use of these mutually specific properties of what they see and hear enables their increasingly rich and precise perception of the musical events of their world.

## Perceiving Meaning in Musical Events

From our experiments we have learned about some aspects of melodic structure young children perceive, and that they become increasingly sensitive to properties of musical events. We have also learned that even very young babies are sensitive to some properties of melodies. Why should children develop skill in detecting the structure of musical events? What might be the function of such an achievement? We believe that the development of sensitivity to the structure of music is the beginning of the discovery of meaning in music.

But what is the meaning that listeners learn to discern in music? James Gibson (1979) wrote about knowledge and language that

> Knowledge that has been put into words can be said to be *explicit* instead of *tacit*. The human observer can verbalize his awareness, and the result is to make it communicable. But my hypothesis is that there has to be an awareness of the world before it can be put into words. You have to see it before you can say it. Perceiving precedes predicating. (p. 260)

Gibson was arguing that what is verbalizable is only part of what there is to be known. One can make the additional hypothesis that all knowledge and meaning are not verbalizable. We think the meaning of music that listeners seek out is, at least partly, of this type. It is not constructed by listeners; it is there, specified in the acoustic array. Composers know it is there, and performers and listeners know it also. It is not verbalizable, but it can be communicated about. It is not vague, like the emotional connotations of a particular passage, although that is part of the meaning, too. It is precise, and in communicating about it, it can be agreed on or argued about. Performers produce music in ways that reveal or conceal its meaning; music critics write about it, and listeners debate it.

That the meaning in music is not a construction of the mind's ear, but instead is available to be heard in a rendition if one is willing to learn to listen for it, is not a matter of doubt for musicians—composers, conductors, performers, scholars. We are less certain about behavioral scientists, but if the idea is at least plausible, then we should ask why children will learn to search for the meaning in music. What does perceiving this meaning provide or afford?

One consequence of learning to perceive the meaning of music or of a particular kind of music may be a social–cultural bonding. A community of people is established who can understand, communicate about, and produce music of various types. The significance of such shared understanding is reflected in the diversity of ways in which music is used to direct and guide human behavior, from soothing babies to controlling adolescents' emotions to summoning warriors to arms.

From another perspective, seeking the meaning of music is an instance of our general sensitivity to the meaning of acoustically specified events. In the natural surround, in the woods or fields, the sounds of brooks bubbling and flowing, of birds warbling, insects croaking, and mosquitoes buzzing, are informative about what creatures are present, and what they are doing. The structure of the sounds changes dramatically when predators are nearby, and the changes specify what is happening. In the habitats we have constructed for ourselves, the sounds likewise are highly informative about the layout of the environments and about the events occurring in it. An impressive example of the specificity of the sounds to their sources, and their availability for guiding action, is the achievement of persons having visual impairments whose locomotion through the layout, including avoiding obstacles, is guided by the sounds of events occurring in the layout.

Eleanor Gibson (1983) noted that the learning of language during infancy and early childhood is a striking accomplishment of differentiation of the structure and meaning of events. Although very young infants distinguish among some intonation patterns and phonetic contrasts, she pointed out that "hearing them as bearers of *meaning* is a matter for learning of deeply embedded relations that extends over years" (p. 14). Clearly the same observation holds for learning the meaning of music.

Finally, at a highest level of human functioning, seeking alternative ways of organizing information, finding economy of structure, in short, seeking the meaning of complex events, is intrinsically pleasurable. Mathemeticians seek not just proofs, but elegant proofs as ways of describing what is known. When we listen to music, we search for its structure. Its aesthetic value is the meaning to be found in all levels of its structure. Musicians and other skilled listeners learn to comprehend it, and we think that is what the babies and children of our experiments are beginning to do too.

## REFERENCES

Dowling, W. J. (1978). Scale and contour: Two components of a theory of memory for melodies. *Psychological Review, 85*, 341–354.

Gibson, E. J. (1969). *Principles of perceptual learning and development.* New York: Appleton-Century-Crofts.

Gibson, E. J. (1982). The concept of affordances in development: The renascence of functionalism. In W. A. Collins (Ed.), *Minnesota symposia on child psychology. Vol. 15: The concept of development* (pp. 55–82). Hillsdale, NJ: Lawrence Erlbaum Associates.

Gibson, E. J. (1983). *Shedding the light of the ecological approach on differentiation and enrichment.* Paper presented at the Second International Conference on Event Perception, Vanderbilt, TN.

Gibson, E. J., & Spelke, E. S. (1983). The development of perception and attention. In J. Flavell & E. Markman (Eds.), *Carmichael's manual of child psychology. Vol. 3: Cognitive development* (pp. 1–76). New York: Wiley.

Gibson, J. J. (1966). *The senses considered as perceptual systems.* Boston: Houghton-Mifflin.

Gibson, J. J. (1979). *The ecological approach to visual perception.* Boston: Houghton-Mifflin.

Gross, D., Miller, M. M., Pick, A. D., & Palmer, C. F. (1987, April). *Children's perception of the unity of musical events.* Paper presented at the meeting of the Society for Research in Child Development, Baltimore, MD.

Hennessy, B. L., Palmer, C. F., Jones, R. K., Richardson, R. M., Unze, M. G., & Pick, A. D. (1983, April). *Do infants recognize transposed melodies?* Paper presented at the meeting of the Society for Research in Child Development, Detroit, MI.

Krumhansl, C. L., & Keil, F. C. (1982). Acquisition of the hierarchy of tonal functions in music. *Memory and Cognition, 10*, 243–251.

Palmer, C. F., Jones, R. K., Hennessy, B. L., Unze, M. G., & Pick, A. D. (1989). How is a trumpet known? The "basic object level" concept and perception of musical instruments. *American Journal of Psychology, 102*, 17–37.

Pick, A. D., Palmer, C. F., Hennessy, B. L., Unze, M. G., Jones, R. K., & Richardson, R. M. (1988). Children's perception of certain musical properties: Scale and contour. *Journal of Experimental Child Psychology, 45*, 28–51.

Shepard, R. N., & Jordan, D. C. (1984). Auditory illusions demonstrating that tones are assimilated to an internalized scale. *Science, 226*, 1333–1334.

Spelke, E. S. (1976). Infants' intermodal perception of events. *Cognitive Psychology, 8*, 553–560.

Spelke, E. S. (1979). Perceiving bimodally specified events in infancy. *Developmental Psychology, 15*, 626–636.

Spelke, E. S., Born, W. S., & Chu, F. (1983). Perception of moving, sounding objects by 4-month-old infants. *Perception, 12*, 719–732.

Walker, A. S. (1982). Intermodal perception of expressive behavior by human infants. *Journal of Experimental Child Psychology, 33*, 514–535.

Walker-Andrews, A. S. (1986). Intermodal perception of expressive behaviors: Relation of eye and voice? *Developmental Psychology, 22,* 373–377.

Ward, W. D. (1970). Musical perception. In J. V. Tobias (Ed.), *Foundations of modern auditory theory* (Vol. 1, pp. 405–447). New York: Academic Press.

# Epilogue
## Implications for Contemporary
## Musical Practice

Jon H. Appleton
*Dartmouth College, Hanover, New Hampshire*

Each year I ask my students if they think music has any survival value. It is easy for them to find the survival value for speech and hearing. But when I suggest to them, partly in jest, that music is merely a vestigial artifact of speech and hearing that we could easily do without, they become demonstrably upset. Music means so much to them, they claim, but they do not understand why. Is it thus the motivation of the authors of this book to explain the meaning of music or simply to describe musical behavior?

Speaking for other composers and performers, I think most of the results of the research in this book are known to us intuitively. It is rewarding to see how these intuitions are confirmed by psychologists and psychoacousticians. However, we have many other questions to ask and I propose to make these queries the focus of this chapter.

What is it that professional musicians want to learn from psychologists? Performers of the traditional, Western classical repertoire have the least to gain from the findings of psychologists except, perhaps, on the level of simple curiosity. These performers have no choice as to the notes they play, these have been determined by the composer. Performers learn the way the notes should be played mostly through nonverbal instruction. They listen to and watch their teachers, by-passing most "right brain" activity. Thus, for example, it is virtually impossible to learn to play the Bach *Chaconne* in a stylistically acceptable manner by solely reading a book on how to play the violin. There are, in fact, very few such books. It would be both informative and amusing to hear a violinist who did not know the repertoire and who learned to play only from an instruction manual.

The rules for what we consider musicality have only recently begun to be studied by psychologists. The most promising work to date has been done by Johan Sundberg in the Department of Speech Communication and Music Acoustics at the Royal Institute of Technology (KTH) in Stockholm, Sweden (see Sundberg, Askenfelt, & Frydèn, 1983). Performers will likely find little value in an accurate description of musicality because its tenets are often expressed in verbose or unfamiliar terms; for example: *a slur between two adjacent quarter notes at quarter note = 60 in a solo clarinet line by Brahms is executed by shortening the second note by 400 milliseconds. This applies to all ascending figures where a constant dynamic of mezzo-forte or louder obtains.* The number of variables is so staggering as to seriously bring into question whether such a "rule book" could even be written. It certainly would not be used by performers who have developed a far more efficient, nonverbal means of conveying the same information.

Perhaps some musicologists might find useful a description of performance practice in detailed and scientific terms. But would it not be more appropriate to study audio and video records of the same phenomena? Why, for musicians, is it necessary to express concepts in one language (written) that can be eloquently expressed in another (gestural or aural)?

Composers, on the other hand, can gain much from the study of musical perception. They usually need to communicate with performers as accurately as possible and this is most often accomplished by means of a written score. Orchestration books summarize the capabilities of the various instruments but most composers learn by example and by trial and error. They see and hear how performers play what they have composed and they modify their succeeding works accordingly. Even this behavior, however, is difficult to describe in psychoacoustic terms because there are no "correct" ways to play music. There are traditions that have evolved, styles and procedures that are understood, but no rules that a composer must follow. In Western culture of the second half of the 20th century, nearly every imaginable approach to musical composition has been tried. We have gone through a period of stylistic pluralism and musical extremes. How then does a composer know where to start? What sounds to use? What notes to choose?

Composers usually do not suddenly appear. They most often have had intense, early experience with music. They may have sung or played a musical instrument. At some point they had a strong emotional experience with a piece of music that made them wish they had composed that piece. They wanted to get closer to the music—almost to become part of it. Other composers are drawn to the art of composition through a fascination with the mechanics of music, the way sounds and notes are put together. It has been observed that this kind of fascination is similar to that of a scientist. This author believes that composers are closer to tinkerers, the term unfortunately having a superficial connotation. Composers are much closer in spirit to Thomas Edison than they are to Albert

Einstein. Composers do not need to know why the note F♯ does not fit the schema called C major nor why a low B♭ on the bassoon sounds differently two octaves higher. Nevertheless, there continues to be the belief in Western culture that the education of composers should contain some theoretical information. We might ask Why? and What information?

It is in the area of electro-acoustic music (music made with tape manipulation, synthesizers, and computers) that composers find most useful the discoveries of psychoacousticians. In this domain, composers must design their own sounds and they are unable to rely on a fixed, instrumental tradition to provide the sounds themselves. Originality in electro-acoustic music is expressed more often in the timbre domain than in the domains of rhythm and pitch. Two composes who are also psychoacousticians, John Chowning and Jean-Claude Risset, have provided valuable ways of thinking to their fellow composers who are involved in digital sound synthesis. The chapter, "Exploration of Timbre by Analysis and Synthesis" shows the complexity of dealing with the variables of timbre (Risset & Wessel, 1982).

Twenty-five years ago this author expressed the view that music consisted of three equal parameters; pitch, rhythm, and timbre, and that composers have usually ordered these parameters, making one more important than another in their work (see Appleton, 1966). The article was written at a time when there was a belief among composers that modes of listening and perception could be determined by the composer himself or herself. Serial (12-tone) composition is a case in point. Composers of this kind of music believed that the entire structure of pitch relationships common to the music of our culture could be abandoned in favor of a new "pitch" logic. Composers of electro-acoustic music, this author included, believed that one could have a music in which the primary organizing force was the development of timbre itself. Today it has been shown that although these habits or modes of listening can be learned, those musics that employ radical stylistic and syntactical procedures have not made any significant inroads into our musical culture. Very little serial music is composed today and even less is performed! Electro-acoustic music has increasingly subjugated timbral exploration to rhythmic and pitch structures.

Would composers have tried to alter the fundamental tenets of Western tonal music if they had read Arlette Zenatti's chapter on "Children's Musical Cognition and Taste," in which it is established that by the age of 6, the organization of the tonal system is fully internalized? The answer is probably affirmative because most educated adults believe that new forms and structures can be learned by attentive listeners. This is an area that needs much attention. We know that uneducated listeners respond to "modern" music by saying "that's just noise." Music is only music when it conforms to their expectations. But what about educated listeners on whom the "art" music tradition has been predicated in recent years? What mechanisms do they use to adapt to (or "understand") a new syntax?

It is in this area that composers need the help of psychologists. Lola L. Cuddy, in her chapter on melody, says "Research findings should have interesting implications for the creating of pitch structures for new music." What are those implications? Dowling (1988) has written "being familiar with the materials presented leads listeners and viewers to perceive things differently from the way they would if they were totally naive" (p. 203). It would help composers to know the relative strengths of rhythm, pitch, and timbre as perceptual models. Can learning occur within the framework of one composition on a first hearing? How are originality and novelty dependent on previous listening habits and on expectations provided by the musical composition itself? Mari Riess Jones begins to address this issue in her chapter on the "Dynamics of Musical Patterns." Her attempt to point out the "right time" for composers or performers to communicate new musical ideas could be developed into a new kind of treatise for musicians.

Psychologist Jamshed J. Bharucha and others have begun to address the even more complex problems of harmonic organization (see Bharucha, 1987). By looking at the internalized representations of structural regularities in music, perhaps composers could better understand the harmonic implications of their music. But do most composers think about the creation of music this calculatingly? A connectionist model of harmony is most certainly specific to a musical style. Harmonic progressions in the music of Thelonious Monk must certainly refer to a slightly different network than that used by W. A. Mozart.

What music lovers, and some musicians, find most wanting in the work of those psychologists who have attempted to deal with music is an account of human emotional response to music. It is not enough to label our feelings to music as simply "happy" and "sad" as Sandra E. Trehub does in her chapter on "The Music Listening Skills of Infants and Young Children." The feelings raised are often difficult to describe. Is it possible that there are areas of human experience that can only crudely be measured or described in words? Perhaps this is why music exists! It reflects our emotions in a wholly separate way. It conveys the subtlety of complex feelings better than words. This author remembers reading Leonard B. Meyer's important book, *Emotion and Meaning in Music*, (1956) and thinking with each succeeding chapter that the answers were closer at hand. Meyer answered some of the questions concerning the "meaning" of music in both aesthetic and cultural terms but he gets no closer to the emotional impact of music than to tell us that our feelings are aroused when expectations are confirmed or violated. Can we come closer than this?

## REFERENCES

Appleton, J. (1966). An approach to twentieth-century music. *The Music Review, 27*(1), 54–58.
Bharucha, J. J. (1987). Music cognition and perceptual facilitation: A connectionist framework. *Music Perception, 5*(1), 1–30.

Dowling, W. J. (1988). Attending to hidden melodies. *Yearbook of Science and the Future*, 192–203.

Meyer, L. B. (1956). *Emotion and meaning in music*. Chicago: University of Chicago Press.

Risset, J. & Wessel, D. L. (1982). Exploration of timbre by analysis and synthesis. In D. Deutsch (Ed.), *The psychology of music* (pp. 25–58). New York: Academic Press.

Sundberg, J., Askenfelt, A., & Frydèn, L. (1983). Musical performance: A synthesis-by-rule approach. *Computer Music Journal, 7*(1), 37–43.

# Author Index

## A

Abeles, H. F., 177, 193, *194*
Amiel-Tison, C., 158, *160*
Appleton, J., 217, *218*
Askenfelt, A., 117, *120*, 216, *219*
Attneave, F., 164, *175*

## B

Badertscher, B., 31, *37*
Balzano, G. J., 139, *151*
Barrière, M., 168, *175*
Bartlett, J. C., 51, 52, 54, 56, 57, *59*, *60*, 182, *194*
Bastide, R., 178, *194*
Berlyne, D., 178, *194*
Bengtsson, I., 110, 111, 112, 113, *119*
Berstein, L., 9, *18*
Bertoncini, J, 158, *160*, 168, *175*
Bharucha, J. J., 24, 25, 37, *37*, 41, 50, 55, 59, *59*, *60*, 127, *151*, 218, *218*
Boltz, M., 74, 85, 88, *91*, 143, 145, *151*, *152*
Born, W. S., 206, *212*
Boyle, J. D., 177, *195*
Bregman, A. S., 125, *152*

## C

Bresson, F., 178, *195*
Bull, D., 57, *61*, 164, 166, *176*
Burns, E. M., 191, *194*
Butterfield, E. C., 157, *160*

## C

Campbell, J., 125, *152*
Capodilupo, S., 169, *175*
Carterette, E. C., 125, 126, 127, 129, 130, 136, 137, 138, 139, 143, 145, 146, 148, *153*
Castellano, M., 50, *60*
Chailley, J., 190, 192, *194*
Chu, F., 206, *212*
Clarke, E. F., 8, *18*, 114, *119*, 127, 130, 132, 133, 135, 136, 137, 138, *152*
Clement, D. E., 46, *60*
Clynes, M., 107, 117, *119*
Cohen, A. J., 23, 36, *37*, *38*, 167, 170, *175*, *176*
Cooper, G. W., 99, *119*, 143, *152*
Cross, I., 40, 41, 42, 43, *60*
Crowder, R. G., 57, *60*
Crozier, J. B., 178, *194*
Cuddy, L. L., 23, 31, 35, 36, *37*, *38*

# Subject Index

## A

Ability, 22, 24, 29, 30, 37
Aristoxenes of Tarente, 121, 142

## B

Bach, J. S., 215
Baroque era, 97
Beethoven, L. van, 23, 117, 178

## C

Celtic melody, 29
Clementi, 182
Culture,
  Balkan, 142
  logocentric, 8
  West African, 142
  western, 142, 216

## D

Development, 155–212
  listening skills, 161–174

music cognition,
  environmental determinants of, 155, 161, 168, 169, 174
  biological determinants of, 155, 161, 168, 169, 174
  musical taste, 182–183
    environmental determinants of, 178–179
    biological determinants of, 178–179
  perception, 155–160, 197–212
Diabelli, 182
Digital synthesizer, 21
Distorted melodies test, 21–24, 35–37
Dragnet, 63, 148, 149
Dyslexia, 186

## E

Education, 8, 16–18, 193, 217
  procedural learning, 16–17
Electro-acoustical music, 217
Emotion, 106–108, 170–171
European music, 8, 64, 123
Event perception,
  meaning of musical events, 210–212
  melody, 197–212
  unity of musical events, 206–210
Experience, 2, 12–19, 22, 28, 29, 42, 75, 161

WITHDRAWN

from

STIRLING UNIVERSITY LIBRARY